# Wildflowers of Mississippi

# Wildflowers
# of Mississippi

Stephen L. Timme

UNIVERSITY PRESS OF MISSISSIPPI   JACKSON

**This book is dedicated
to William Clayton Timme and
to Linda, Caleb, Zachary, Clifford, Bill, Esther, Flossie,
and the people of Mississippi.**

www.upress.state.ms.us

The University Press of Mississippi is a member of the Association
of American University Presses.

Copyright © 2007 by University Press of Mississippi

Manufactured in China

First edition 1989
Illustrations by Sam Minor

Library of Congress Cataloging-in-Publication Data

Timme, S. Lee.
  Wildflowers of Mississippi / S. Lee Timme.
    p. cm.
  Includes bibliographical references (p. ) and index.
  ISBN-13: 978-1-57806-969-9 (pbk. : alk. paper)
  ISBN-10: 1-57806-969-6 (pbk. : alk. paper)
  1. Wildflowers—Mississippi—Identification. I. Title.
QK169.T56 2007
582.13′09762—DC22

                                        2006047076

British Library Cataloging-in-Publication Data available

# Note on Nomenclature

Since the publication of *Wildflowers of Mississippi* more than fifteen years ago, several taxa have undergone name changes that reflect the results of phylogenetic and molecular taxonomic studies. These studies have provided a better picture of the evolutionary history and relationships among plants. Not all botanical taxonomists agree with the changes, but they are given here as current information. The name changes follow nomenclature given by the United States Department of Agriculture's Natural Resources Conservation Service Plants Database (http://www.plants.usda.gov/). Recent molecular studies indicate that some families should be transferred to other families and new ones formed (W. S. Judd, C. S. Campbell, E. A. Kellogg, and P. F. Stevens, *Plant Systematics: A Phylogenetic Approach* [Sunderland, MA: Sinauer Associates, Inc., 1999]). The traditional Milkweed family (Asclepidaceae), that includes *Asclepias*, *Cynanchum*, and *Matelea*, is now placed in the family Apocynaceae. The genera *Veronica*, *Penstemon*, *Mimulus*, *Linaria*, *Gratiola*, and *Veronicastrum* (all formerly in the Scropulariaceae) have been placed in the family Plantaginaceae. The Liliaceae has been divided to form the Trilliaceae, Uvulariaceae, Alliaceae, Hemerocallidaceae, Melanthiaceae, and Liliaceae. The genus *Hypoxis* has been placed in its own family, the Hypoxidaceae.

| NAME IN BOOK | NEW NAME | PAGE |
| --- | --- | --- |
| *Agave virginica* L. | *Manfreda virginica* (L.) Salisb. *ex* Rose | 5 |
| *Aster ericoides* L. | *Symphyotrichum eriocoides* (L.) Nesom | 59 |
| *Aster linariifolius* L. | *Ionactis linariifolius* (L.) Greene | 59 |
| *Aster paludosus* Ait. | *Eurybia hemispherica* (Alexander) G. L. Nesom | 60 |
| *Aster patens* Ait. | *Symphyotrichum patens* (Ait.) Nesom | 60 |
| *Aster pilosus* Willd. | *Symphyotrichum pilosum* (Willd.) Nesom | 60 |
| *Aster sericocarpoides* (Small) K. Schum | *Symphyotrichum umbellatus* var. *latifolius* Gray | 61 |
| *Aster shortii* Lindl. | *Symphyotrichum shortii* (Lindl.) Nesom | 61 |
| *Aster tortifolius* Michx. | *Sericocarpus tortifolius* (Michx.) Nees | 61 |
| *Baptisia lacteal* (Raf.) Thieret | *Baptisia alba* (L.) Vent. | 138 |
| *Cacalia ovata* Walt. | *Arnoglossum ovatum* (Walt.) H. E. Robins. | 64 |
| *Calopogon pulchellus* (Salis.) R. Br. | *Calopogon tuberosus* (L.) B.S.P. | 28 |
| *Campanula americana* L. | *Campanulastrum americana* (L.) Small | 110 |
| *Cassia marilandica* L. | *Senna marilandica* (L.) Link | 108 |
| *Cassia obtusifolia* L. | *Senna obtusifolia* (L.) Irwin & Barneby | 108 |
| *Chrsanthemum leucanthemum* L. | *Leucanthemum vulgare* Lam. | 67 |
| *Chrysopsis camporum* Greene | *Heterotheca camporum* (Greene) Shinners | 68 |
| *Chrysopsis graminifolia* (Michx.) Ell. | *Pityopsis graminifolia* (Michx.) Nutt. | 68 |
| *Cleistes divaricata* (L.) Ames | *Cleistes bifaria* (Fern.) Catling & Gregg | 28 |
| *Cleome spinosa* Jacq. | *Cleome hassieriana* Chod. | 113 |
| *Cnidoscolus stimulosus* (Michx.) Engelm. & Gray | *Cnidoscolus urens* var. *stimulosus* (Michx.) Govaerts | 135 |
| *Coronilla varia* L. | *Securigera varia* (L.) Lassen | 139 |
| *Epidendrum conopseum* R. Br. | *Epidendrum magnoliae* Muhl. | 29 |
| *Euthamia minor* (Michx.) Greene | *Euthamia caroliniana* (L.) Greene *ex* Porter & Britt. | 76 |
| *Euthamia tenuifolia* (Pursh) Mitt. | *Euthamia caroliniana* (L.) Greene *ex* Porter & Britt. | 76 |
| *Gaura parviflora* Doug. | *Gaura mollis* James | 188 |
| *Haplopappus divaricatus* (Nutt.) Gray | *Croptilon divaricatum* (Nutt.) Raf. | 78 |
| *Hedyotis crassifolia* Raf. | *Houstonia pusilla* Schoepf | 217 |
| *Hedyotis caerulea* (L.) T. & G. | *Houstonia caerulea* L. | 217 |
| *Hepatica americana* (DC.) Ker-Gawl. | *Hepatica nobilis* var. *obtusa* (Pursh) Steyermark | 208 |
| *Hibiscus militaris* Cav. | *Hibiscus laevis* Ait. | 178 |

| | | |
|---|---|---|
| *Hymenocallis eulae* auct. non Shinners | *Hymenocallis liriosme* (Raf.) Shinners | 18 |
| *Hymenocallis occidentalis* (Le Conte) Kunth | *Hymenocallis caroliniana* (L.) Herbert | 18 |
| *Hypericum denticulatum* Walt. | *Hypericum virgatum* Lam. | 122 |
| *Hypoxis micrantha* Pollard | *Hypoxis wrightii* (Baker) Brackett | 19 |
| *Ipomoea stolonifera* (Cyr.) Gmel. | *Ipomoea imperati* (Vahl) Griseb. | 127 |
| *Isopyrum biternatum* (Raf.) T. & G. | *Enemion biternatum* Raf. | 208 |
| *Kuhnia eupatorioides* L. | *Brickellia eupatorioides* (L.) Shinners | 83 |
| *Linaria canadensis* (L.) Dumont | *Nuttallanthus canadensis* (L.) D. A. Sutton | 228 |
| *Marshallia tenuifolia* Raf. | *Marshallia graminifolia* var. *cynanthera* (Ell.) Beadle & F. E. Boynt. | 85 |
| *Melilotus alba* Medikus | *Melilotus officinalis* (L.) Lam. | 143 |
| *Nasturtium officinale* R. Br. | *Rorippa nasturtium-aquaticum* (L.) Hayek | 104 |
| *Oenothera tetragona* Roth | *Oenothera fruticosa* L. | 190 |
| *Psoralea psoralioides* (Walt.) Cory | *Orbexilum pedunculatum* (P. Mill.) Rydb. | 143 |
| *Rhododendron serrulatum* (Sm.) Mill. | *Rhododendron viscosum* (L.) Torr. | 134 |
| *Salicornia virginica* L. | *Salicornia depressa* Standl. | 119 |
| *Schrankia microphylla* (Dry.) MacBr. | *Mimosa quadrivalvis* L. | 183 |
| *Senecio aureus* L. | *Packera aurea* (L.) A. & D. Löve | 89 |
| *Senecio glabellus* Poir. | *Packera glabella* (Poir.) C. Jeffrey | 89 |
| *Senecio smallii* Britt. | *Packera anonyma* (Wood) W. A. Weber & A. Löve | 89 |
| *Sesbania macrocarpa* Muhl. *ex* Raf. | *Sesbania herbacea* (P. Mill.) McVaugh | 146 |
| *Smilacina racemosa* (L.) Desf. | *Maianthemum racemosum* (L.) Link | 22 |
| *Swertia caroliniensis* (Walt.) Ktze | *Frasera caroliniensis* Walt. | 154 |
| *Toxicodendron toxicarium* Salisb. | *Toxicodendron pubescens* P. Mill. | 44 |
| *Trifurcia lahue* ssp. *caerulea* (Herb.) Goldbl. | *Herbertia lahue* (Molina) Goldblatt | 14 |
| *Viola floridana* Brainerd | *Viola sororia* Willd. | 240 |
| *Viola rafinesquii* Greene | *Viola bicolor* Pursh | 242 |
| *Xyris iridifolia* Chapm. | *Xyris laxifolia* var. *iridifolia* (Chapman) Kral | 38 |

## Other Corrections

*Anemone caroliniaa* = *A. caroliniana*
*Cardiospermum halicababum*, page 219 (not 218)
*Euonymus amereicanus* = *Euonymus americanus*
*Helianthus heterophylus* = *Helianthus heterophyllus*
*Hypericum denticulatum* Walt. (pg. 122) should be *Hypericum pseudomaculatum* Bush
*Lachnanthes caroliniana* = *Lachnanthes caroliana*
*Nuphar luteum* = *Nuphar lutea*
*Opuntia humifusa* Raf. (pg. 107) should be *O. macrorhiza* Engelm.
*Pinquicula caerulea* = *Pinguicula caerulea*
*Rhododendron serrulatim* = *Rhododendron viscosum*
*Sebastiana fruticosa* = *Sebastiania fruticosa*
*Sarracenia leucohylla* = *S. leucophylla*
*Solidago sempivirens* should be *Solidago nemoralis* Aiton (Gray Goldenrod)
*Stillingia sylatica* = *S. sylvatica*
*Styrax americana* = *S. americanus*
*Styrax grandifolia* = *S. grandifolius*
*Zephyranthes atamasco* = *Z. atamasca*

# Contents

# Preface

Wildflowers have long intrigued both the professional and nonprofessional botanist. The records of early explorers and settlers of North America reveal that they were impressed by the beauty and often the abundance of wildflowers, and, like the American Indians, they were dependent on plants for food, shelter, and medicine. This fascination with plants, especially those we call wildflowers, continues today. Several organizations have been established to advance the study and preservation of plants. Intensive forest clearing and prairie plowing have made preservation an especially vital issue for many of these groups.

Nearly every state has an established native plant or wildflower society. The Mississippi Native Plant Society was established in 1980 to further knowledge about native and naturalized plant species of the state and to encourage an attitude of respect and appreciation for these plants. These goals are accomplished through organized, informative field trips throughout the state, led by competent professional or nonprofessional botanists. Prior to the publication of this book, Mississippi was the only state in the southeast with no wildflower guide available to the public. Members of the Mississippi Native Plant Society acknowledged this void, and as a direct result of their effort, this field guide became a reality.

Many people have contributed to the success of this book. The following are acknowledged for their financial contribution: The Oktibbeha Audubon Society, The Garden Clubs of Mississippi, Edith Anderson, Robert D. Bowling, Mary H. Butler, Betty Duckworth, Halla Joe Ellis, Mrs. Lynn Crosby Gammill, Mrs. William L. Gill, Jerry F. Hall, Dawn Lacoste Herring, Dr. and Mrs. H. J. Jacobs, Sr., Cathryn Kever, Mrs. Gray Layton, David and Jo Ann Lee, Mrs. James E. Lloyd, Bryant Mather, E. W. Permenter, Mrs. I. N. Roberts, Mrs. J. C. Rochester, Mary Evelyn Stringer, Eugenia Summer, Pat and Faye Swan, Thomas and Glenda Thorne, and William E. and Esther Timme.

I also wish to recognize several other individuals who contributed to this project. First, sincere gratitude is extended to Joseph Werner, who first showed me the real beauty and fascination of plants. Thanks go to Paul Redfearn, Jr., Wallace Weber, Grant Pyrah, and Russel Rhodes of Southwest Missouri State University for instilling the biology of plants in me through coursework and field trips and for their guidance as I furthered my career as a botanist. Thanks also go to Sid-

ney McDaniel, Keith Clancy, Timothy Smith, and Randall
Warren for their many enlightening and stimulating discus-
sions on Mississippi's flora and additionally to Dr. Sidney
McDaniel for his assistance in species identifications and his
professional contribution. Anne S. Bradburn, Edward L. Blake,
Dr. Robert Daly, and Christopher J. Wells also made most
helpful comments on the manuscript. I would also like to
thank Faye Swan for her continued encouragement throughout this project; it was greatly appreciated. A special thanks is
extended to Samuel Minor for his excellent line drawings,
which play a major role in the use of this book. To the Mississippi Native Plant Society and Dr. Richard Abel of the University Press of Mississippi, I extend my thanks and appreciation for their encouragement, advice, and foresight to see a
need for a guide to Mississippi's wildflowers. I also thank the
many people who submitted slides for review. The photos in
this book are mine, except for those contributed by the following: Keith Clancy, James Cummins, Edwin Gregory, Robert Haynes, Carl Hunter, H. J. Jacobs, Sidney McDaniel, Paul
Nace, Travis Salley, John Allen Smith, and Timothy Smith.
To Andreas Daehnick, Wendy Gowder, Darryl Worley, Linda
D. Jackson, and my many botany students at the University
of North Alabama, thanks are given for field assistance and
the stamina to listen to my lectures on the beauty and impor-
tance of plants. Appreciation is extended to John and Nancy
Cook, Garland Owens, Janet Hicks, and Timothy Smith for
accompanying me on many field trips. Finally, I extend a sincere thanks to my wife, Linda, for without her encouragement and her patience on the many field excursions, this
book would never have been completed.

The flora of Mississippi includes some 2,500 species of ferns and fern allies, sedges, rushes, grasses, woody plants, and forbs. This diversity of plant life can be found in a variety of habitats ranging from the floodplains in the western part of the state to the mountainous areas in the northeast and the dunes and savannas along the coast. A number of these species have been introduced from other areas or have escaped cultivation and become naturalized. Such species may become an established part of the flora for a particular area. Although the flora of some counties is well known, other areas have yet to be adequately inventoried.

## Purpose

The goal of this book is to provide both professional and amateur botanists with a source to use in identifying more than five hundred species of Mississippi's wildflowers. The challenge of identifying plants is enjoyable and rewarding. Learning to identify plants, helps one gain a greater appreciation of their beauty, as well as a better understanding of how each species associates with its environment. A further purpose of this book, then, is to enhance the reader's understanding and appreciation of Mississippi's diverse wildflowers and bring about an awareness of the need for plant protection.

It is impossible to present all of the flowering plants or even all the forbs that occur in Mississippi in a pictorial field guide. The plants pictured in this book were chosen because the author and other botanists consider them to be the most common species found in the state. A few of the species pictured are rarely found, however, but were included because of their interesting and showy flowers. The plants presented here are mostly forbs, with a few woody species represented. Although the ferns, grasses, sedges, rushes, and many woody species are excluded, the reader should remember that they represent an important part of Mississippi's flora.

Because plants do not adhere to state boundaries, this field guide will also serve well for the identification of plants in eastern Louisiana and Arkansas, southwest and southcentral Tennessee, and western Alabama.

## Plant Names

Carolus Linnaeus, a Swedish naturalist, is credited with the development of the binomial system of nomenclature, which gives every known organism a name consisting of two words, the genus and the species. This combination constitutes the scientific name, which is Latin or Latinized. A plant family is composed of one or more genera (plural); the genus (singular) is composed of one or more species. Plants are placed in taxonomic categories (such as genus, family, order) based on characteristics common for a particular category. This system allows botanists and biologists around the world to communicate, although the scientists sometimes disagree on some plant names.

All known plants have a scientific name, and most also have a common name. Common names usually are based on some characteristic of the plant. The common name may be derived from the flower color, leaf shape, medicinal use, edibility, or location of the plant. For example, Self-heal (*Prunella vulgaris* L.) was held by some Indians to be a cure for most ailments; Crimson Clover (*Trifolium incarnatum* L.) was so named because of its brilliant crimson-red flowers. The common name of a plant may be limited to a particular locality or it may be a name well known throughout North America. A common name of a plant in one area of the country may not be the same for that species in some other area. A plant thus may have many different common names. For example, one species of *Trillium* has at least eighteen common names. Furthermore, different species may share a common name. For example, members of the genus *Ranunculus* are commonly called buttercups, and some members of the genus *Oenothera* are called buttercups as well.

## How to Use This Book

The plants presented in "Plates and Descriptions" are divided into two major groups, or classes—the Liliopsida (monocots) and the Magnoliopsida (dicots). The monocots and dicots differ by a number of characteristics, but most can be correctly categorized by using only two of the characteristics—the number of flower parts and the type of leaf venation. Monocots have flower parts in threes or multiples of three and have leaves with parallel veins. Dicots have flower parts in twos, fours, or fives or multiples of these numbers and have leaves with net venation. (These characteristics are not always consistent within the two groups, but they will be for nearly all the species found in Mississippi.)

The plants in this book are arranged alphabetically by the scientific family name, genus, and species within each class. Brief family descriptions follow the scientific and common family names, and these include information on growth habit, leaf arrangement, flower structure, and fruit type.

DE Delta
NE Northeast
EC East Central
SW Southwest
SE Southeast
CO Coast

Map 1 Distribution Map for Species

This book will assist the user in identifying 520 species of Mississippi's wildflowers and provide a reference to nearly 100 additional species. It is designed to enable identification through color photographs and brief species descriptions. Each photograph is accompanied by the scientific name for the species, the common name or names, and a brief description. The plant descriptions are consistently organized for quick reference and comparisons. A number of important closely related species are mentioned in some of the descriptions.

The geographic distributions given are broad because information on all the counties is incomplete for the species presented. The state has been divided into six areas to facilitate identifying species' distributions (see Map 1.). The areas given in the descriptions are those in which the species are commonly found. However, plants do not adhere to boundaries; therefore, a species may be found in an area not indicated in the description.

An attempt has been made to keep the amateur botanist from being overwhelmed with botanical terminology. Scientific terms are generally used to avoid a lengthy description of a particular characteristic. However, a working knowledge of

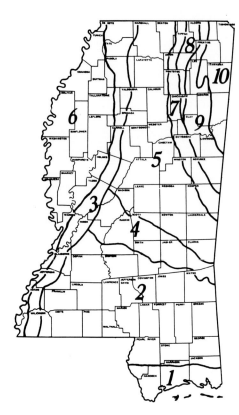

1. Coastal
2. Pine Hills
3. Loess Hills
4. Jackson Prairies
5. North Central Plains
6. Mississippi Alluvial Plain
7. Flatwoods
8. Pontotoc Hills
9. Black Prairie
10. Fall Line Hills

Map 2 Physiographic Regions of Mississippi

some botanical terms will be helpful in studying and understanding plants. For this reason an extensive glossary and numerous line drawings of vegetative and floral characteristics have been included following the "Plates and Descriptions" section.

Few tools are needed for identifying plants. The most useful tools for field identifications are a hand magnifying lens for observing minute plant parts and a small ruler for measuring structures. Becoming familiar with plant characteristics will quickly make recognition of characters easier. Successful, confident identifications are made possible by understanding and continually studying plants.

This book is not a complete guide to the flora of Mississippi, but it can be the starting point for a better understanding of the native plants in the state. References to other field guides for areas surrounding Mississippi and selected technical manuals can be found in the back of this book. The index serves both as an index and a checklist, providing the user a means for keeping track of species seen and identified.

## Physiographic Regions of Mississippi

The natural vegetation found in an area is a result of topography and soils, which are influenced by geological structure and climate. Rainfall amount and distribution, temperature, humidity, and soil composition play an important role in where plants grow. Plants have adapted to certain areas because of the interaction of physical factors. Most important are the amount of water held in the soil, the types and quantity of soil nutrients, slope and aspect of an area, day/night temperature fluctuations, and atmospheric humidity.

The topography of Mississippi is quite diverse, ranging from only a few feet above sea level along the Gulf of Mexico to an elevation of 805 feet at Woodall Mountain in Tishomingo County. In Lowe's *Plants of Mississippi*, the combination of soil characteristics, topography, and vegetation was used to divide Mississippi into nine regions and one subregion. The state's ten physiographic regions (see Map 2) are variously divided and named, according to geological formations, topography, and soils; they all fall within the larger Gulf Coastal Plain Province.

Following are the ten provinces and their soil and vegetative characteristics. The plants listed represent only common or characteristic species for each province.

COASTAL   The Coastal province includes the barrier islands and coastal counties, which are characterized by beaches, dunes, marshes, and savannas. Plants typical of the beaches include numerous species of grasses and sedges, sea-rocket, and beach morning glory. The dunes are typified by such plants as bush goldenrod, rosemary, yaupon, saw palmetto, dune greenbrier, sea oats, slash pine, wax myrtle, scarlet oak, and sand live oak. The marshes are characterized largely by marsh pinks, sea-rocket, seaside goldenrod, sea ox-eye, and species of grasses and sedges. Plants typical of savannas include pitcher plants, sundews, southern magnolia, sweet bay, the yellow-eyed grasses (not true grasses), pipeworts, meadow beauties, St. John's-worts, candy roots, longleaf pine, and numerous species of oaks.

PINE HILLS   The Pine Hills province lies adjacent to the Coastal and is flat to hilly. In the drier areas, loblolly and longleaf pine, southern magnolia, sourwood, sweetleaf, oaks, candy roots, meadow beauties, St. John's-worts, and asters are typical. Gallberry, yaupon, tupelos, titis, rhododendrons, saw palmetto, and mallows are characteristic of wetter sites.

LOESS HILLS   The Loess Hills province consists of a relatively narrow strip bordering the eastern edge of the Mississippi Alluvial Plain. The soil in this region consists of wind-deposited, nonstratified, calcareous silt. The woody vegetation is quite diverse, with magnolias, oaks, hickories, elms, hackberry, beech, tupelos, ash, baldcypress, tulip poplar, Cherokee rose, witch hazel, spicebush, hydrangea, wild grapes, dogwood, and hawthorns common to the area. Characteristic herbs include jack-in-the-pulpit, Indian pink, wild petunia, May apple, goldenrods, asters, beggar's ticks, bedstraw, seedbox, cardinal flower, bellworts, milkweeds, asters, and sunflowers.

JACKSON PRAIRIES    The Jackson Prairies province is distinguished by rolling to hilly topography with soils consisting of sand, loam, or clay. Small prairie remnants, with typical prairie flora, are scattered throughout the area. Plants commonly found in this region are sumac, longleaf and shortleaf pine, oaks, penstemons, indigo, compass plant, rosin weed, Illinois bundle flower, asters, goldenrods, black-eyed Susan, milkweeds, and sunflowers.

NORTH CENTRAL PLAINS    The topography of the North Central Plains is mostly hilly with some ridges. The soils consist of clays, sands, and silt loam. Loblolly and shortleaf pine represent the main tree growth of the upland areas of this province. Other common woody plants include elms, wild plum, sassafras, persimmon, dogwood, hickories, oaks, hydrangea, witch hazel, wild grapes, and sumac. Among the herbaceous plants common to the North Central Plains are bluets, buttercups, anemone, milkweeds, morning glories, pussy toes, wild petunia, bedstraw, asters, and sunflowers.

In the lowland areas, oaks, elms, maples, sycamore, baldcypress, river birch, button bush, pawpaw, bladder nut, strawberry bush, Japanese honeysuckle, and hazel alder are among the common woody plants. Common herbaceous plants are phlox, trilliums, bellworts, jack-in-the-pulpit, fringed orchids, Indian cucumber root, bonesets, mallow, meadow beauties, rattlebox, buttercups, and asters.

MISSISSIPPI ALLUVIAL PLAIN    The Mississippi Alluvial Plain lies between the Mississippi River and the Loess Hills region and is characterized by a relatively flat topography. Swamps also characterize the area. The soil is mostly clay, except along streams, where it consists of sandy loam. These soils (termed alluvium) were deposited by the Mississippi River. In this province, hardwoods are predominant. Pines characterize only some areas of secondary growth (areas once forested, then cleared, and now abandoned). Oaks, cucumber tree, southern magnolia, ashes, gums, baldcypress, hickories, maples, cottonwood, and sweet gum are among the more common woody plants. Common herbaceous plants include bedstraw, smartweeds, rattlebox, cardinal flower, clearweed, false nettle, Spanish moss, lizard's tail, asters, and sunflowers.

FLATWOODS  Topography in the Flatwoods province is flat to slightly hilly, with soils of clay and some sand. Many plants found in the Flatwoods are the same species as those of the North Central Plains. Some of the common woody plants are loblolly and shortleaf pine, oaks, hawthorns, wild plums, wild cherries, sumac, hydrangea, hickories, dogwood, sassafras, and New Jersey tea. Herbaceous plants common to this province are trilliums, phlox, buttercups, jack-in-the-pulpit, ladies' tresses, squaw weed, asters, bonesets, and sunflowers.

PONTOTOC HILLS  The topography of Pontotoc Hills consists of hills and ridges with sandy loam soils. The province is predominantly characterized by a pine/oak mixture. Shortleaf and loblolly pine are mixed with such oaks as post, black, southern red, red, chestnut, chinquapin, and white. Other commonly found woody plants are beech, maples, sweet gum, walnut, tulip poplar, greenbriers, buckeye, and hydrangea. Some common herbaceous plants include wild geraniums, fire pink, Jacob's ladder, spring beauties, trilliums, dwarf iris, toothwort, saxifrage, asters, and sunflowers.

BLACK PRAIRIE  The Black Prairie province has a gently rolling topography with mostly calcareous, loamy clay soils. Chalk cedar glades are prevalent in the southern portion, where eastern red cedar is the dominant woody vegetation. Some common showy plants of the open prairies are coreopsis, compass plant, rosin weed, butterfly weed, black-eyed Susan, blue-eyed grass, green-flowered milkweed, purple prairie clover, and blazing stars.

Oaks, shortleaf pine, sand plum, wild roses, sassafras, sumac, persimmon, Samson's snakeroot, New Jersey tea, goat's rue, spiderwort, and Indian pink are some of the common plants found in higher areas scattered throughout the prairies. Along stream bottoms, white oak, black oak, water oak, pawpaw, buckeye, ash-leaf maple, sugar maple, tulip poplar, phlox, violets, clematis, and coral honeysuckle represent a few of the common plants.

FALL LINE HILLS  In the northeastern counties of Fall Line Hills, the topography is characterized by outcrops of limestone, sandstone, and shale. Moving south, the topography becomes hilly. The soil of this province consists mostly of sand and clay loam. This area represents a transition zone between the Appalachian Mountains and the Gulf Coastal Plain, and it contains habitats that harbor some northern and southern species. Some of the common plants of the upper slopes and ridge tops are chestnut oak, red oak, chinquapin oak, scrub pine, wild blueberries, rhododendrons, cedar, yellow-eyed grass, bird's-foot violet, fire pink, larkspur, pucoon, hawkweed, bonesets, and asters.

The lower slopes and ravines are characterized by cucumber tree, tulip poplar, shortleaf pine, liverleaf, wild ginger, trilliums, dwarf iris, violets, Jacob's ladder, wild geraniums, alum root, stonecrop, Virginia saxifrage, and asters. The larger river bottoms contain white oak, water oak, willow oak, sycamore, beech, black gum, sweet gum, baldcypress, hackberry, ash, redbud, pawpaw, goldenrods, and asters.

# Wildflowers of Mississippi

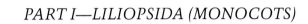

*PART I—LILIOPSIDA (MONOCOTS)*

# AGAVACEAE [= AMARYLLIDACEAE]
Agave Family

Plants perennial, often with a stem that becomes woody. Leaves alternate, generally linear to elliptic; margins entire or fraying to filaments. Sepals and petals similar, white to greenish white, united, in some only at the base; flowers tubular or bell shaped; six stamens; ovary superior in *Yucca* and inferior in *Agave.* Fruit a capsule.

## *Agave virginica* L.
### Agave, American Aloe, False Aloe, Rattlesnake-Master

Plants: Upright, glabrous perennial from thick, fleshy roots.
Leaves: Basal and alternate on the stem; basal leaves succulent, lanceolate, entire, acute to acuminate; stem leaves reduced upward, clasping.
Inflorescence: Spike or raceme; calyx and corolla united, greenish to purplish; stamens long, exerted, and conspicuous.
Fruit: Capsule.
Flowering Date: April–August.
Habitats: Rocky areas of woodland edges, dry roadsides.
Distribution: NE, EC.
Comments: The flowers are very fragrant.

## *Yucca flaccida* Haw.
### Ear-Grass, Yucca, Spanish Bayonets, Adam's Needle

Plants: Upright, glabrous perennial from a rhizome.
Leaves: Mostly basal, linear, entire, reduced upward.
Inflorescence: Terminal panicle or raceme; perianth white to yellowish white, with perianth segments less than 5 mm long and each having a single green gland (gland occasionally absent).
Fruit: Capsule.
Flowering Date: April–June.
Habitats: Savannas, pinelands.
Distribution: CO.

## ALISMATACEAE
Water-Plantain Family

Plants perennial. Leaves alternate, linear to spatulate, mostly basal, with netted venation and petioles sheathing the stem; margins entire. Three petals, white; ovary superior. Fruit an aggregrate of achenes.

### *Sagittaria latifolia* Willd.
**Arrowhead, Duck-Potato, Wapato**

Plants: Upright, glabrous or hairy, marsh or aquatic perennial with stolons and producing tubers.

Leaves: Basal, ovate or occasionally linear, petiolate, with base usually sagittate.

Inflorescence: Raceme, with flowers in whorls of three per node; imperfect, female flowers below, male flowers above; three sepals; three petals, white.

Fruit: Achene.

Flowering Date: June–September.

Habitats: Swamps, ditches, marshes, ponds, lakes.

Distribution: Throughout.

Comments: The tubers are edible after cooking for a half hour. *S. graminea* is similar but has linear to lanceolate leaves.

# ARACEAE
## Arum Family

Plants perennial from rhizomes or corms. Leaves simple or compound; petioles long, sheathing the stem. Inflorescence a spadix, with or without a spathe; ovary superior. Fruit a berry.

*Arisaema triphyllum* (L.)
Schott
**Jack-in-the- Pulpit, Indian Turnip,
Lords and Ladies, Wild Turnip,
Devil's Ear, Wild Pepper,
Dragon Turnip, Priest's Pintle**

Plants: Upright, glabrous perennial from corms.
Leaves: One or two, divided into five leaflets or segments, petiolate.
Inflorescence: Cylindrical with spadix to green-and-purple-striped spathe that spreads at the top; flowers imperfect, with female flowers below, male flowers above; sepals and petals absent.
Fruit: Red berries in sphere-shaped to slightly elongated clusters.
Flowering Date: March–April.
Habitats: Hardwoods, floodplains.
Distribution: DE, NE, EC, SW, SE.

*Arisaema dracontium* (L.)
Schott
**Green Dragon, Dragon Root**

Plants: Upright, glabrous perennial from corms.
Leaves: Solitary, palmately lobed with seven to fifteen leaflets or segments, petiolate.
Inflorescence: Cylindrical with spadix enclosed in a light green, tubular spathe tapering to a point; flowers imperfect, with female flowers below, male flowers above; sepals and petals absent; two to five stamens.
Fruit: Red berries in sphere-shaped to slightly elongated clusters.
Flowering Date: March–April.
Habitats: Hardwoods, floodplains.
Distribution: DE, NE, EC, SW, SE.
Comments: The entire plant contains crystals of calcium oxalate, which produces a burning sensation if eaten. The crystals will dissipate after long exposure to heat. The starchy corms, after drying, may be ground and used as a flour.

*Peltandra sagittifolia* (Michx.)
Morong
**Arrow Arum, White Arum, Spoon
Flower**

Plants: Upright, glabrous perennial
from a short rootstock.
Leaves: Basal, sagittate or hastate with
three main nerves or veins; petiolate.
Inflorescence: Spadix surrounded by a
white spathe that spreads at the top;
flowers imperfect, with female flowers below, male flowers above; sepals
and petals absent.
Fruit: Red berry.
Flowering Date: April–June.
Habitats: Pineland bogs.
Distribution: CO.
Comments: *P. virginica* has a green or
greenish white spathe and a green to
blackish berry.

*Orontium aquaticum* L.
**Golden Club, Golden Torch**

Plants: Upright, glabrous, aquatic perennial; in clumps from a rhizome.
Leaves: Basal, ovate to elliptic, entire,
acute to obtuse, petiolate, with base
cuneate.
Inflorescence: Cylindrical with spadix
that's yellow above, white below;
spathe basal, not noticeable; flowers
perfect, regular.
Fruit: Berry.
Flowering Date: March–November.
Habitats: Bogs, streams.
Distribution: CO, NE, EC, SE.

# COMMELINACEAE
## Spiderwort Family

Plants annual or perennial. Leaves alternate; margins entire. Flowers of three petals, with one sometimes much reduced; blue or white; ovary superior. Fruit a capsule.

### *Commelina communis* L.
### Day Flower

Plants: Upright to prostrate, mostly glabrous annual, rooting at the nodes or stems.

Leaves: Alternate, entire, ovate, with basal portion sheathing stem.

Inflorescence: Flowers in terminal clusters subtended by a spathe; irregular, perfect; three sepals; three petals, with two blue and one smaller and white.

Fruit: Capsule.

Flowering Date: April–November.

Habitats: Woods, waste areas, yards, pinelands, roadsides.

Distribution: Throughout.

Comments: *C. virginica* is similar but is hairy and has lanceolate leaves.

### *Tradescantia ohiensis* Raf.
### Spiderwort

Plants: Upright, glabrous to hairy perennial.

Leaves: Alternate, linear to lanceolate, entire, sheathing at the base.

Inflorescence: Flowers regular, perfect, in a terminal cluster subtended by bracts that are similar to the stem leaves; three sepals, glabrous or hairy at the margins; three petals, blue, purple, rose, or pink; six stamens.

Fruit: Capsule.

Flowering Date: April–August.

Habitats: Woods, prairies, waste areas, roadsides.

Distribution: Throughout.

Comments: *T. virginiana* has densely hairy sepals.

# ERIOCAULACEAE
## Pipewort Family

Plants perennial. Leaves in basal rosettes. Inflorescence a solitary head; flowers white to grayish and minute; two or three sepals and petals that are similar; ovary superior; two to six stamens. Fruit a two- or three-seeded capsule.

### *Eriocaulon decangulare* L.
**Pipewort, Hard Heads**

Plants: Upright, glabrous, monoecious perennial.
Leaves: Basal rosette, linear, entire.
Inflorescence: Solitary, with very hard head; scape twisted or ribbed; sepals and petals similar, white or grayish white; female flower petals smooth.
Fruit: Capsule.
Flowering Date: May–November.
Habitats: Bogs, savannas, pinelands, ditches.
Distribution: CO.
Comments: *E. compressum* is similar but has a softer head and hairy female flower petals.

# HAEMODORACEAE
## Redroot Family

Plants perennial from rhizomes. Leaves mostly basal, linear. Sepals and petals similar, yellowish; ovary inferior or nearly so; three stamens in *Lachnanthes* and six in *Lophiola*. Fruit a capsule enclosed by the perianth.

### *Lachnanthes caroliniana* (Lam.) Dandy
**Redroot**

Plants: Upright, hairy perennial from rhizomes.

Leaves: Mostly basal, linear with overlapping bases, entire; stem leaves clasping and becoming reduced upward.

Inflorescence: Flowers terminal, perfect, regular, hairy, with three sepals and three petals that are similar and yellowish to brownish; three stamens.

Fruit: Capsule.

Flowering Date: June–October.

Habitats: Bogs, ditches, pinelands, savannas.

Distribution: CO.

### *Lophiola americana* (Pursh) Wood
**Gold-Crest**

Plants: Upright, hairy perennial from rhizomes.

Leaves: Mostly basal, linear with overlapping bases, entire; stem leaves clasping and becoming reduced upward.

Inflorescence: Flowers terminal, perfect, regular, hairy, with three sepals and three petals that are similar and bright yellow; six stamens.

Fruit: Capsule.

Flowering Date: June–September.

Habitats: Bogs, ditches, pinelands, savannas.

Distribution: CO.

# IRIDACEAE
Iris Family

Plants annual or perennial. Leaves alternate, linear. Sepals and petals usually similar, but sometimes different in color; ovary inferior; three stamens. Fruit a capsule.

## *Belamcanda chinensis* (L.) DC.
### Blackberry Lily

Plants: Upright, glabrous perennial from a rhizome.
Leaves: Alternate, linear, entire, clasping.
Inflorescence: Terminal panicle or clusters; flowers regular, perfect, orange spotted with red.
Fruit: Capsule.
Flowering Date: June–August.
Habitats: Woods, thickets, roadsides, pastures.
Distribution: NE, EC.
Comments: Introduced from Asia.

## *Iris cristata* Ait.
### Crested Iris

Plants: Upright, glabrous perennial from beadlike rhizomes.
Leaves: Alternate, linear, entire.
Inflorescence: Flowers terminal, subtended by leaflike bracts, regular, perfect; petals violet to bluish white; sepals crested, violet to bluish white, with the basal portion having a yellowish band bordered by white, which is bordered by purple.
Fruit: Capsule.
Flowering Date: April–May.
Habitats: Wooded areas along streams, wooded slopes.
Distribution: NE, SW, SE.
Comments: This species can be grown easily in shaded rock gardens.

## *Iris fulva* Ker
### Copper Iris, Red Iris

Plants: Upright, glabrous perennial
  from rhizomes.
Leaves: Alternate and basal, linear, entire.
Inflorescence: Flowers terminal, subtended by leaflike bracts, regular,
  perfect; copper, red, or orange petals
  often drooping; sepals often spreading.
Fruit: Capsule.
Flowering Date: March–May.
Habitats: Marshes, stream banks, wet
  ditches, swamps.
Distribution: DE.

## *Iris verna* L.
### Dwarf Iris

Plants: Upright, glabrous perennial
  from rhizomes.
Leaves: Alternate, linear, entire.
Inflorescence: Flowers terminal, subtended by leaflike bracts, regular,
  perfect, violet to bluish white; sepals
  not crested, with yellowish band bordered by white, which is bordered by
  purple.
Fruit: Capsule.
Flowering Date: April–May.
Habitats: Rocky woods.
Distribution: NE, EC.
Comments: This species can be transplanted easily.

## *Iris virginica* L.
### Blue Flag

Plants: Upright, glabrous perennial
  from rhizomes.
Leaves: Alternate, mostly basal, entire.
Inflorescence: Flowers terminal, subtended by leaflike bracts, regular,
  perfect; violet, lavender, or white
  with dark veins; petals shorter than
  sepals, which have a yellow patch toward the base.
Fruit: Capsule.
Flowering Date: March–May.
Habitats: Marshes, swamps, wet
  ditches, wet pastures.
Distribution: DE, NE, EC.
Comments: *I. brevicaulis* (Zigzag or
  Short-stemmed Iris) has a stem that
  zigzags, and the flowers in the lower
  part appear to be hidden among the
  leaves. Both species can be easily
  transplanted.

## *Nemastylis geminiflora* Nutt.
**Celestrial Lily**

Plants: Upright, glabrous perennial from a bulb; produces new bulbs below the old bulbs.

Leaves: Alternate, linear, entire, somewhat folded.

Inflorescence: Flowers terminal, subtended by leaflike bracts, regular, perfect, light blue with a white base; open in the morning and wilt by early afternoon.

Fruit: Capsule.

Flowering Date: March–May.

Habitats: Prairies, rocky woods, grassy areas, pinelands.

Distribution: EC.

## *Sisyrinchium angustifolium* Mill.
**Blue-Eyed Grass**

Plants: Upright, glabrous perennial with fibrous roots.

Leaves: Alternate and basal, linear, entire.

Inflorescence: Flowers terminal; flowering stem branched, each with two to five spathes; flowers on peduncles, regular, perfect, blue to violet or occasionally white with a yellow center.

Fruit: Capsule.

Flowering Date: March–June.

Habitats: Prairies, woods and woodland edges, roadsides.

Distribution: EC, SW, SE.

Comments: This is a very difficult genus for determining some species. Some taxonomists recognize numerous species while others tend to conserve the number and develop varieties. A yellow-flowered species, if indeed it is a good species, found along the coast is *S. exile*. Several other species are found in the state.

## *Trifurcia lahue* ssp. *caerulea* (Herb.) Goldbl.
**Herbertia**

Plants: Upright, glabrous perennial from a bulb.

Leaves: Alternate and basal, linear, entire, and sheathing the bulb.

Inflorescence: Flowers terminal and solitary, regular, perfect; sepals pale to dark violet and whitish at the base with purple spots and much larger than the three purple inner petals.

Fruit: Capsule.

Flowering Date: April–May.

Habitats: Grassy areas and prairies.

Distribution: Known from the Vicksburg and Picayune area.

# LILIACEAE
## Lily Family

Plants perennial from bulbs or rhizomes. Leaves alternate, whorled, or basal. Sepals and petals usually similar, with segments united or separate; ovary superior or nearly so; six stamens. Fruit a capsule or berry.

### *Aletris farinosa* L.
**Colic Root, Star Grass**

Plants: Upright, glabrous perennial from a rhizome.
Leaves: Mostly basal, lanceolate to oblanceolate, acute, entire; stem leaves reduced upward.
Inflorescence: Raceme; flowers tubular to bell shaped and constricted just below the apex; calyx and corolla united, white.
Fruit: Capsule.
Flowering Date: April–July.
Habitats: Pinelands, savannas, open woods, bogs.
Distribution: CO, EC.

### *Aletris lutea* Small
**Colic Root, Star Grass**

Plants: Upright, glabrous perennial from a rhizome.
Leaves: Mostly basal, lanceolate to oblanceolate, acute, entire; stem leaves reduced upward.
Inflorescence: Raceme; flowers tubular to bell shaped and slightly constricted just below the apex; calyx and corolla united, yellow.
Fruit: Capsule.
Flowering Date: June–July.
Habitats: Savannas, pinelands, roadsides, bogs.
Distribution: CO.
Comments: *A. aurea* Walt. has flowers that appear closed because the perianth lobes are folded inward.

## *Amianthium muscaetoxicum* (Walt.) Gray
**Fly Poison**

Plants: Upright, glabrous perennial from a bulb.

Leaves: Mostly basal, linear; apexes obtuse to notched; stem leaves reduced upward.

Inflorescence: Raceme; pedicels with bracts; flowers white to greenish white.

Fruit: Capsule.

Flowering Date: May–July.

Habitats: Wooded slopes, open grassy areas, dry upland woods, savannas.

Distribution: CO, NE, EC.

Comments: The entire plant is poisonous.

## *Allium canadense* L.
**Wild Onion**

Plants: Upright, glabrous perennial from a bulb that has a fibrous covering, aromatic.

Leaves: Basal, linear, flat, entire, sheathing at the base.

Inflorescence: Terminal umbel subtended by membranous spathes; flowers often mixed with bulblets, rotate or bell shaped, white or pink.

Fruit: Capsule.

Flowering Date: March–June.

Habitats: Roadsides, yards, prairies, woodlands, fields.

Distribution: DE, NE, EC, SW, SE.

## *Camassia scilloides* (Raf.) Cory
### Wild Hyacinth

Plants: Upright, glabrous perennial from a bulb.
Leaves: Basal, linear, entire, acute, with one or two reduced leaves on the stalk.
Inflorescence: Raceme; pedicels with bracts; flowers deep blue to bluish white.
Fruit: Capsule.
Flowering Date: April–May.
Habitats: Prairies, roadsides, open woods.
Distribution: EC.

## *Chamaelirium luteum* (L.) Gray
### Fairy Wand, Blazing Star, Devil's Bit

Plants: Upright, glabrous perennial from a rhizome; dioecious.
Leaves: Basal rosette, evergreen, elliptic to oblanceolate, entire, obtuse, with the base attenuate.
Inflorescence: Spike or raceme; flowers imperfect, white.
Fruit: Capsule.
Flowering Date: March–May.
Habitats: Moist or dry woods, roadsides adjacent to woods.
Distribution: EC, SE.

## *Crinum americanum* L.
### Swamp Lily, String Lily

Plants: Upright, glabrous perennial from a bulb.
Leaves: Mostly basal, linear, entire, becoming reduced upward.
Inflorescence: Umbel subtended by a spathe; flowers white.
Fruit: Capsule.
Flowering Date: March–November.
Habitats: Marshes, swamps.
Distribution: CO.

### *Erythronium albidum* Nutt.
### Trout Lily, Fawn Lily, Dogtooth Violet

Plants: Upright, glabrous perennial from a bulb.

Leaves: Two, basal, dark green mottled with purple, elliptic or oblong to lanceolate, entire, somewhat fleshy.

Inflorescence: Flowers terminal, solitary, often nodding, white; sepals and petals often reflexed.

Fruit: Capsule.

Flowering Date: February–April.

Habitats: Wooded, rocky slopes and ravines.

Distribution: EC.

Comments: The leaves can be cooked as a vegetable, and the bulbs can be eaten raw or cooked. The bulbs have also been reported to cause vomiting.

### *Hemerocallis fulva* (L.) L.
### Day Lily, Orange Day Lily

Plants: Upright, glabrous perennial from thick, fleshy roots with tuberous swellings.

Leaves: Mostly basal, linear, reduced upward, entire.

Inflorescence: Flowers terminal, solitary, orange, broadly bell shaped.

Fruit: Capsule.

Flowering Date: May–July.

Habitat: Roadsides.

Distribution: NE, EC.

Comments: Escaped cultivation. The buds or flowers can be cooked as a fritter or added to soups. The fleshy roots can be boiled and eaten and the young roots can be eaten raw, especially in salads.

## *Hypoxis hirsuta* (L.) Coville
**Yellow Star Grass**

Plants: Upright, hairy perennial from a corm.
Leaves: Basal, linear, entire.
Inflorescence: Flowers terminal, solitary or clustered, subtended by two to several linear or pointed bracts, yellow.
Fruit: Capsule with black seeds.
Flowering Date: March–May.
Habitats: Rocky dry areas, prairies, pinelands, grassy roadsides.
Distribution: CO, NE, EC, SW, SE.
Comments: *H. micrantha* has brown seeds.

## *Hymenocallis occidentalis* (Le Conte) Kunth
**Spider Lily**

Plants: Upright, glabrous perennial from a bulb.
Leaves: Basal, linear, entire, present at flowering.
Inflorescence: Umbel; usually three to seven flowers per umbel; sepals and petals united below and flaring upward to form a cuplike corona, white.
Fruit: Capsule.
Flowering Date: April–June.
Habitats: Moist woods, wet roadsides.
Distribution: DE, NE, EC.
Comments: *H. eulae.* lacks leaves at flowering time.

## *Lilium catesbaei* Walt.
**Pine Lily, Southern Pine Lily**

Plants: Upright, glabrous perennial from a bulb.
Leaves: Alternate, linear to elliptic, acute or obtuse, entire.
Inflorescence: Flowers terminal, solitary; perianth parts well parted to the base, have reflexed tips, orange to red-orange, and spotted toward the base.
Fruit: Capsule.
Flowering Date: August–September.
Habitats: Savannas, pinelands, bogs, wet roadside ditches.
Distribution: CO.

*Medeola virginiana* L.
**Indian Cucumber Root**

Plants: Upright, glabrous perennial
from a rhizome.
Leaves: In whorls of three to eleven per
node; the lower whorl has leaves that
are oblong to elliptic, with bases attenuate or sessile; the upper whorl
usually has three to four leaves that
are elliptic to ovate, acuminate or
acute, with bases rounded to cuneate.
Inflorescence: Flowers terminal, somewhat nodding and usually below the
upper whorl of leaves, yeallowish to
greenish; stamens purple.
Fruit: Berry; fruit stalks becoming
erect.
Flowering Date: April–June.
Habitats: Moist, rocky, wooded slopes
and along streams.
Distribution: NE.
Comments: The succulent rhizome
may be eaten raw, taste resembling
that of a cucumber.

*Lilium superbum* L.
**Turk's Cap Lily**

Plants: Upright, glabrous perennial
from a bulb.
Leaves: In whorls of five to twenty per
node, lanceolate to elliptic, entire.
Inflorescence: Terminal panicle of one
to twenty-five flowers; perianth parts
separate to base, orange to reddish
orange, spotted toward the base,
strongly reflexed; stamens less than
5.5 cm long.
Fruit: Capsule.
Flowering Date: July–August.
Habitats: Moist or wet shaded areas.
Distribution: NE, EC.
Comments: *L. michauxii.* (Carolina
Lily) usually has one to six flowers
per inflorescence and oblanceolate,
obovate, or spatulate leaves, with
four to fifteen leaves per node. Stamens are longer than 5.5 cm.

## *Melanthium virginicum* L.
### Bunchflower

Plants: Upright, glabrous to hairy perennial from a bulb.

Leaves: Alternate, overlapping, linear, entire, clasping.

Inflorescence: Paniclelike; flowers cream turning greenish to purplish with age; perianth segments clawed.

Fruit: Capsule.

Flowering Date: June–August.

Habitats: Savannas, bogs, woodland margins.

Distribution: CO, EC.

## *Nothoscordum bivalve* (L.) Britt. [ = *Allium bivalve* (L.) Ktze.]
### False Wild Garlic

Plants: Upright, glabrous perennial from a bulb encompassed with a membranous covering; not aromatic.

Leaves: Basal, linear, round to flat, entire.

Inflorescence: Umbel subtended by a spathe; flowers yellowish white or white with greenish or purplish midrib, bell-shaped.

Fruit: Capsule.

Flowering Date: February–May; October.

Habitats: Prairies, roadsides, yards, pinelands, savannas.

Distribution: Throughout.

## *Polygonatum biflorum* (Walt.) Ell.

### Solomon's Seal, Sealwort, Conquer-John, Lady's Seal, St. Mary's Seal, Drop-Berry

Plants: Upright, glabrous perennial from a rhizome.

Leaves: Alternate, lanceolate to ovate, entire.

Inflorescence: Axillary, with one to nine flowers per leaf axil; flowers nodding, greenish white or yellowish white to white, cylindrical to slightly bell-shaped; calyx and corolla fused.

Fruit: Berry.

Flowering Date: April–June.

Habitat: Woodlands.

Distribution: NE, EC.

Comments: The root has been used medicinally for centuries to lighten the skin, to lessen menstrual irregularities and cramps, and to help bruises heal. It has also been used for stomach and bowel problems.


## *Smilacina racemosa* (L.) Desf.

### False Solomon's Seal, False Lily of the Valley, Scurvy Berries, Zigzag Solomon's Seal

Plants: Upright, glabrous to slightly hairy perennial from a rhizome.

Leaves: Alternate, elliptic to lanceolate, entire, acute or acuminate, with base cuneate or rounded.

Inflorescence: Terminal panicle; flowers white or greenish; stamens petal-like.

Fruit: Berry.

Flowering Date: April–June.

Habitats: Wooded slopes, low woods.

Distribution: NE, EC.

Comments: The young shoots can be cooked and eaten, tasting similar to asparagus. The berries are edible but somewhat bitter tasting. The rhizome has been used medicinally as a poultice and for making a tea to regulate menstrual disorders.

*Trillium cuneatum* Raf.
**Little Sweet Betsy**

Plants: Uright, glabrous perennial from a rhizome.

Leaves: In one whorl of three, lanceolate to ovate to widely elliptic, acuminate, mostly sessile, green mottled with a lighter green and purplish spots.

Inflorescence: Flowers terminal; sepals horizontally spreading or erect; petals erect, maroon, occasionally light yellow.

Fruit: Berry.

Flowering Date: March–April.

Habitats: Wooded slopes, floodplains, along streams.

Distribution: DE, NE, EC, SW, SE.

Comments: The rhizomes of *Trillium* were once used by the American Indians to help stop the bleeding during childbirth. When powdered and made into a "milk," it has been used for diarrhea. The leaves when boiled have been used as a poultice.

*Stenanthium gramineum* (Ker) Morong
**Featherbells**

Plants: Upright, glabrous perennial from a bulb.

Leaves: Basal and alternate on the stem, linear, entire, clasping.

Inflorescence: Paniclelike; flowers white to yellowish white; perianth segments free nearly to base.

Fruit: Capsule.

Flowering Date: July–September.

Habitats: Edges of woods, open woods, open areas.

Distribution: CO, NE, EC, SW, SE.

*Tofieldia racemosa* (Walt.) B.S.P.
**False Asphodel**

Plants: Upright, slightly hairy perennial from a rhizome.

Leaves: Mostly basal, overlapping, becoming reduced upward, linear, entire.

Inflorescence: Racemelike; flowers white to greenish white; anthers red to black and conspicuous.

Fruit: Capsule.

Flowering Date: June–September.

Habitats: Savannas, pinewoods.

Distribution: CO.

## *Trillium flexipes* Raf.
### Bent Trillium, White Wake Robin, White Trillium

Plants: Upright, glabrous perennial from a rhizome.

Leaves: In one whorl of three, ovate to nearly diamond shaped, nearly as broad as long, sessile, acute to slightly acuminate, light green.

Inflorescence: Flowers terminal, with one borne on a single elongated stalk, usually nodding or slightly so; sepals lanceolate; petals reflexed or spreading with tips reflexed, white.

Fruit: Berry.

Flowering Date: April–May.

Habitat: Wooded rocky slopes.

Distribution: Known only from Tishomingo County.

## *Trillium recurvatum* Beck
### Recurved-Sepal Trillium, Purple Trillium

Plants: Upright, glabrous perennial from a rhizome.

Leaves: In a whorl of three, elliptic to ovate, acuminate, sessile, mottled with dark shades of green and purple.

Inflorescence: Flowers terminal, solitary; sepals reflexed; petals erect, mostly maroon.

Fruit: Berry.

Flowering Date: March–April.

Habitats: Wooded slopes, ravine bottoms.

Distribution: NE.

Comments: Same as for *T. cuneatum* Raf.

## *Trillium stamineum* Harb.
### Twisted Trillium

Plants: Upright, glabrous perennial
   from a rhizome.
Leaves: In a whorl of three, ovate to
   lanceolate, acuminate, sessile,
   lightly mottled.
Inflorescence: Flowers terminal, solitary; sepals horizontally spreading;
   petals maroon, twisted, and horizontally spreading.
Fruit: Berry.
Flowering Date: March–April.
Habitats: Wooded slopes, ravine bottoms.
Distribution: NE, EC.
Comments: Same as for *T. cuneatum*.

## *Uvularia grandiflora* Sm.
### Bellwort

Plants: Upright, glabrous perennial
   from a rhizome; often several stalks
   per rhizome.
Leaves: Alternate, perfoliate, entire, elliptic to ovate.
Inflorescence: Flowers axillary or appearing alternate a leaf, nodding; perianth segments separate to base, yellow.
Fruit: Capsule.
Flowering Date: April–May.
Habitat: Wooded slopes.
Distribution: NE, EC.

## *Uvularia perfoliata* L.
### Small Bellwort

Plants: Upright, glabrous perennial
   from a rhizome.
Leaves: Alternate, perfoliate, entire, elliptic.
Inflorescence: Flowers terminal, solitary, and subtended by a large, perfoliate bract; perianth segments separate to the base, yellow to cream.
Fruit: Capsule.
Flowering Date: April–May.
Habitats: Wooded slopes, woods, ravine
   bottoms.
Distribution: NE, EC.
Related Species: *U. sessilifolia* is similar but does not have perfoliate
   leaves.

### *Zephyranthes atamasco* (L.) Herb.
**Atamasco Lily, Easter Lily**

Plants: Upright, glabrous perennial from a bulb.
Leaves: Basal, linear, entire.
Inflorescence: Flowers terminal, solitary, white.
Fruit: Capsule.
Flowering Date: March–April.
Habitats: Woods, sandy pinelands.
Distribution: sw, CO

### *Zigadenus glaberrimus* Michx.
**Camass, Death Camass**

Plants: Upright, glabrous perennial from a rhizome.
Leaves: Mostly basal, linear, entire, reduced upward.
Inflorescence: Terminal panicle; petals clawed; sepals can be clawed; perianth white to yellowish white, with each segment having a pair of green glands.
Fruit: Capsule.
Flowering Date: June–September.
Habitats: Savannas, pinelands, bogs.
Distribution: CO.
Comments: The entire plant is poisonous.

### *Zigadenus densus* (Desr.) Fern.
**Black Snakeroot, Crow Poison, Death Camass**

Plants: Upright, glabrous perennial from a rhizome.
Leaves: Mostly basal, linear, entire, reduced upward.
Inflorescence: Terminal panicle or raceme; perianth white to yellowish white, with perianth segments less than 5 mm long and each having a single green gland (gland occasionally absent).
Fruit: Capsule.
Flowering Date: April–June.
Habitats: Savannas, pinelands.
Distribution: CO.

# MARANTACEAE
## Arrowroot Family

Plants perennial from rhizomes. Leaves alternate, lanceolate, long petiolate. Flowers irregular, with purple petals; ovary inferior; three stamens, with one normal and two purple and petaloid. Fruit a capsule.

### *Thalia dealbata* Roscoe
**Powdery Thalia**

Plants: Upright, glabrous perennial from a rhizome; stems covered with a white, powdery material.

Leaves: Alternate, ovate to lanceolate, petiolate, entire, and covered with a white, powdery material.

Inflorescence: Terminal panicle; flowers irregular, perfect, with a pair of spathelike bracts subtending two flowers; three sepals, pale purple; three petals, longer and darker purple than the sepals.

Fruit: Capsule.

Flowering Date: June–October.

Habitat: Wet ditches.

Distribution: DE.

# ORCHIDACEAE
Orchid Family

Plants perennial; most terrestrial; one an epiphyte; a few lacking chlorophyll (saprophyte). Flower irregular, with the parts in some highly modified in shape; ovary inferior. Fruit a capsule with numerous, minute seeds.

## *Calopogon pulchellus* (Salis.) R. Br.
**Grass-Pink Orchid**

Plants: Upright, glabrous perennial from a corm.
Leaves: Basal, linear, entire.
Inflorescence: Raceme; sepals and petals similar, pink or occasionally white.
Fruit: Capsule.
Flowering Date: April–June.
Habitats: Savannas, pinewoods, wet open sites.
Distribution: CO, EC.

## *Cleistes divaricata* (L.) Ames
**Spreading Pogonia, Rosebud Orchid**

Plants: Upright, glabrous perennial with fibrous roots.
Leaves: Solitary, lanceolate to elliptic, acuminate, with a translucent, entire margin.
Inflorescence: Flowers terminal, usually solitary, occasionally two to three subtended by a leaflike bract; sepals linear to lanceolate, up to nearly three inches long, brownish purple; petals forming a tube, pink, occasionally white, with lip prominent, three lobed, and strongly veined.
Fruit: Capsule.
Flowering Date: May–July.
Habitats: Savannas, swamps, moist pinelands.
Distribution: CO.

## *Corallorhiza wisteriana* Conrad
### Spring Coral Root

Plants: Upright, glabrous, saprophytic perennial from a rhizome; stems yellowish or purplish.
Leaves: Reduced to thin sheaths.
Inflorescence: Raceme; sepals and petals greenish yellow to purplish brown; lip white, spotted with purple.
Fruit: Capsule.
Flowering Date: April–May.
Habitat: Woods.
Distribution: NE, EC, SW, SE.
Comments: *C. odontorhiza* (Late Coral Root) blooms from July to October.

## *Cypripedium calceolus* L.
### Yellow Lady's Slipper

Plants: Upright, hairy perennial from a rhizome.
Leaves: Basal and alternate on stem, ovate to lanceolate, distinctly ribbed, entire.
Inflorescence: Flowers terminal, numerous, subtended by leaflike bracts; sepals and petals greenish yellow to purple, with lateral sepals united nearly to apex and petals spreading; lip slipper shaped or pouch shaped, bright yellow.
Fruit: Capsule.
Flowering Date: April–May.
Habitat: Wooded slopes.
Distribution: EC.

## *Epidendrum conopseum* R. Br.
### Green-Fly Orchid

Plants: Epiphytic, glabrous perennial.
Leaves: Alternate, elliptic, entire, with base sheathing.
Inflorescence: Raceme; flowers numerous; sepals and petals yellowish green, with sepals oblanceolate and petals narrowly oblanceolate; lip three lobed.
Fruit: Capsule.
Flowering Date: Mostly September–November.
Habitat: Swamps.
Distribution: CO.

### *Goodyera pubescens* (Willd.) R. Br.
**Downy Rattlesnake Plantain**

Plants: Upright, hairy perennial.
Leaves: Basal and alternate, petiolate, oblong to ovate, entire, acute to obtuse, with base cuneate to rounded; green with white veins.
Inflorescence: Raceme; flowers numerous, white to greenish white; lip sac-like with three nerves.
Fruit: Capsule.
Flowering Date: June–August.
Habitat: Woods.
Distribution: NE, EC.

### *Habenaria repens* Nutt.
**Water Spider Orchid, Floating Orchid**

Plants: Upright, glabrous perennial.
Leaves: Alternate, linear to lanceolate, three ribbed, entire, clasping.
Inflorescence: Raceme; flowers numerous; sepals and petals similar, greenish, with petals two parted to base, lip three parted, and lateral segments filiform.
Fruit: Capsule.
Flowering Date: April–November.
Habitats: Edges of streams, ponds, and lakes; bogs, marshes, wet ditches.
Distribution: CO, EC.

## *Isotria verticillata* (Muhl. ex Willd.) Raf.
### Large Whorled Pogonia, Five-Leaves

Plants: Upright, glabrous perennial from long, filamentous roots.

Leaves: Five to six whorled just below the flower, oblong to elliptic, acute or acuminate, entire.

Inflorescence: Flowers terminal, usually one, occasionally two; sepals lanceolate to linear, nearly 3 inches long, yellowish purple at the base, becoming purple near apex; petals yellowish green; lip yellowish green with purple streaks, three lobed.

Fruit: Capsule.

Flowering Date: April–July.

Habitats: Wooded slopes, edges of streams.

Distribution: SE.

## *Listera australis* Lindl.
### Southern Twayblade, Long-Lip Twayblade

Plants: Upright, slightly hairy, delicate plants with fibrous roots.

Leaves: Two, opposite, ovate to kidney shaped, acute to acuminate, entire.

Inflorescence: Raceme; flowers numerous; sepals and petals similar, reddish purple; lip two parted to three-fourths its length, with segments linear.

Fruit: Capsule.

Flowering Date: April–June.

Habitats: Moist woods, pinelands, bogs.

Distribution: DE, CO, EC, SW, SE.

## *Malaxis unifolia* Michx.
### Green Adder's Mouth

Plants: Upright, glabrous, bright green plants with fibrous roots; stem swollen at the base.

Leaves: Solitary, ovate, clasping, bright green, entire, with tip obtuse to acute.

Inflorescence: Raceme; flowers numerous; sepals and petals similar, with sepals spreading, petals curved backward; lip heart shaped or auriculate at the base and mostly three toothed at the tip.

Fruit: Capsule.

Flowering Date: April–June.

Habitats: Woods, bogs, wet open sites.

Distribution: NE, EC.

## *Platanthera ciliaris* (L.) Lindl.
**Yellow Fringed Orchid**

Plants: Upright, glabrous perennial from tuberous roots.
Leaves: Two to four alternate, glossy green, lanceolate, reduced upward, entire.
Inflorescence: Raceme; flowers numerous; sepals and petals similar, yellow to deep orange; lip oblong, fringed.
Fruit: Capsule.
Flowering Date: July–September.
Habitats: Bogs, savannas, pinewoods, sandy areas of mixed woods.
Distribution: NE, EC, SW, SE.
Comments: *P. cristata* has a lip that is ovate and much less fringed. *P. blephariglottis* (Willd.) Lindl. has white flowers with a fringed lip.

## *Platanthera clavellata* (Michx.) Luer.
**Small Green Wood Orchid**

Plants: Upright, glabrous perennial with angled to slightly winged stems.
Leaves: One to two, alternate, near the middle, oblanceolate, entire, reduced upward to bracts.
Inflorescence: Raceme; sepals and petals similar, greenish, yellow-green to yellowish white; lip oblong to truncate, slightly toothed at the apex.
Fruit: Capsule.
Flowering Date: June–September.
Habitats: Bogs, swamps, wet woods.
Distribution: CO, EC, SE.

## *Platanthera flava* (L.) Lindl.
**Southern Rein Orchid**

Plants: Upright, glabrous perennial from fleshy roots.
Leaves: Mostly basal, dark green, linear to lanceolate, entire.
Inflorescence: Raceme; flowers numerous; sepals and petals similar, yellowish green; lip ovate, round, or nearly square and lobed.
Fruit: Capsule.
Flowering Date: June–September.
Habitats: Wet open sites, marshes, moist alluvial woods.
Distribution: NE, EC.

## *Platanthera integra* (Nutt.) Gray ex Beck.
### Yellow Fringeless Orchid

Plants: Upright, glabrous perennial from tapering, fleshy roots.

Leaves: One to two alternate, lanceolate, entire.

Inflorescence: Raceme; flowers numerous; sepals and petals similar, lemon orange or deep orange; lip ovate, toothed.

Fruit: Capsule.

Flowering Date: July–September.

Habitats: Savannas, pinewoods, swamps, hardwoods.

Distribution: CO.

## *Platanthera lacera* (Michx.) G. Don
### Ragged Orchid

Plants: Upright, glabrous perennial from fleshy roots.

Leaves: Two to five, alternate, elliptic to lanceolate, entire.

Inflorescence: Raceme; flowers numerous; sepals and petals similar, yellowish green to whitish green; lip divided into shallow and deep segments.

Fruit: Capsule.

Flowering Date: June–August.

Habitats: Wet prairies, bogs, marshes.

Distribution: EC.

*Pogonia ophioglossoides* (L.)
   Juss.
**Rose Pogonia**

Plants: Upright, glabrous plants with
   fibrous roots.
Leaves: Solitary, occasionally two,
   ovate to elliptic, obtuse at tip, entire.
Inflorescence: One to three terminal
   flowers; sepals and petals similar,
   pink to white, fragrant; lip fringed.
Fruit: Capsule.
Flowering Date: April–June.
Habitats: Savannas, bogs, wet ditches.
Distribution: CO, EC.

*Platanthera peramoena* Gray
**Purple Fringeless Orchid**

Plants: Upright, glabrous perennial
   from fleshy roots.
Leaves: Two to five, alternate, elliptic
   to lanceolate, sheathing the stem,
   entire, reduced upward.
Inflorescence: Raceme; flowers numerous; sepal and petals similar, purple
   lips divided in 3 deep segments.
Fruit: Capsule.
Flowering Date: June–October.
Habitats: Low moist areas of woods,
   near streams.
Distribution: NE, EC.

## *Spiranthes cernua* (L.) Rich.
### Nodding Ladies' Tresses, Fragrant Ladies' Tresses

Plants: Upright, glabrous to hairy perennial with fleshy roots.

Leaves: Three to six, mostly basal, linear to lanceolate, entire, becoming bractlike and sheathing above.

Inflorescence: Spike; flowers slightly nodding; sepals and petals similar, white with a yellowish center; lip white with a greenish yellow center, slightly toothed at the apex.

Fruit: Capsule.

Flowering Date: July–November.

Habitats: Marshes, bogs, wet open sites, stream edges.

Distribution: NE, EC, SW, SE.

Comments: *S. odorata* has very fragrant flowers, is aquatic to semiaquatic, and is found in the southern half of the state. Several other species occur in Mississippi. It is often difficult to determine the species of *Spiranthes*.

## *Spiranthes magnicamporum* Sheviak
### Great Plain's Ladies' Tresses

Plants: Upright, hairy perennial.

Leaves: Basal, linear to lanceolate, entire, becoming bractlike above, persisting for only a short time.

Inflorescence: Spike; densely flowered, spiraled; sepals and petals similar, white to cream; lip white, yellowish at the center.

Fruit: Capsule.

Flowering Date: August–November.

Habitats: Calcareous prairies or glades.

Distribution: EC.

## *Tipularia discolor* (Pursh) Nutt.
### Crane-Fly Orchid

Plants: Upright, glabrous perennial from a tuber.

Leaves: Solitary, green with purple blotches, purple below, cordate to elliptic, entire, produced in the autumn and decaying in the summer.

Inflorescence: Raceme; flowers numerous; sepals and petals similar, greenish, yellowish, reddish, or purplish; lip three lobed.

Fruit: Capsule.

Flowering Date: July–September.

Habitat: Wet sites in woods.

Distribution: DE, NE, EC.

## *Triphora trianthophora* (Sw.) Rydb.
### Three Birds Orchid

Plants: Upright, glabrous perennial with a succulent stem and fleshy roots forming round tubers.

Leaves: Two to eight alternate, ovate, entire, clasping.

Inflorescence: Racemelike; flowers one to two to numerous; sepals and petals similar, pink to white or white tinged with pink; lip three lobed.

Fruit: Capsule.

Flowering Date: July–September.

Habitat: Moist woods.

Distribution: NE, EC.

# PONTEDERIACEAE
## Pickerelweed Family

Plants perennial aquatics. Leaves alternate or a basal rosette; sheathing. Sepals and petals similar; ovary superior; three or six stamens fused to the perianth. Fruit a capsule or achene.

### *Eichornia crassipes* (Mart.) Solms.
**Water Hyacinth**

Plants: Aquatic and stoloniferous; stem base swollen.
Leaves: Rosettes, mostly elliptic, occasionally orbicular, entire, with apex rounded.
Inflorescence: Spike; flowers nearly regular to irregular, perfect; sepals and petals similar, light to dark blue.
Fruit: Capsule.
Flowering Date: June–October.
Habitats: Lakes, freshwater marshes.
Distribution: CO.

### *Heteranthera reniformis* R. & P.
**Mud Plantain**

Plants: Aquatic, glabrous annual or perennial.
Leaves: Rosette, petiolate, cordate, with tip rounded to broadly acute.
Inflorescence: Flowers solitary or several, subtended by a spathe; sepals and petals similar, white; three stamens.
Fruit: Capsule.
Flowering Date: June–October.
Habitats: Shallow standing water and shallow streams.
Distribution: NE, DE, EC, SE.

### *Pontederia cordata* L.
**Pickerelweed**

Plants: Aquatic perennial from a rhizome.
Leaves: Basal, ovate to lanceolate, entire, with base cordate to truncate and tip obtuse.
Inflorescence: Spike; flowers irregular, perfect; sepals and petals similar, blue marked with yellow.
Fruit: Achene.
Flowering Date: April–November.
Habitats: Lakes, freshwater marshes, streams, ponds.
Distribution: CO.

# XYRIDACEAE
## Yellow-eyed Grass Family

Plants annual or perennial. Leaves mostly basal and linear. Inflorescence a solitary, terminal head; flowers irregular and enclosed by evenly overlapping brown to reddish brown bracts; petals yellow; ovary superior; three stamens. Fruit a capsule.

### *Xyris iridifolia* Chapm.
**Yellow-Eyed Grass**

Plants: Upright, glabrous perennial.
Leaves: Basal, linear, flat or twisted, with bases overlapping.
Inflorescence: Sphere-shaped head; flowers subtended by a scale; three sepals; three petals, yellow,
Fruit: Capsule.
Flowering Date: June–August.
Habitats: Bogs, marshes, savannas, wet ditches, stream banks.
Comments: Numerous species of *Xyris* occur in Mississippi and are often difficult to determine to species.

*PART II   MAGNOLIOPSIDA (DICOTS)*

# ACANTHACEAE
## Acanthus Family

Plants perennial. Leaves opposite. Flowers irregular or regular, with corolla funnel shaped in *Ruellia*; ovary superior; two stamens in *Justicia* and four in *Ruellia*. Fruit a capsule.

### *Dicliptera brachiata* (Pursh) Spreng.
**Dicliptera**

Plants: Upright, minutely hairy annual; stems diffusely branched.

Leaves: Opposite, petiolate, ovate, acuminate, entire, with base attenuate.

Inflorescence: Axillary clusters; flowers perfect, irregular, funnelform; calyx five lobed; corolla five lobed and two lipped, pink to blue; two stamens.

Fruit: Capsule.

Flowering Date: August–October.

Habitats: Stream banks, moist shaded woods, thickets.

Distribution: NE, SE.

### *Justicia americana* (L.) Vahl.
**Water Willow, American Dianthera**

Plants: Aquatic, trailing to erect perennial from rhizomes.

Leaves: Opposite, petiolate to sessile, linear or lanceolate to nearly elliptic, acute, entire, with base attenuate.

Inflorescence: Axillary, headlike spike; flowers perfect, irregular, bilabiate; calyx five lobed; corolla two lipped with the upper lip notched and the lower lip three lobed, light purple to white, often spotted with purple; two stamens.

Fruit: Capsule.

Flowering Date: May–October.

Habitats: Streams, lakes, and ditches with standing water.

Distribution: NE, EC.

*Ruellia caroliniensis* (Gmel.) Steud.
**Wild Petunia**

Plants: Upright, hairy perennial.
Leaves: Opposite, petiolate; ovate, lanceolate, or elliptic; acute or nearly so; entire; base cuneate to attenuate.
Inflorescence: Axillary; flowers perfect, regular or nearly so, funnelform; calyx five lobed; corolla with 5 unequal lobes in blue, light purple, pink, or occasionally white; four stamens.
Fruit: Capsule.
Flowering Date: May–October.
Habitats: Dry woods, fields, roadsides, prairies.
Distribution: EC.
Comments: *R. humilis* is similar but has leaves that are sessile or nearly so.

# AMARANTHACEAE
## Amaranth Family

Plants annual or perennial. Leaves alternate or opposite. Five
sepals; petals absent; ovary superior or nearly so; stamens five
to many. Fruit a capsule.

### *Alternanthera philoxeroides* (Mart.) Griseb.
#### Chaff-Flower, Alligator Weed

Plants: Perennial; lower stems lying on
   the ground and upper stems ascending.
Leaves: Opposite, petiolate, spatulate
   to elliptic.
Inflorescence: Headlike spikes that are
   axillary or terminal on the branches;
   flowers perfect; calyx four or five
   lobed; petals absent; five stamens.
Fruit: Capsule.
Flowering Date: April–November.
Habitats: In or near streams, ditches,
   lakes, and ponds.
Distribution: DE, CO, EC, SE.

### *Froelichia floridana* (Nutt.) Moq.
#### Cottonweed

Plants: Upright, whitish annual with
   hairy stems.
Leaves: Opposite, lanceolate, entire,
   with base attenuate.
Inflorescence: Terminal spikes; flowers
   perfect; calyx 5 parted; petals absent;
   five stamens.
Fruit: Capsule.
Flowering Date: June–November.
Habitats: Pinelands, fields, roadsides.
Distribution: CO.

# ANACARDIACEAE
Sumac Family

Plants woody vine, shrub, or small tree. Leaves compound. Flowers usually have both male and female structures; some plants have only male flowers; four to five sepals; four to five petals; ovary superior; four to five stamens. Fruit a drupe.

## *Toxicodendron radicans* (L.) Ktze.
### Poison Ivy

Plants: Upright, climbing, or trailing perennial with adventitious roots.

Leaves: Alternate, ternate with the three leaflets ovate to elliptic, acute to acuminate; margins toothed or lobed, rarely entire; base cuneate.

Inflorescence: Axillary panicle; flowers perfect, regular; five sepals; five petals, greenish yellow; five stamens.

Fruit: Drupe.

Flowering Date: April–June.

Habitats: Woods, waste areas, fence rows, roadsides.

Distribution: Throughout.

Comments: The volatile oils this plant produces give some people skin irritations, ranging from redness to severe blistering. *T. toxicarium* (Poison Oak) is a more erect plant without adventitious roots and has leaves with lobes that are usually much more rounded than those of *T. radicans* (like oak leaves).

# ANNONACEAE
## Pawpaw Family

Plants a shrub or tree. Leaves simple, alternate, foul smelling when crushed. Three sepals; six petals in two series; ovary superior; many stamens. Fruit, an aromatic berry.

## *Asimina triloba* (L.) Dun.
### Pawpaw, Ozark Banana

Plants: Trees to 30 feet tall.

Leaves: Alternate, obovate, acuminate, entire, nearly sessile, with base cuneate.

Inflorescence: Solitary; flowers perfect, regular, bell- shaped; three sepals; six petals, reddish brown, purple-brown, purple-green; stamens numerous.

Bruit: Bananalike berry.

Flowering Date: March–May.

Habitats: Alluvial woods, wooded slopes along streams, ravines.

Distribution: Throughout.

Comments: In September, edible sweet fruits ripen that resemble small, fat bananas. Some people may develop a dermatitis after handling the fruit. The trees are easily grown from seeds, which contain an alkaloid that may cause depression if eaten. *A. parviflora* (Dwarf Pawpaw) grows to no more than 7 feet tall and has flowers that are much smaller than *A. triloba.*

# APIACEAE [= UMBELLIFERAE]
## Parsley Family

Plants annual, biennial, or perennial. Leaves alternate, compound, simple or lobed, often deeply so that they appear compound. Inflorescence a simple or compound umbel or compact head (*Eryngium*); sepals minute; corolla usually regular; ovary inferior; five stamens. Fruit a schizocarp.

### *Cicuta maculata* L.
### Water Hemlock

Plants: Upright, glabrous perennial with fleshy or tuberous roots.
Leaves: Alternate, pinnately or bipinnately divided, with leaflets lanceolate to elliptic and toothed.
Inflorescence: Terminal compound umbel; flowers perfect, regular; five petals, white.
Fruit: Ovoid schizocarp.
Flowering Date: April–September.
Habitats: Stream banks, moist ditches, marshes, wet disturbed sites.
Distribution: Throughout.
Comments: All parts of this plant are **extemely poisonous.** It has been reported that a mouthful swallowed can cause death. *Conium maculatum* is somewhat similar but has leaves that are bipinnately compound. All parts of this species are also **extremely poisonous.**

### *Daucus carota* L.
### Queen Anne's Lace, Wild Carrot

Plants: Upright, hairy perennial with a taproot.
Leaves: Alternate, pinnately decompound, with segments linear to lanceolate or ovate and lobed.
Inflorescence: Compound umbel that's terminal, axillary, or opposite a leaf; flowers perfect, regular; five petals, white.
Fruit: Ovoid or elliptical schizocarp.
Flowering Date: April–October.
Habitats: Roadsides, prairies, fields, waste areas.
Distribution: Throughout.
Comments: When handled, this species may give some people a dermatitis.

## *Eryngium integrifolium* Walt.
**Eryngo**

Plants: Upright perennial with a taproot.
Leaves: Alternate, with basal leaves
lanceolate, elliptic, or triangular, and
petiolate, usually toothed and with
upper leaves sessile or nearly so, lanceolate, elliptic, or linear, and
toothed to spinose.
Inflorescence: Terminal umbel subtended by toothed bracts; flowers in
a head subtended by bractlets, perfect, regular; five petals, light blue.
Fruit: Ovoid schizocarp with protrub-
erances.
Flowering Date: August–October.
Habitats: Pinelands, savannas.
Distribution: CO, EC.

## *Eryngium prostratum* Nutt.
**Sprawling Eryngo**

Plants: Prostrate to slightly erect, glabrous perennial.
Leaves: Alternate, ovate to lanceolate,
petiolate, entire to toothed, acute,
with base cuneate; mostly basal.
Inflorescence: Head, subtended by
linear bracts; flowers perfect, regular; five petals, light blue.
Fruit: Ovoid schizocarp with protru-
berances.
Habitats: Waste areas, roadsides,
ditches, open sites.
Distribution: Throughout.

## *Eryngium yuccifolium* Michx.
**Rattlesnake Master, Button
Snakeroot**

Plants: Upright perennial with a taproot.
Leaves: Alternate, linear, leathery tex-
tured, and parallel veined; margins
toothed to nearly spinose.
Inflorescence: Terminal umbel; flowers
perfect, regular, in heads subtended
by ovate to lanceolate bractlets; five
petals, white.
Fruit: Ovoid schizocarp with protru-
berances.
Habitats: Prairies, roadsides, woods,
pinewoods.
Distribution: CO, NE, EC, SE.
Comments: The leaves were once
thought to be a remedy for rattlesnake bite.

## *Hydrocotyle bonariensis* Lam.
### Pennyworts, Dollar Grass

Plants: Upright, glabrous perennial rooting from the nodes.

Leaves: Simple, petiolate, peltate, orbicular, with margins slightly toothed.

Inflorescence: Branched umbels with flowers whorled on the branches; flowers perfect, regular; petals greenish.

Fruit: Flattened schizocarp.

Flowering Date: April–September.

Habitats: Wet ditches, edges of ponds, wet lawns.

Distribution: CO, EC.

Comments: *H. umbellata* has a simple umbel. *H. verticillata* has whorled umbels that are simple and unbranched.

## *Osmorhiza longistylis* (Torr.) DC.
### Wild Sweet Cicely, Anise-Root, Wild Licorice

Plants: Upright, glabrous to slightly hairy perennial with fleshy roots.

Leaves: Alternate, bipinnately or ternately compound, with segments ovate and toothed or lobed.

Inflorescence: Compound umbel subtended by lanceolate to filiform bracts; flowers perfect, regular to irregular; three to five petals, white.

Fruit: Elliptical schizocarp.

Flowering Date: April–May.

Habitats: Ravines, wooded slopes, alluvial woods.

Distribution: EC, NE.

Comments: The roots smell and taste like licorice and can be eaten raw or used as a flavoring.

## *Oxypolis filiformis* (Walt.) Britt.
### Hog-Fennel, Cowbane

Plants: Upright, glabrous perennial with fibrous roots.

Leaves: Alternate, simple, flattened, linear, hollow, entire.

Inflorescence: Compound umbel subtended by filiform bracts; flowers perfect, regular; five sepals; five petals, white.

Fruit: Oval or elliptic schizocarp.

Flowering Date: July–August.

Habitats: Wet ditches, prairies, bogs, marshes, pinelands.

Distribution: CO.

## *Torilis arvensis* (Huds.) Link
### Hedge Parsley, Hemlock Chervil

Plants: Upright, hairy annual.

Leaves: Alternate, with lower leaves pinnately or bipinnately compound, upper leaves ternately compound, and leaflets linear to lanceolate, toothed; petioles sheathing.

Inflorescence: Terminal or lateral compound umbel; flowers perfect, regular; five to nine petals, white.

Fruit: Elliptical schizocarp.

Flowering Date: June–August.

Habitats: Roadsides, fields.

Distribution: NE, EC.

# APOCYNACEAE
## Dogbane Family

Plants herbaceous perennial or woody vine with white sap (latex). Leaves alternate or opposite. Corolla salverform or funnel shaped; five stamens. Fruit a follicle.

## *Amsonia tabernaemontana* Walt.
### Blue Star, Willow Amsonia

Plants: Upright, glabrous perennial with milky sap and a woody rootstock.

Leaves: Alternate, simple, sessile, lanceolate, entire, acuminate, with base cuneate.

Inflorescence: Terminal cluster; flowers perfect, regular; calyx five lobed; corolla salverform, with five lobes, separate in part, light blue.

Fruit: Follicle.

Flowering Date: April–May.

Habitats: Roadsides, woods, along railroad tracks, stream edges.

Distribution: Throughout.

Comments: *A. ciliata* has similar flowers but has leaves that are filiform to linear.

## *Apocynum androsaemifolium* L.
### Indian Hemp

Plants: Upright, glabrous perennial with a rhizome.

Leaves: Opposite, simple, sessile or short petiolate, ovate, entire, acute, with base cuneate.

Inflorescence: Terminal or axillary cluster; flowers perfect, regular; calyx five lobed; corolla bell shaped, five lobed with lobes reflexed, white to pinkish or white marked with pink.

Fruit: Follicle.

Flowering Date: June–August.

Habitats: Woods, fields, roadsides, waste areas.

Distribution: DE, NE, EC.

## *Apocynum cannabinum* L.
**Indian Hemp, Dogbane, Prairie Dogbane**

Plants: Upright, glabrous perennial with a rhizome.

Leaves: Opposite, simple, sessile or petiolate, elliptic to lanceolate, entire, acute, with base cuneate.

Inflorescence: Terminal cluster; flowers perfect, regular; calyx five lobed; corolla uruolate or cylindrical, five lobed, white to greenish.

Fruit: Follicle.

Flowering Date: May–July.

Habitats: Roadsides, woodland edges, waste sites.

Distribution: DE, NE, EC.

Comments: The plant is poisonous but has been used as an emetic, cathartic, and diuretic. The stems were once used to make rope.

## *Trachelospermum difforme* (Walt.) Gray
**Climbing Dogbane**

Plants: Woody twining vine.

Leaves: Opposite, simple, petiolate to nearly sessile, lanceolate to elliptic, entire, acuminate, with base cuneate.

Inflorescence: Axillary or terminal clusters; flowers perfect, regular; calyx five lobed; corolla funnel shaped, five lobed, yellow to greenish.

Fruit: Follicle.

Flowering Date: May–July.

Habitats: Woods, stream edges, alluvial woods, marshes, swamp edges.

Distribution: DE, NE, EC, SE, SW.

Comments: The flowers are very fragrant.

# ARALIACEAE
## Ginseng Family

Plants perennial herb or shrub. Leaves alternate or whorled, mostly compound. Flowers regular, in umbels or umbels in racemes; five sepals; five petals; ovary inferior; usually five stamens. Fruit a drupe.

### *Aralia spinosa* L.
**Devil's Walking Stick, Hercules' Club, Angelica Tree, Tear Blanket**

Plants: Upright shrubs.

Leaves: Decompound, with leaflets elliptic to ovate, petiolate, and having toothed margins.

Inflorescence: Terminal panicle of umbels; flowers imperfect; sepals five or absent; five petals, white to greenish white; five stamens.

Fruit: Drupe.

Flowering Date: June–September.

Habitats: Woodland edges, savannas.

Distribution: Throughout.

Comments: The fruits were once used for dying hair black. Some people develop a dermatitis after handling the plant.

### *Panax quinquefolius* L.
**Ginseng**

Plants: Upright, glabrous perennial with a fleshy root.

Leaves: Whorled, palmately compound, petiolate; leaflets elliptic, acuminate, with margins toothed and base often unequal.

Inflorescence: Solitary, terminal umbel; flowers imperfect and perfect on the same plant; sepals reduced; five petals, white to greenish; five stamens.

Fruit: Drupe.

Flowering Date: May–June.

Habitat: Rocky wooded slopes.

Distribution: NE, EC.

Comments: The roots are reported to be used for a number of medicinal properties and as an aphrodisiac.

# ARISTOLOCHIACEAE
## Birthwort Family

Plants perennial herb or woody vine. Leaves alternate. Flowers axillary; three sepals, united at least at the base; petals absent; ovary inferior or superior; six to twelve stamens. Fruit a capsule.

## *Aristolochia tomentosa* Sims
### Dutchman's Pipe, Pipe-Vine

Plants: Woody climbing vine.
Leaves: Alternate, simple, cordate, petiolate, entire.
Inflorescence: Solitary or paired in leaf axils; flowers perfect, irregular (pipe shaped); sepals three lobed, yellowish or tan with purplish lobes and mouth; petals absent; six stamens.
Fruit: Capsule.
Flowering Date: May–July.
Habitat: Woods, usually near streams.
Distribution: NE, EC.
Comments: *A. serpentaria* is herbaceous and is erect to reclining.

## *Hexastylis arifolia* (Michx.) Small
### Heart Leaf, Wild Ginger

Plants: Perennial from a rhizome with no aboveground stem.
Leaves: Two, simple, triangular, sagittate or hastate, entire.
Inflorescence: Flowers usually in clusters of two or more, arising from between the two leaves, usually hidden beneath or just barely emerged above the leaf litter; flowers perfect, irregular; sepals jug shaped or flask shaped, three lobed, brownish to yellowish brown; petals absent; twelve stamens.
Fruit: Fleshy capsule.
Flowering Date: March–May.
Habitat: Woods.
Distribution: CO, NE, EC, SE.

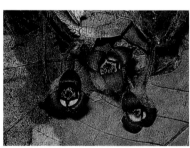

## *Asarum canadense* L.
### Wild Ginger

Plants: Perennial from a rhizome with no aboveground stem.
Leaves: Two, simple, cordate, petiolate, entire.
Inflorescence: Flowers usually in clusters of two or more, arising from between the two leaves, usually hidden beneath the leaf litter; flowers perfect, irregular; sepals three lobed, bell shaped, brown to maroon; petals absent; twelve stamens.
Fruit: Fleshy capsule.
Flowering Date: March–May.
Habitats: Wooded slopes and ravines.
Distribution: CO, NE, EC, SE.

## ASCLEPIADACEAE
Milkweed Family

Plants erect or twining perennial with milky sap. Leaves alternate, opposite, or whorled. Inflorescence an umbel or flowers have five petals that are reflexed, with five stamens and a five-lobed corona, each lobe consisting of a hood and horn fused to either or both (see fig. 24, page 256). In other genera, the flowers consists of a five-lobed calyx and a five-lobed corolla that is rotate or bell shaped. Ovary superior. Fruit a follicle.

### *Asclepias incarnata* L.
**Swamp Milkweed**

Plants: Upright, glabrous to slightly hairy perennial.
Leaves: Opposite, simple, short petiolate, lanceolate to elliptic, entire.
Inflorescence: Terminal umbels; corolla pink or rose; hoods pink or rose.
Fruit: Follicle.
Flowering Date: July–September.
Habitats: Stream banks, wet ditches, moist fields.
Distribution: DE, CO.
Comments: The silky part of the fruit was once used as a substitute for kapok in life preservers. The young shoots when cooked are edible, as are the young flowers and leaves.

### *Asclepias lanceolata* Walt.
**Milkweed**

Plants: Upright, glabrous perennial.
Leaves: Opposite, simple, short petiolate, linear to lanceolate, entire.
Inflorescence: Terminal umbel; corolla red; hoods orange to reddish orange.
Fruit: Follicle
Flowering Date: May–August.
Habitats: Pinelands, savannas.
Distribution: CO.
Comments: *A. rubra* is similar but has leaves that are less than 6 inches long while *A. lanceolata* has longer leaves.

## *Asclepias longifolia* Michx.
### Milkweed

Plants: Upright, hairy perennial.
Leaves: Opposite to nearly alternate, simple, sessile, entire.
Inflorescence: Axillary umbels; corolla greenish white with rose-colored tips; hoods greenish with top purplish; horns absent.
Fruit: Follicle.
Flowering Date: May–June.
Habitats: Pinewoods, savannas, bogs.
Distribution: CO.

## *Asclepias tuberosa* L.
### Butterfly Weed, Pleurisy Root

Plants: Upright, hairy perennial with a woody rootstock.
Leaves: Alternate, simple, short petiolate, linear to oblanceolate, entire.
Inflorescence: Terminal, coiled umbels; corolla yellow, orange, or red; hoods yellow to red.
Fruit: Follicle.
Flowering Date: May–August.
Habitats: Dry roadsides, prairies, woodland edges, pastures, fields.
Distribution: Throughout.
Comments: This species does well in cultivation. The root has been used medicinally as an emetic and diuretic. The aboveground parts are reported to be poisonous.

## *Asclepias viridis* Walt.
### Antelope-Horn, Spider Milkweed, Green Milkweed

Plants: Upright, glabrous to sparsely hairy perennial.
Leaves: Alternate to nearly opposite, simple, short petiolate, entire.
Inflorescence: Terminal umbels; corolla green; hoods purple; horns inconspicuous.
Fruit: Follicle.
Flowering Date: April–September.
Habitats: Roadsides, prairies, mixed woods, pinelands.
Distribution: NE, EC.
Comments: *A. viridiflora* has terminal and lateral umbels with yellowish green corolla lobes, and lacks horns.

## *Asclepias variegata* L.
### White-Flowered Milkweed

Plants: Upright, hairy to glabrous perennial.
Leaves: Opposite, simple, short petiolate, ovate to nearly lanceolate, entire.
Inflorescence: Terminal, compact umbels; corolla white; hoods white.
Fruit: Follicle.
Flowering Date: May–July.
Habitats: Woods, woodland edges.
Distribution: NE, EC, SE, SW.
Comments: *A. humistrata* is similar but has leaves that clasp the stem.

## *Cynanchum laeve* (Michx.) Pers.
### Anglepod, Sand Vine, Blue Vine, Honey Vine, Climbing Milkweed

Plants: Twining, glabrous perennial with milky sap.
Leaves: Opposite, simple, petiolate, triangular to ovate, entire, acuminate.
Inflorescence: Axillary, umbel-like; flowers perfect, regular; corolla white tinged with green.
Fruit: Follicle.
Flowering Date: July–August.
Habitats: Waste sites, roadsides, thickets.
Distribution: Throughout.

# ASTERACEAE [= COMPOSITAE]
## Sunflower Family

Plants annual biennial, or perennial vine or shrub. Leaves alternate, opposite, whorled, or basal rosettes. Inflorescence a head(s) consisting of both ray and disc flowers or of only one of these; heads subtended by bracts (phyllaries); ovary inferior. Fruit an achene.

## *Achillea millefolium* L.
### Yarrow, Milfoil, Nosebleed

Plants: Upright, hairy perennial from a rhizome.

Leaves: Basal rosettes and alternate on the stem, simple, pinnately dissected (fernlike) with segments linear.

Inflorescence: Terminal; flowers perfect, regular; ray and disc flowers white, occasionally pink; ray flowers female and disc flowers perfect.

Fruit: Achene.

Flowering Date: April–November.

Habitats: Prairies, roadsides, pastures, waste sites.

Distribution: Throughout.

Comments: Europeans use the plant as an ornamental. The plant has been used medicinally for colds, as a blood tonic, and to control hemorrhages. The name Nosebleed comes from the belief that if the leaves are placed in the nostrils, the nose will bleed.

## *Anthemis cotula* L.
### Dog Fennel, May Weed, Stinking Chamomile

Plants: Upright to asending, hairy to glabrous annual.

Leaves: Alternate, simple, bipinnately or tripinnately dissected with segments linear.

Inflorescence: Flowers terminal on long peduncles; perfect, regular; disc flowers yellow; ray flowers usually white, occasionally yellow, three toothed.

Fruit: Achene.

Flowering Date: May–July.

Habitats: Roadsides, fields, waste sites.

Distribution: DE.

Comments: The plant is a native of Europe. It has been reported to cause skin irritation to some.

## *Antennaria plantaginifolia* (L.) Richards.
### Pussy-Toes, Ladies' Tobacco, Indian Tobacco

Plants: Upright, woolly, stoloniferous perennial.

Leaves: Mostly basal rosettes; alternate on the stem; simple; elliptic, ovate or obovate; three veined; entire; tip rounded or acute; base attenuate or cuneate.

Inflorescence: Flowers terminal, solitary or clustered, imperfect, regular; disc flowers white to purplish; involucral bracts white.

Fruit: Achene.

Flowering Date: March–May.

Habitats: Prairies, dry woods.

Distribution: NE, EC, SE.

Comments: The rosette of leaves remains green through winter.

## *Arctium minus* Bernh.
### Burdock

Plants: Upright, glabrous to sparsely hairy perennial.

Leaves: Alternate, petiolate with petioles hollow, simple, ovate; margins toothed; base cordate to truncate.

Inflorescence: Heads in panicles or racemes flowers perfect; disc flowers numerous, purple; ray flowers absent; involucral bracts spine tipped and hooked; pappus barbed.

Fruit: Achene.

Flowering Date: June–December.

Habitats: Disturbed sites, waste sites, fields.

Distribution: NE, EC.

Comments: Naturalized from Europe. The young leaves and peeled roots can be boiled or baked for a vegetable, tasting like salsify. The root can be dried, ground and mixed with coffee. The plant was once used medicinally as a diuretic and in ointment form as a treatment for sores and burns.

## *Aster ericoides* L.
### Wreath Aster

Plants: Upright, glabrous to slightly hairy perennial.

Leaves: Alternate, simple, elliptic, rough feeling above, acute to attenuate, with margins toothed and base attenuate to cuneate.

Inflorescence: Panicle; flowers regular; disc flowers perfect, yellow or red; ray flowers female, numerous, white.

Fruit: Achene.

Flowering Date: September–November.

Habitat: Woodlands.

Distribution: NE, EC.

## *Aster linariifolius* L.
### Aster

Plants: Upright, slightly hairy perennial.

Leaves: Alternate, linear to narrowly lanceolate, entire.

Inflorescence: Terminal cluster of heads; flowers regular; disc flowers perfect, yellowish; ray flowers female, white.

Fruit: Achene.

Flowering Date: August–October.

Habitat: Dry sandy woods.

Distribution: SE, EC, NE.

## *Aster novae- angliae* L.
### New England Aster

Plants: Upright, hairy perennial.

Leaves: Alternate, simple, lanceolate, sessile, rough feeling above, entire, acute to acuminate, with base rounded to auriculate.

Inflorescence: Panicle; flower regular; disc flower perfect, yellow; ray flowers female, numerous, violet.

Fruit: Achene.

Flowering Date: September–November.

Habitats: Roadsides, fence rows, along railroad tracks, bogs.

Distribution: NE, EC.

Comments: This species does well in cultivation.

### *Aster paludosus* Ait.
**Aster**

Plants: Upright, glabrous to hairy perennial from a rhizome.

Leaves: Alternate, simple, upper leaves sessile and lower leaves petiolate, entire to slightly toothed, acute, with base cuneate to attenuate.

Inflorescence: Flowers terminal, sometimes clustered, regular; disc flower perfect yellow; ray flowers female, numerous, blue to violet.

Fruit: Achene.

Flowering Date: July–November.

Habitats: Prairies, roadsides, woodland edges.

Distribution: NE, EC, SE, SW.

### *Aster patens* Ait.
**Purple Daisy, Spreading Aster**

Plants: Upright, colonial perennial with a rhizome.

Leaves: Alternate, simple, sessile, lanceolate to oblanceolate, entire, acute, with base auriculate.

Inflorescence: Panicle; flowers regular; disc flowers perfect, yellow or purple; ray flowers female, numerous, blue to violet.

Fruit: Achene.

Flowering Date: September–November.

Habitats: Woodlands, fields.

Distribution: Throughout.

### *Aster pilosus* Willd.
**White Heath Aster**

Plants: Upright, glabrous to hairy perennial with a rhizome.

Leaves: Alternate, simple, sessile, elliptic to linear, acute; margins entire to slightly toothed; base attenuate.

Inflorescence: Panicle; flowers regular; disc flowers perfect, yellow; ray flowers female, white.

Fruit: Achene.

Flowering Date: September–November.

Habitats: Roadsides, fields, waste sites.

Distribution: DE, NE, EC, SE, SW.

## *Aster sericocarpoides* (Small) K. Schum.
**Aster**

Plants: Upright, glabrous to slightly hairy perennial with a rhizome.

Leaves: Alternate, simple, nearly sessile, lanceolate to elliptic, entire or nearly so, acute to acuminate, with base cuneate.

Inflorescence: Flowers compact, terminal cluster, regular; disc flowers perfect, yellowish white; ray flowers female.

Fruit: Achene.

Flowering Date: August–October.

Habitats: Moist pinelands, wet areas.

Distribution: SW.

## *Aster tortifolius* Michx.
**White-Top Aster**

Plants: Upright, hairy perennial from a rhizome.

Leaves: Alternate, simple, sessile, obovate to oblanceolate, entire, acute to acuminate, with base attenuate.

Inflorescence: Panicle; flowers regular; disc flowers perfect, white; ray flowers female, white.

Fruit: Achene.

Flowering Date: June–August.

Habitats: Woodlands, fields, roadsides.

Distribution: NE, EC, SE, SW.

## *Aster shortii* Lindl.
**Aster**

Plants: Upright, nearly glabrous perennial.

Leaves: Alternate, simple, petiolate, lanceolate to ovate, acute to acuminate, entire or few toothed, with base cordate.

Inflorescence: Paniclelike; flowers perfect, blue, white, or rose; ray flowers female.

Fruit: Achene.

Flowering Date: August–October.

Habitat: Woods.

Distribution: NE, EC.

*Baccharis halimifolia* L.
## Groundsel Tree, Silverling, Sea Myrtle, Consumption Weed

Plants: Shrub to about 15 feet tall; dioecious.

Leaves: Alternate, simple, sessile, fleshy, elliptic to obovate; margins toothed, occasionally entire.

Inflorescence: Flowers axillary, pedunculate to sessile, regular; disc flowers numerous, white to yellowish white.

Fruit: Achene.

Flowering Date: September–October.

Habitats: Roadsides, fence rows, woodland edge, fields, freshwater marshes, edges of ponds, edges of salt marshes.

Distribution: DE, CO, EC, SE, SW.

### *Balduina uniflora* Nutt.
**Balduina**

Plants: Upright, hairy, perennial with fibrous roots.

Leaves: Alternate, simple, sessile, linear, reduced upward, entire, acute or obtuse, with base attenuate.

Inflorescence: Flowers terminal and solitary, regular; disc flowers perfect, yellow to purplish; ray flowers sterile, three to five toothed, yellow, more than 1 inch long.

Fruit: Achene.

Flowering Date: July–October.

Habitats: Savannas, pinelands, bogs.

Distribution: CO.

### *Balduina angustifolia* (Pursh) Robins.
**Honeycomb Head**

Plants: Upright, hairy to glabrous perennial with a taproot.

Leaves: Alternate, simple, nearly linear, entire.

Inflorescence: Flowers terminal, regular; disc flowers perfect, yellow; ray flowers sterile, three to five toothed, yellow, less than 1 inch long.

Fruit: Achene.

Flowering Date: March–December.

Habitat: Pinelands.

Distribution: CO.

### *Bidens aristosa* (Michx.) Britt.
**Beggar Ticks, Sticktight**

Plants: Upright, glabrous to hairy annual with a taproot.

Leaves: Alternate, simple, petiolate, pinnately dissected, with segments lanceolate and toothed or lobed.

Inflorescence: Flowers solitary, on long peduncles, regular; disc flowers perfect, yellow; ray flowers female, to eight to ten, yellow.

Fruit: Achene.

Flowering Date: September–October.

Habitats: Ditches, roadsides, fields, waste sites, along railroad tracks.

Distribution: Throughout.

Comments: *B. frondosa* L. does not have ray flowers. *B. laevis* (L.) B.S.P. has simple, serrate, and unlobed leaves. *B. pilosa* L. (White Bidens) has white ray flowers.

## *Bigelowia nudata* (Michx.) DC.
### Rayless Goldenrod

Plants: Upright, glabrous perennial.
Leaves: Basal leaves simple, spatulate, petiolate, entire; stem leaves linear to spatulate to filiform.
Inflorescence: Flowers in terminal clusters, perfect, regular; disc flowers yellow; ray flowers absent.
Fruit: Achene.
Flowering Date: September–October.
Habitat: Pinelands.
Distribution: CO.

## *Boltonia diffusa* Ell.
### Boltonia

Plants: Upright, glabrous perennial from a rhizome.
Leaves: Alternate, sessile, mostly linear, entire or nearly so, acute, with base attenuate.
Inflorescence: Panicle; flowers terminal, regular; disc flowers perfect, yellow; ray flowers female, numerous, white.
Fruit: Achene.
Flowering Date: August–October.
Habitats: Along railroad tracks, prairies, roadsides, savannas, fields.
Distribution: Throughout.

## *Borrichia frutescens* (L.) DC.
### Sea Ox- Eye

Plants: Shrub from a rhizome.
Leaves: Opposite, simple, sessile, obovate to oblanceolate, entire, acute, with base attenuate.
Inflorescence: Flowers terminal, solitary, regular; disc flowers perfect, yellow; ray flowers female, numerous, yellow.
Fruit: Achene.
Flowering Date: May–September.
Habitats: Salt and brackish marshes.
Distribution: CO.

## *Brintonia discoidea* (Ell.) Greene
**Brintonia**

Plants: Upright, hairy perennial from a rhizome.

Leaves: Alternate, simple, petiolate, reduced upward, lanceolate to elliptic, with margins toothed or entire.

Inflorescence: Paniclelike; flowers perfect, regular; disc flowers white to greenish white; ray flowers absent.

Fruit: Achene.

Flowering Date: August–October.

Habitat: Woods.

Distribution: CO, NE, EC, SE.

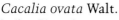

## *Cacalia ovata* Walt.
**Indian Plantain**

Plants: Upright, glabrous perennial.

Leaves: Alternate, simple, with seven to nine prominent longitudinal veins that converge toward the tip, elliptic to ovate, with margins toothed.

Inflorescence: Paniclelike, flat topped; flowers perfect, regular; disc flowers white to greenish white; ray flowers absent.

Fruit: Achene.

Flowering Date: May–August.

Habitats: Prairies, floodplains, rocky woods, fields.

Distribution: CO, NE, EC, SE.

## *Carduus nutans* L.
**Musk Thistle, Nodding Thistle**

Plants: Upright biennial with winged stems, wings spiny.

Leaves: Alternate, simple, decurrent, elliptic to lanceolate; margins toothed, teeth spiny.

Inflorescence: Heads terminal, solitary; flowers perfect, regular; disc flowers numerous, purple; involucral bracts spine tipped pappus capillary; ray flowers absent.

Fruit: Achene.

Flowering Date: May–Frost.

Habitats: Waste sites, roadsides.

Distribution: DE.

Comments: Naturalized from Europe.

## *Carphephorus odoratissimus* (Gmel.) Herb.
### Deer's Tongue, Vanilla-Plant, Hound's Tongue

Plants: Upright, glabrous perennial.
Leaves: Alternate and basal, simple, basal leaves petiolate and upper leaves sessile, elliptic to oblanceolate, entire, with tip obtuse and base attenuate.
Inflorescence: Flowers terminal, flat-topped cluster of heads; flowers perfect, regular; disc flowers purple; ray flowers absent.
Fruit: Achene.
Flowering Date: July–October.
Habitats: Sandy pinelands, savannas.
Distribution: CO.

## *Carphephorus pseudoliatris* Cass.
### False Liatris

Plants: Upright, hairy perennial.
Leaves: Alternate, simple, sessile; lower leaves spatulate to linear, entire; upper leaves becoming linear.
Inflorescence: Flat-topped or rounded cluster of heads; flowers regular, perfect; disc flowers numerous, purple; ray flowers absent.
Fruit: Achene.
Flowering Date: June–October.
Habitats: Savannas, pinelands.
Distribution: CO.

## *Centaurea cyanus* L.
### Bachelor's Button, Blue Bottle, Cornflower, Raggedy Sailors

Plants: Upright, hairy annual.
Leaves: Alternate, simple, sessile; lower leaves entire to deeply lobed; upper leaves linear, entire to toothed.
Inflorescence: Flowers terminal on long peduncles, regular, perfect; disc flowers numerous, with tip toothed to fringed, blue, violet, occasionally white; ray flowers absent.
Fruit: Achene.
Flowering Date: April–June.
Habitats: Abandoned fields, roadsides, waste sites.
Distribution: DE, NE, EC.
Comments: Naturalized from Europe.

## *Chaptalia tomentosa* Vent.
**Sunbonnets**

Plants: Upright, hairy perennial.
Leaves: Basal rosette, simple, spatulate, entire.
Inflorescence: Heads terminal, solitary, usually nodding; flowers regular; disc flowers perfect, white; ray flowers female, numerous, white, often pinkish below.
Fruit: Achene.
Flowering Date: February–May.
Habitats: Savannas, pinelands.
Distribution: CO.

## *Chrysanthemum leucanthemum* L.
**Ox-Eye Daisy**

Plants: Upright, glabrous to slightly hairy perennial from a rhizome.
Leaves: Alternate, simple, sessile, oblanceolate to spatulate below, becoming reduced upward, with margins entire to toothed or lobed.
Inflorescence: Heads terminal on long peduncles; flowers regular; disc flowers perfect, yellow; ray flowers female, numerous, white.
Fruit: Achene.
Flowering Date: April–July.
Habitats: Roadsides, fields, pastures.
Distribution: DE, NE, EC, SE, SW.

## *Chrysoma pauciflosculosa* (Michx.) Greene
**Goldenrod**

Plants: Upright shrub.
Leaves: Alternate, simple, petiolate, oblong to oblanceolate, entire, with tip obtuse and base attenuate.
Inflorescence: Paniclelike; flowers perfect, regular; disc and ray flowers yellow.
Fruit: Achene.
Flowering Date: July–November.
Habitat: Dunes, sandy woodlands.
Distribution: CO.

## *Chrysopsis camporum* Greene
**Golden Asters**

Plants: Upright, coarsely hairy perennial with a taproot.
Leaves: Alternate, elliptic to ovate, sessile or nearly so, with margins finely toothed.
Inflorescence: Heads numerous; flowers regular; disc flowers perfect, yellow; ray flowers female, numerous, golden yellow.
Fruit: Achene.
Flowering Date: July–October
Habitats: Prairies, roadside.
Distribution: NE, EC.

## *Chrysopsis mariana* (L.) Ell.
**Golden Asters**

Plants: Upright perennial with fibrous roots, initially having soft hairs but becoming glabrous at maturity.
Leaves: Alternate, simple; lower leaves oblanceolate or obovate, petiolate; upper leaves lanceolate to elliptic, sessile, entire to slightly toothed.
Inflorescence: Terminal cluster of heads; disc flowers perfect, yellow; ray flowers female, numerous, golden yellow.
Fruit: Achene.
Flowering Date: June–October.
Habitats: Fields, edges of woods, roadsides, pinelands.
Distribution: NE, EC, SE, SW.

## *Chrysopsis graminifolia* (Michx.) Ell.
**Golden Asters**

Plants: Upright, hairy perennial with fibrous roots.
Leaves: Alternate, linear to narrowly lanceolate, becoming reduced upward, entire.
Inflorescence: Heads terminating branches; flowers regular; disc flowers perfect, yellow; ray flowers female, numerous, yellow.
Flowering Date: July-October.
Habitats: Dry pinelands, roadsides.
Distribution: CO, SE.

## *Cirsium carolinianum* (Walt.) Fern. & Schub.
### Thistle

Plants: Upright biennial.
Leaves: Alternate, simple, sessile, elliptic; margins pinnately lobed with spiny tips.
Inflorescence: Terminal heads; flowers perfect, regular; disc flowers numerous, purple; ray flowers absent; involucral bracts spine tipped; pappus featherlike.
Fruit: Achene.
Flowering Date: May–August.
Habitats: Roadsides, woods.
Distribution: Northern half of state.
Comments: *C. muticum* Michx. is similar but lacks spine-tipped involucral bracts.

## *Cichorium intybus* L.
### Common Chicory, Blue Sailors

Plants: Upright, freely branching perennial with a taproot.
Leaves: Alternate, simple, sessile; basal leaves lanceolate to oblanceolate; margins toothed to dissected; stem leaves reduced upward.
Inflorescence: Heads terminal, solitary; flowers regular; disc flowers absent; ray flowers perfect, numerous, blue to purple, occasionally white.
Fruit: Achene.
Flowering Date: May–November.
Habitats: Roadsides, fields, waste sites.
Distribution: DE, NE.
Comments: The dried root can be ground and use as a strong coffee or mixed with coffee. In the spring, the young leaves can be cooked as a green. Chicory was introduced to the United States from Europe.

## *Conoclinium coelestinum* (L.) DC.
### Mist-Flower, Ageratum

Plants: Upright to reclining, hairy perennial with a rhizome.
Leaves: Opposite, simple, petiolate, ovate to lanceolate, acute to obtuse, with margins toothed and base cuneate.
Inflorescence: Terminal, flat-topped cluster of heads; flowers tubular, perfect, regular, light blue to purple.
Fruit: Achene.
Flowering Date: July–October.
Habitats: Edges of streams, woods, ditches.
Distribution: Throughout.
Comments: Easily cultivated.

### *Coreopsis auriculata* L.
**Coreopsis**

Plants: Upright or ascending, hairy perennial with stolons terminating in rosettes, usually no more than two to three nodes below the inflorescence.

Leaves: Alternate, simple, lower leaves petiolate and upper leaves sessile, acute, with margins entire to ternately lobed, and base cuneate to rounded.

Inflorescence: Heads terminal, solitary or few flowered; flowers regular; disc flowers perfect, yellow; ray flowers female, yellow, with tip toothed.

Fruit: Achene.

Flowering Date: April–June.

Habitat: Woods.

Distribution: NE, EC.

Comments: *C. pubescens* Ell. is not stoloniferous and has up to eleven nodes below the inflorescence.

### *Coreopsis lanceolata* L.
**Coreopsis**

Plants: Upright, glabrous to hairy perennial from rhizomes.

Leaves: Alternate, simple, sessile to long petiolate; basal leaves pinnately divided; upper leaves entire, acute, with base attenuate.

Inflorescence: Heads terminal, solitary or few flowered; flowers regular with long peduncles; disc flowers perfect, yellow; ray flowers female, yellow, with tip toothed.

Fruit: Achene.

Flowering Date: April–June.

Habitats: Roadsides, fields, waste sites, woodland edges.

Distribution: Throughout.

### *Coreopsis major* Walt.
**Coreopsis**

Plants: Upright, glabrous to slightly hairy perennial from a rhizome.

Leaves: Opposite, trifoliate to the base thus appearing whorled, with segments lanceolate and margins usually toothed, occasionally entire.

Inflorescence: Terminal, flat-topped cluster of heads; flowers regular; disc flowers perfect, yellow or red; ray flowers female, numerous, tips entire or slightly toothed, yellow.

Fruit: Achene.

Flowering Date: June–August.

Habitats: Roadsides, woods and woodland edges, fields.

Distribution: NE, EC, SW.

## *Coreopsis nudata* Nutt.
### Pink Coreopsis

Plants: Upright, glabrous perennial from a rhizome.
Leaves: Alternate, simple, sessile, linear, entire.
Inflorescence: Solitary heads on peduncles; flowers regular; disc flowers perfect, yellow; ray flowers female, numerous, pink to pale purple.
Fruit: Achene.
Flowering Date: April–June.
Habitats: Savannas, pinelands.
Distribution: CO.

## *Coreopsis tinctoria* Nutt.
### Calliopsis

Plants: Upright, glabrous annual or perennial.
Leaves: Opposite, simple, pinnately to bipinnately dissected, with segments linear.
Inflorescence: Open, somewhat flat-topped cluster of heads; flowers regular; disc flowers perfect, red; ray flowers female, numerous, yellow with a red spot at the base, three lobed at the tip.
Fruit: Achene.
Flowering Date: May–July.
Habitats: Fields, roadsides, waste sites.
Distribution: Throughout.
Comments: Easily cultivated. *C. linifolia* Nutt. is similar but has entire leaves and rays that are four lobed at the apex, and it is found in savannas, ditches, bogs, and pinewoods of the Coastal province.

## *Coreopsis tripteris* L.
### Coreopsis

Plants: Upright, glabrous perennial.
Leaves: Opposite, trifoliate, petiolate; leaflets lanceolate, entire.
Inflorescence: Terminal heads; flowers regular; disc flowers perfect, yellow becoming red or purple; ray flowers female, yellow.
Flowering Date: July–September.
Habitats: Roadsides, waste areas, woods.
Distribution: NE, EC, SE.

## *Dracopis amplexicaulis* (Vahl) Cass.
### Coneflower

Plants: Upright, glabrous annual.

Leaves: Alternate, simple, sessile, ovate to lanceolate, entire, with tip acute to attenuate and base cordate, clasping.

Inflorescence: Terminal, solitary heads on long peduncles; flowers regular; disc flowers perfect, elongated, brown to reddish brown; ray flowers female, numerous, yellow tipped, reddish to reddish purple toward the base.

Fruit: Achene.

Flowering Date: June–July.

Habitats: Old fields, prairies, waste sites, roadsides, ditches.

Distribution: DE, NE, EC, SE.

## *Echinacea purpurea* (L.) Moench
### Pale Purple Coneflower

Plants: Upright, hairy to glabrous perennial.

Leaves: Alternate, simple, petiolate, lanceolate to ovate, entire to slightly toothed, acute.

Inflorescence: Terminal, solitary heads on long peduncles; flowers regular; disc flowers perfect, dark brown to purple; ray flowers female, numerous, usually more than 2 inches long.

Fruit: Achene.

Flowering Date: June–July.

Habitats: Prairies, roadsides, woodland edges.

Distribution: EC.

## *Elephantopus carolinianus* Raeusch.
### Elephant's Foot

Plants: Upright, hairy, freely branched perennial.

Leaves: Alternate, simple; basal leaves ovate to lanceolate, acute to acuminate, with margins slightly toothed and base attenuate; stem leaves well developed.

Inflorescence: Terminal, solitary heads on long peduncles; flowers perfect, regular; disc flowers purple, pink, occasionally white; ray flowers absent; outer involucral bracts ovate.

Fruit: Achene.

Flowering Date: August–November.

Habitat: Woodlands.

Distribution: Throughout.

Comments: *E. tomentosus* has reduced stem leaves.

## *Erigeron strigosus* Muhl. ex Willd.
### Daisy Fleabane

Plants: Upright, freely branching glabrous to slightly hairy annual.

Leaves: Alternate, simple; basal leaves oblanceolate to elliptic, entire to toothed, with base attenuate; upper leaves linear to narrowly lanceolate, mostly entire.

Inflorescence: Terminal, flat-topped cluster of heads; flowers regular; disc flowers perfect, yellow; ray flowers female, numerous, white to pale pink.

Fruit: Achene.

Flowering Date: May–October.

Distribution: Throughout.

## *Erigeron philadelphicus* L.
### Philadelphia Fleabane

Plants: Upright hairy biennial or short-lived perennial.

Leaves: Alternate, simple; basal leaves oblanceolate to elliptic, petiolate, acute or obtuse, with margins toothed or shallowly lobed and base cuneate or attenuate; stem leaves reduced, often clasping.

Inflorescence: Terminal, flat-topped cluster of heads; flowers regular; disc flowers perfect, yellow; ray flowers female, seventy-five to one hundred, white to lavender.

Fruit: Achene.

Flowering Date: April–June.

Habitats: Yards, waste sites, old fields.

Distribution: DE, NE, EC.

Comments: *E. pulchellus* Michx. (Robin's Plantain) is stoloniferous, has fifty or fewer ray flowers, and is found in rich woods.

*Eupatorium capillifolium*
(Lam.) Small
**Dog Fennel**

Plants: Upright, hairy annual or short-
lived perennial.
Leaves: Alternate, often opposite at the
stem base, simple, pinnately to bipinnately dissected into filiform segments.
Inflorescence: Panicle of heads; flowers
regular, perfect; flowers yellowish
white to purplish white.
Fruit: Achene.
Flowering Date: September–November.
Habitats: Roadsides, fields, woods.
Distribution: Throughout.

*Eupatoriadelphus fistulosus*
(Barr.) King & H. E. Robins.
**Joe-Pye Weed**

Plants: Upright, nearly glabrous perennial with hollow stems.
Leaves: Whorled, four to seven per
node, lanceolate, petiolate, entire,
acute to acuminate, with base attenuate.
Inflorescence: Paniclelike; heads terminal; flowers of disc flowers only,
perfect, with corolla five lobed, pink,
lavender, or purple.
Fruit: Achene.
Flowering Date: July–October.
Habitats: Ditches, alluvial woods,
fields.
Distribution: Throughout.

## *Eupatorium hyssopifolium* L.
**Boneset**

Plants: Upright, hairy perennial.
Leaves: In whorls of 3 or 4 four, some-
   times opposite or alternate; mostly
   sessile, narrowly lanceolate to linear,
   entire; principal leaves subtending
   axillary clusters of smaller leaves.
Inflorescence: Terminal heads; flowers
   tubular, regular, perfect, white.
Fruit: Achene.
Flowering Date: July–October.
Habitats: Waste sites, roadsides, fields.
Distribution: NE, EC, SE, SW.

## *Eupatorium perfoliatum* L.
**Boneset**

Plants: Upright, hairy perennial.
Leaves: Opposite, but attached at the
   base, therefore appearing perfoliate;
   lanceolate, with margins toothed and
   tip long acuminate.
Inflorescence: Terminal, flat-topped
   cluster of heads; flowers perfect, reg-
   ular; disc flowers white.
Fruit: Achene.
Flowering Date: August–October.
Habitat: Woods.
Distribution: Throughout.

## *Eupatorium rotundifolium* L.
**Boneset**

Plants: Upright, hairy perennial.
Leaves: Opposite, simple, sessile, ovate
   to nearly round; margins toothed;
   apex obtuse, acute, to rounded; base
   rounded to truncate.
Inflorescence: Terminal, flat-topped
   cluster of heads; flowers perfect, reg-
   ular; disc flowers white.
Fruit: Achene.
Flowering Date: August–October.
Habitats: Woods, savannas.
Distribution: CO, NE, EC, SE.

### *Eupatorium serotinum* Michx.
**Boneset**

Plants: Upright, hairy perennial.

Leaves: Opposite, lanceolate to elliptic, acuminate to acute, with margins toothed and base cuneate to truncate.

Inflorescence: Terminal, flat-topped cluster of heads; flowers perfect, regular; disc flowers white.

Fruit: Achene.

Flowering Date: August–October.

Habitats: Waste sites, roadsides, along railroad tracks, fields.

Distribution: Throughout.

### *Euthamia leptocephala* (T. & G.) Greene
**Flat-Topped Goldenrod**

Plants: Upright, glabrous or hairy perennial with angular stems and rhizomes.

Leaves: Alternate, simple, sessile, linear, with three prominent veins (not dotted with resin).

Inflorescence: Terminal, flat-topped cluster of heads; flowers regular; disc flowers perfect, yellow; ray flowers female, yellow.

Fruit: Achene.

Flowering Date: September–October.

Habitat: Fields, glades, roadsides, prairies.

Distribution: EC, DE, CO.

Comments: *E. minor* and *E. tenuifolia* have leaves that are resin dotted. The two species differ from one another in that the former has a prominent midvein, while the latter usually has a faint vein parallel to the midvein on both sides. Some botanists consider these species to be the same.

## *Gaillardia pulchella* Foug.
### Blanket Flower, Indian Blanket, Fire Wheels.

Plants: Upright, hairy annual or short-lived perennial with ribbed stems.

Leaves: Alternate, simple; leaves petiolate, lanceolate to oblanceolate, acute, with margins toothed or slightly lobed and base attenuate.

Inflorescence: Terminal, solitary head on a long peduncle; flowers regular; disc flowers perfect, dark brown to deep red; ray flowers sterile, numerous, red tipped with yellow in various degrees.

Fruit: Achene.

Flowering Date: April–December.

Habitats: Sandy roadsides, sandy fields, dunes, prairies.

Distribution: CO.

### *Gnaphalium obtusifolium* L.
**Sweet Everlasting, Rabbit Tobacco, Pearly Everlasting, Catfoot, Old-Field Balsam**

Plants: Upright, densely hairy annual.

Leaves: Alternate, simple, lanceolate to nearly linear, entire, acute, with base attenuate.

Inflorescence: Panicle of heads; disc flowers perfect, regular; flowers whitish; rays absent.

Fruit: Achene.

Flowering Date: August–October.

Habitats: Woods, roadsides, disturbed sites.

Distribution: NE, EC.

Comments: *G. purpureum* has basal leaves and fewer stem leaves.

### *Haplopappus divaricatus* (Nutt.) Gray
**Haplopappus**

Plants: Upright, hairy annual with a taproot.

Leaves: Alternate, simple, sessile, elliptic to oblanceolate, with margins toothed, base attenuate, and tip spine tipped.

Inflorescence: Paniclelike; heads on peduncles; flowers regular; disc flowers perfect, yellow; ray flowers female, yellow.

Fruit: Achene.

Flowering Date: August–October.

Habitats: Roadsides, open woods.

Distribution: NE.

### *Helenium amarum* (Raf.) H. Rock
**Sneeze Weed, Bitterweed**

Plants: Upright, glabrous, branching annual with a taproot.

Leaves: Alternate, simple, sessile, linear.

Inflorescence: Terminal, solitary head on a peduncle; flowers regular; disc flowers perfect, yellow; ray flowers female, ten to fifteen, three lobed at the tip, yellow.

Fruit: Achene.

Flowering Date: May–December.

Habitats: Roadsides, pastures, abandoned fields.

Distribution: Throughout.

Comments: The plants contain a narcotic poison. Cows that graze on the plants produce bitter-tasting milk.

## *Helenium flexuosum* Raf.
### Sneeze Weed

Plants: Upright, glabrous, branching perennial.

Leaves: Alternate, simple, elliptic to oblanceolate, entire to toothed; lower leaves with bases attenuate, petiolate; upper leaves smaller, sessile, with bases decurrent and forming wings on the stem.

Inflorescence: Terminal, solitary head on a peduncle; flowers regular; disc flowers perfect, reddish; ray flowers female, three lobed at the tip, yellow.

Fruit: Achene.

Flowering Date: September–October.

Habitats: Roadsides, woodland edges, fields, ditches.

Distribution: Throughout.

Comments: *H. autumnale* L. has yellow disc flowers. The two species contain a bitter substance that gives a bitter taste to the milk of cows that have grazed on the plants. It is reported that some Indians used the plant to treat colds by rubbing the plant to produce sneezing.

## *Helenium vernale* Walt.
### Sneeze Weed

Plants: Upright, glabrous to hairy annual with a taproot.

Leaves: Alternate, simple, sessile, linear, with base slightly decurrent.

Inflorescence: Terminal, solitary head on a peduncle; flowers regular; disc flower perfect, yellow; ray flowers female, numerous, three lobed at tip, yellow.

Fruit: Achene.

Flowering Date: April–May.

Habitats: Pinelands, savannas.

Distribution: CO.

## *Helianthus anqustifolius* L.
**Helianthus**

Plants: Upright, hairy perennial from a
   short rhizome.
Leaves: Lower leaves opposite and upper leaves alternate, linear to narrowly lanceolate, entire.
Inflorescence: Terminal, solitary head
   on a peduncle; flowers regular; disc
   flowers perfect, reddish brown; ray
   flowers female, numerous, yellow.
Fruit: Achene
Flowering Date: July–December.
Habitats: Roadsides, savannas, woodland and pineland edges.
Distribution: Throughout.

## *Helianthus annuus* L.
**Common Sunflower**

Plants: Upright, hairy annual with a
   taproot.
Leaves: Lower leaves opposite and upper leaves alternate, simple, sessile,
   ovate to triangular, acute to acuminate, with margins toothed and base
   truncate to cordate.
Inflorescence: Terminal, solitary head
   per peduncle; flowers regular; disc
   flowers perfect, reddish brown; ray
   flowers female, numerous, yellow.
Fruit: Achene.
Flowering Date: June–October.
Habitats: Roadsides, pastures, old
   fields, waste areas.
Distribution: DE, NE, EC, SE, SW.

## *Helianthus heterophyllus* Nutt.
### Sunflower

Plants: Upright, hairy perennial.

Leaves: Opposite, mostly on the lower part of the stem; lanceolate or elliptic to linear; entire to toothed; base cuneate to attenuate; leaves reduced upward.

Inflorescence: Terminal, solitary head per peduncle; flowers regular; disc flowers perfect, reddish to purple; ray flowers female, yellow.

Fruit: Achene.

Flowering Date: August–October.

Habitats: Savannas, pinewoods.

Distribution: CO.

## *Helianthus hirsutus* Raf.
### Sunflower

Plants: Upright, hairy perennial from rhizomes.

Leaves: Opposite, simple, sessile, lanceolate, entire to toothed, acuminate, with base rounded or truncate.

Inflorescence: Terminal, solitary head per peduncle; flowers regular; disc flowers perfect, yellow; ray flowers female, numerous, yellow.

Fruit: Achene.

Flowering Date: June–August.

Habitats: Woods and woodland edges, roadsides.

Distribution: CO, NE, EC, SE, SW.

Comments: *H. divaricatus* L. is similar but has glabrous stems.

## *Helianthus microcephalus* T. & G.
### Small-Flowered Helianthus

Plants: Upright, glabrous perennial.

Leaves: Opposite, simple, petiolate, lanceolate, entire or toothed, with base cuneate.

Inflorescence: Terminal, solitary head per peduncle; flowers regular; disc flowers perfect, yellow; ray flowers female yellow.

Fruit: Achene.

Flowering Date: August–October.

Habitats: Edges of woods, roadsides, fields.

Distribution: EC, NE.

Comments: The flower heads of this species are much smaller than those of any other member of *Helianthus.*

### *Helianthus mollis* Lam.
**Ashy Sunflower**

Plants: Upright, hairy perennial from rhizomes.

Leaves: Opposite, simple, sessile, ovate to lanceolate, densely hairy, acute, with margins toothed and base rounded or cordate.

Inflorescence: Terminal, solitary head on a peduncle; flowers regular; disc flowers perfect, yellow; ray flowers female, numerous, yellow.

Fruit: Achene.

Flowering Date: June–August.

Habitats: Prairies, woodland edges, roadsides.

Distribution: EC.

### *Helianthus strumosus* L.
**Sunflower**

Plants: Upright, mostly glabrous perennial from rhizomes.

Leaves: Opposite, simple, petiolate, lanceolate, acuminate, with margins toothed and base cuneate to nearly rounded.

Inflorescence: Terminal, solitary head on a peduncle; flowers regular; disc flowers perfect, yellow; ray flowers female, numerous, yellow.

Fruit: Achene.

Flowering Date: July–September.

Habitats: Woodland edges, thickets.

Distribution: NE, EC.

### *Heterotheca subaxillaris* (Lam.) Britt. & Rusby
**Golden Aster**

Plants: Upright to ascending, hairy perennial.

Leaves: Alternate, simple, lower leaves petiolate and upper leaves sessile, ovate to elliptical, acute, with margins toothed, base attenuate, and leaves becoming reduced upward.

Inflorescence: Heads in panicles or clusters; flowers regular; disc flowers perfect, yellow; ray flowers female, numerous, yellow.

Fruit: Achene.

Flowering Date: June–November.

Habitats: Roadsides, fields, dunes.

Distribution: CO.

## *Hieracium gronovii* L.
### Hawkweed

Plants: Upright, hairy perennial from a rhizome.

Leaves: Mostly basal or on the lower part of the stem, reduced upward, simple, elliptic to oblanceolate, hairy, entire to toothed, with tip acute to obtuse and base cuneate to attenuate.

Inflorescence: Compact panicle of heads; flowers perfect, regular; disc flowers absent; ray flowers numerous, yellow.

Fruit: Achene.

Flowering Date: July–December.

Habitats: Woods and woodland edges, roadsides, fields.

Distribution: NE, EC, SW, SE.

## *Krigia dandelion* (L.) Nutt.
### Dwarf Dandelion

Plants: Upright, mostly glabrous perennial with a tuber.

Leaves: Basal, simple, sessile; lanceolate to oblanceolate or linear; margins toothed or lobed; base attenuate.

Inflorescence: Head on stalk lacking leaves; flowers perfect, regular; disc flowers absent; ray flowers numerous, yellow.

Fruit: Achene.

Flowering Date: April–May.

Habitats: Prairies, rocky woods, roadsides, fields, yards.

Distribution: Mostly northern half of state.

Comments: *K. virginica* is much smaller and is an annual. *K. biflora* has stem leaves that are sessile or clasping.

## *Kuhnia eupatorioides* L.
### False Boneset

Plants: Upright, hairy perennial.

Leaves: Alternate to nearly opposite on lower leaves, sessile or nearly so, linear to narrowly lanceolate, entire to toothed, acute to acuminate, with base cuneate to rounded.

Inflorescence: Heads in panicles or clusters; disc flowers perfect, cream to dull whitish yellow; ray flowers absent.

Fruit: Achene.

Flowering Date: June–October.

Habitats: Prairies, woods.

Distribution: NE, EC, SE.

### *Lactuca floridana* (L.) Gaertn.
**Wild Lettece**

Plants: Upright, glabrous biennial.
Leaves: Alternate, simple, sessile, lanceolate to triangular, dissected to nearly entire, with base attenuate.
Inflorescence: Panicle of heads; flowers perfect, regular; disc flowers absent; ray flowers numerous, light to dark blue.
Fruit: Achene.
Flowering Date: July–November.
Habitats: Prairies, roadsides, edges of woods.
Distribution: Throughout.
Comments: *L. canadensis* L. has yellow flowers.

### *Liatris aspera* Michx.
**Blazing Star, Gay Feather**

Plants: Upright, hairy to glabrous perennial.
Leaves: Alternate, simple, sessile, linear to narrowly elliptic, entire.
Inflorescence: Spike of heads; flowers perfect, regular; flowers numerous, pink to light purple; bracts purplish toward the tip; ray flowers absent.
Fruit: Achene.
Flowering Date: July–August.
Habitats: Prairies, rocky woods.
Distribution: NE, EC, SE.

### *Liatris elegans* (Walt.) Michx.
**Blazing Star, Gay Feather**

Plants: Upright, hairy perennial with corms.
Leaves: Alternate, linear, entire.
Inflorescence: Spike or raceme of heads; flowers perfect, regular; flowers white to pinkish; bracts petaloid, pink or white; ray flowers absent.
Fruit: Achene.
Flowering Date: September–October.
Habitats: Woods, prairies, savannas.
Distribution: CO, SE.

## *Liatris squarrosa* (L.) Michx.
### Blazing Star, Gay Feather

Plants: Upright, mostly hairy perennial.

Leaves: Alternate, simple, sessile, linear to narrowly lanceolate.

Inflorescence: Terminal and axillary heads; flowers on peduncles, regular, numerous, pink to light purple; ray flowers absent.

Fruit: Achene.

Flowering Date: June–August.

Habitats: Prairies, roadsides, woodland edges.

Distribution: CO, NE, EC, SE.

Comments: *L. spicata* (L.) Willd. has a spiked inflorescence with bracts that are purplish to straw colored at the margins.

## *Marshallia tenuifolia* Raf.
### Marshallia, Barbara's Buttons

Plants: Upright, glabrous to hairy perennial.

Leaves: Alternate, linear to lanceolate, entire.

Inflorescence: Terminal head; flowers perfect; corolla white or pinkish to purplish.

Fruit: Achene.

Flowering Date: July–September.

Habitats: Savannas, pinewoods, ditches.

Distribution: CO.

Comments: *M. trinervia* has ovate leaves and blooms in the spring.

## *Melanthera nivea* (L.) Small
### Melanthera

Plants: Erect to arching, hairy perennial.

Leaves: Opposite, simple, petiolate, ovate to lanceolate, acuminate, with margins lobed to toothed and base cuneate.

Inflorescence: Heads terminal or in clusters; disc flowers perfect, white; ray flowers absent.

Fruit: Achene.

Flowering Date: June–November.

Habitats: Roadsides, woodland edges.

Distribution: NE, EC.

## *Mikania scandens* (L.) Willd.
### Climbing Hempweed

Plants: Climbing vine with nearly four-angled stems.

Leaves: Opposite, simple, petiolate, ovate to nearly triangular, entire, acuminate, with base cordate.

Inflorescence: Terminal or axillary flat-topped cluster of heads; flowers perfect, regular; disc flowers numerous, white; ray flowers absent.

Fruit: Achene.

Flowering Date: July–October.

Habitats: Fence rows, thickets, woods.

Distribution: Throughout.

## *Parthenium integrifolium* L.
### Wild Quinine

Plants: Upright, glabrous to hairy perennial.

Leaves: Alternate and basal, simple, petiolate, elliptic to lanceolate, with margins toothed or occasionally lobed.

Inflorescence: Terminal heads; flowers regular; disc flowers sterile, white; ray flowers female, tip toothed, white.

Fruit: Achene.

Flowering Date: June–August.

Habitats: Woodland edges, roadsides, fields.

Distribution: Mostly northern half of state.

## *Pluchea rosea Godfrey*
### Marsh Fleabane

Plants: Upright, hairy, branching annual or short-lived perennial.

Leaves: Alternate, simple, elliptic to lanceolate, obtuse to acute, with margins toothed and base clasping.

Inflorescence: Panicle of heads; flowers perfect, regular; disc flowers purple; ray flowers absent.

Fruit: Achene.

Flowering Date: August–October.

Habitats: Edges of streams, wet ditches.

Distribution: Throughout.

Comments: The plant produces a strong camphorlike odor.

## *Polymnia uvedalia* L.
### Bearsfoot, Leaf-Cup

Plants: Upright, glabrous to hairy perennial with hollow, angulate stems.

Leaves: Lower leaves opposite and upper leaves alternate, simple, petiolate, pinnately or palmately lobed or dissected, with margins toothed.

Inflorescence: Panicle of heads; flowers regular; disc flowers with stamens and pistils but sterile, yellow; ray flowers female, yellow.

Fruit: Achene.

Flowering Date: July–October.

Habitats: Alluvial or upland woods.

Distribution: DE, NE, EC.

## *Prenanthes altissima* L.
### Rattlesnake Root

Plants: Upright, glabrous biennial.

Leaves: Alternate, simple, entire, toothed, dissected or palmately lobed, with upper leaves nearly sessile and lower leaves petiolate.

Inflorescence: Paniclelike, with heads drooping; flowers yellowish, nine or more per head; involucre green to purplish.

Fruit: Achene.

Flowering Date: August–November.

Habitat: Woods.

Distribution: NE.

Comments: *P. serpentaria* (Gall-of-the-Earth, Lion's Foot) is similar but has eight or fewer flowers per head.

## *Pyrrhopappus carolinianus* (Walt.) DC.
### False Dandelion

Plants: Upright, branching biennial; glabrous below, hairy above.

Leaves: Alternate and basal, with basal leaves petiolate and upper leaves sessile, oblanceolate to elliptic, acute to acuminate, with margins toothed to dissected.

Inflorescence: Terminal, solitary heads on a peduncle; flowers perfect, regular; disc flowers absent; ray flowers numerous, yellow.

Fruit: Achene.

Flowering Date: April–June.

Habitats: Roadsides, pastures, fields, waste sites.

Distribution: DE, NE, EC, SE, SW.

## *Ratibida pinnata* (Vent.) Barnh.
### Gray-Head Coneflower, Drooping Coneflower, Prairie Coneflower

Plants: Upright, hairy perennial from a rhizome.

Leaves: Alternate, simple, petiolate but upper leaves often sessile, entire or toothed; margins deeply dissected, with segments lanceolate.

Inflorescence: Terminal, solitary head on a long peduncle; flowers regular; disc flowers perfect, gray before maturity and turning dark brown with age; ray flowers female, drooping, eight to ten, tip notched or lobed, yellow.

Fruit: Achene.

Flowering Date: May–September.

Habitats: Prairies, roadsides, woodland edges.

Distribution: NE, EC.

## *Rudbeckia hirta* L.
### Black-Eyed Susan

Plants: Upright, hairy perennial or biennial with a taproot.

Leaves: Alternate and basal, simple, petiolate, entire to toothed, acute; elliptic or ovate to lanceolate; base cuneate to rounded.

Inflorescence: Terminal, solitary head per peduncle; flowers regular; disc flowers perfect, dark brown; ray flowers sterile, yellow.

Fruit: Achene.

Flowering Date: May–August.

Habitats: Prairies, roadsides, woodland edges.

Distribution: Throughout.

*Senecio glabellus* Poir.
## Groundsel, Butterweed, Squaw-Weed

Plants: Upright, glabrous annual.
Leaves: Basal and alternate, simple, with lower leaves petiolate and upper leaves sessile, elliptic to oblanceolate, pinnately dissected.
Inflorescence: Terminal cluster of heads; flowers regular; disc flowers perfect, yellow; ray flowers female, numerous, yellow.
Fruit: Achene.
Flowering Date: March–June.
Habitats: Alluvial woods, wet roadside ditches.
Distribution: Throughout.
Comments: *S. smallii* Britt. is a perennial with mostly basal leaves that is usually found in drier habitats than *S. glabellus* Poir. *S. aureus* L. (Golden Ragwort) usually has a cluster of stems from rhizomes or stoloniferous basal offshoots.

*Rudbeckia triloba* L.
## Coneflower

Plants: Upright, hairy to glabrous perennial.
Leaves: Alternate, simple, ovate, acute to acuminate; lower leaves three lobed, pinnately dissected, or toothed; upper leaves usually not lobed or dissected; base truncate, cuneate, or rounded.
Inflorescence: Terminal, solitary head per peduncle; flowers regular; disc flowers perfect, deep purple to black; ray flowers sterile, yellow.
Fruit: Achene.
Flowering Date: July–October.
Habitats: Roadsides, edges of woods, fields.
Distribution: DE, EC, NE.

*Silphium integrifolium* Michx.
## Rosin Weed

Plants: Upright, perennial with a rhizome.
Leaves: Opposite but occasionally alternate, sessile, often clasping, ovate to lanceolate, entire to toothed.
Inflorescence: Terminal cluster of heads, occasionally only one; flowers regular; disc flowers sterile, dark brown; ray flowers numerous, perfect, tip notched, yellow.
Fruit: Achene.
Flowering Date: July–September.
Habitats: Rocky woods, prairies.
Distribution: EC, SE.

*Silphium perfoliatum* L.
**Cup Plant**

Plants: Upright, glabrous perennial
with a taproot.
Leaves: Perfoliate, lanceolate, acumi-
nate, with margins toothed.
Inflorescence: Panicle of heads; flowers
regular; disc flowers sterile, dark
brown; ray flowers perfect, numer-
ous, yellow.
Fruit: Achene.
Flowering Date: June–August.
Habitats: Wet ditches, alluvial woods.
Distribution: NE, EC, SE, SW.

*Silphium laciniatum* L.
**Compass Plant**

Plants: Upright, hairy perennial with a
taproot.
Leaves: Basal and alternate, simple, reduced upward, sessile, with margins
pinnately dissected.
Inflorescence: Open raceme of heads;
flowers regular; disc flowers sterile,
dark brown; ray flowers perfect, numerous, yellow.
Fruit: Achene.
Flowering Date: July–September.
Habitats: Prairies, chalk outcrops,
along railroad tracks.
Distribution: NE, EC.

## *Silphium terebinthinaceum* Jacq.
### Prairie Dock

Plants: Upright, mostly glabrous perennial with a taproot.

Leaves: Basal and alternate, simple, lower leaves petiolate and upper leaves sessile, ovate, mostly entire, with tip obtuse to rounded and base cordate.

Inflorescence: Panicle of heads; flowers regular; disc flowers sterile, dark brown; ray flowers perfect, numerous, tip notched, yellow.

Fruit: Achene.

Flowering Date: July–September.

Habitats: Prairies, roadsides.

Distribution: NE, EC.

## *Silphium trifoliatum* var. *latifolium* Gray
### Rosin Weed

Plants: Upright, glabrous perennial.

Leaves: Opposite, sessile to petiolate, lanceolate, entire to slightly toothed, acute to acuminate, with base cuneate.

Inflorescence: Open, paniclelike heads, few to numerous; flowers regular; disc flowers sterile, dark brown; ray flowers perfect, numerous, yellow.

Fruit: Achene.

Flowering Date: June–September.

Habitats: Roadsides, edges of woods, fields.

Distribution: EC.

## *Solidago caesia* L.
### Bluestem Goldenrod

Plants: Glabrous perennial with arching stems and rhizomes.

Leaves: Alternate, simple, sessile or short petiolate, elliptic, acuminate, with margins toothed and base cuneate.

Inflorescence: Flowers in axillary clusters, regular; disc flowers perfect, yellow; ray flowers female, yellow.

Fruit: Achene.

Flowering Date: September–October.

Habitats: Alluvial woods, edges of streams.

Distribution: NE, EC, SE, SW.

*Solidago odora* Ait.
**Goldenrod**

Plants: Upright, glabrous to slightly
    hairy perennial.
Leaves: Alternate, simple, sessile, lan-
    ceolate to elliptic, entire, acute to
    acuminate, with base cuneate to
    rounded.
Inflorescence: Panicle of heads, usually
    bent to one side, with base broader
    than the tip; flowers regular; disc
    flowers perfect, yellow; ray flowers
    female, yellow.
Fruit: Achene.
Flowering Date: July–October.
Habitats: Savannas, pinelands, road-
    sides, dry woods.
Distribution: CO, NE, EC, SE, SW.

*Solidago gigantea* Ait.
**Giant Goldenrod**

Plants: Upright, glabrous perennial
    with rhizomes.
Leaves: Alternate, simple, lower leaves
    petiolate and upper leaves sessile, el-
    liptic, acuminate, with margins
    toothed and base cuneate.
Inflorescence: Panicle of heads; flowers
    regular; disc flowers perfect, yellow;
    ray flowers female, yellow.
Fruit: Achene.
Flowering Date: July–October.
Habitats: Fields, roadsides, stream
    banks.
Distribution: Throughout.
Comments: *S. canadensis* L. is similar
    but has hairy stems. *S. nemoralis*
    Ait. has basal, spatulate leaves that
    become reduced upward.

### *Solidago rigida* L.
**Prairie Goldenrod**

Plants: Upright, densely hairy perennial.

Leaves: Alternate and basal; basal leaves petiolate, lanceolate to elliptic, acute to rounded, with base cuneate; upper leaves sessile, somewhat clasping, with tip rounded and margins toothed.

Inflorescence: Terminal cluster of heads, flat-topped to somewhat rounded; flowers regular; disc flowers perfect, yellow; ray flowers female, yellow.

Fruit: Achene.

Flowering Date: August–October.

Habitats: Prairies; dry rocky roadsides; mostly restricted to basic soils.

Distribution: EC.

### *Solidago sempervirens* L.
**Seaside Goldenrod**

Plants: Upright, glabrous to slightly hairy perennial; somewhat succulent.

Leaves: Alternate, simple; lower leaves petiolate, elliptic; upper leaves sessile, elliptic to ovate, often appressed to the stem; entire to slightly toothed.

Inflorescence: Compact, paniclelike heads; flowers regular; disc flowers perfect, yellow; ray flowers female, yellow.

Fruit: Achene.

Flowering Date: August–November.

Habitats: Salt and brackish marshes, dunes.

Distribution: CO.

### *Solidago ulmifolia* Muhl.
**Elm-Leaf Goldenrod**

Plants: Upright, glabrous to hairy perennial.

Leaves: Alternate, elliptic, petiolate or sessile, acute to acuminate, with margins toothed and bases cuneate to attenuate.

Inflorescence: Paniclelike heads with up to twelve regular flowers; disc flowers perfect, yellow; ray flowers female, yellow.

Fruit: Achene.

Flowering Date: September–November.

Habitats: Woods, stream banks.

Distribution: NE, EC.

### *Stokesia laevis* (Hill) Greene
**Stokesia**

Plants: Upright, glabrous to hairy perennial.

Leaves: Alternate, simple, sessile, thick; lower leaves elliptic, leaves becoming lanceolate upward; margins toothed.

Inflorescence: Terminal, solitary head on a short peduncle; flowers perfect, regular; disc flowers blue; ray flowers numerous, tip five lobed, dark to light blue.

Fruit: Achene.

Flowering Date: June–August.

Habitats: Pinelands, roadsides.

Distribution: CO.

### *Verbesina alternifolia* (L.) Britt.
**Crown-Beard**

Plants: Upright, glabrous to slightly hairy perennial.

Leaves: Alternate, simple, petiolate, lanceolate to ovate, with margins toothed to nearly entire.

Inflorescence: Panicle of heads; flowers regular; disc flowers perfect, yellow; ray flowers sterile, two to 10, yellow, drooping or nearly so.

Fruit: Capsule.

Flowering Date: August–September.

Habitats: Alluvial woods, roadside ditches, marshes.

Distribution: NE, EC, SE, SW.

Comments: *V. helianthoides* Michx. has eight to fifteen ray flowers and leaves with decurrent bases producing conspicuously winged stems.

## *Verbesina virginica* L.
### White Crown-Beard

Plants: Upright, hairy perennial with
fleshy roots.
Leaves: Alternate, simple, petiolate
and winged, ovate to nearly lanceolate, with margins toothed and base
cuneate to rounded.
Inflorescence: Terminal, flat-topped
cluster of heads; flowers regular; disc
flowers perfect, white; ray flowers female, one to five, white.
Fruit: Capsule.
Flowering Date: July–October.
Habitats: Woods, fields, roadsides.
Distribution: DE, NE, EC, SE, SW.

## *Vernonia angustifolia* Michx.
### Ironweed

Plants: Upright, hairy to glabrous perennial.
Leaves: Alternate, simple, sessile,
linear to narrowly lanceolate, entire
to slightly toothed.
Inflorescence: Open, paniclelike, usually flat topped; flowers perfect, regular; disc flowers purple; ray flowers
absent.
Fruit: Capsule.
Flowering Date: June–September.
Habitats: Pinelands, dunes.
Distribution: CO, SW.

## *Vernonia gigantea* (Walt.) Trel.
### ex Branner & Coville.
### Ironweed

Plants: Upright, glabrous to hairy perennial.
Leaves: Alternate, simple, petiolate,
lanceolate to oblanceolate, acute to
acuminate, with margins toothed
and base attenuate.
Inflorescence: Terminal, flat-topped
cluster of heads; flowers perfect, regular; disc flowers purple; ray flowers
absent.
Fruit: Capsule.
Flowering Date: August–October.
Habitats: Roadsides, prairies, woods,
stream edges.
Distribution: Throughout.

# BALSAMINACEAE
## Touch- Me-Not Family

Plants annual or perennial with somewhat succulent stems. Leaves alternate and simple. Flowers irregular; three sepals, two forming a saclike structure with a spur; five petals, orange or yellow; ovary superior; five stamens. Fruit a capsule that springs open upon being touched or moved at maturity.

### *Impatiens capensis* Meerb.
### Spotted Touch- Me-Not, Jewel Weed

Plants: Upright, glabrous, branched annual with hollow stems.

Leaves: Alternate, simple, petiolate, elliptic to ovate, with margins toothed and base rounded.

Inflorescence: Axillary clusters; flowers perfect, irregular; three sepals, with middle sepal saccate and modified into a spur; five petals; both sepals and petals orange to red, usually spotted; five stamens.

Fruit: Capsule.

Flowering Date: May–November.

Habitats: Edges of streams, wet alluvial woods, marshes.

Distribution: DE, NE, EC, SE, SW.

Comments: The fruit at maturity snaps open suddenly upon the slightest touch, dispersing the seeds. The name Jewel Weed comes from the shiny, silvery appearance of the leaf when placed under water. It is reported that rubbing the leaves on the skin will relieve the pain of stinging nettle and prevent poison ivy dermatitis.

# BATACEAE
## Saltwort Family

Plants perennial, somewhat woody, dioecious, restricted to salt marshes and salt flats. Leaves simple, succulent. Fruit multiple berries.

### *Batis maritima* L.
### Saltwort

Plants: Trailing, dioecious, succulent perennial that becomes somewhat woody with age.

Leaves: Opposite, succulent, sessile, narrowly lanceolate to linear, somewhat cylindrical, acute, with base attenuate.

Inflorescence: Flowers axillary, cone-like, sessile or stalked, imperfect, with subtending, fleshy scales.

Fruit: Berrylike.

Flowering Date: June–July.

Habitats: Salt marshes, salt flats.

Distribution: CO.

# BERBERIDACEAE
## Barberry Family

Plants perennial from a usually extensive rhizome system. Leaves opposite. Flower solitary and occurring at the axis of the two leaves; sepals and petals similar; ovary superior; stamens usually twice as many as the petals. Fruit a berry.

## *Podophyllum peltatum* L.
### Mayapple, Mandrake

Plants: Upright, glabrous perennial with rhizomes; forms large populations.

Leaves: Opposite, simple, orbicular, palmately deeply parted, with segments dentate, at least at the tip.

Inflorescence: Flowers terminal, solitary from between the two leaves, regular, perfect; six sepals; six to nine petals, white; twelve to eighteen stamens, noticeably yellow.

Fruit: Berry.

Habitats: Woodlands and woodland edges, roadsides, mixed woods.

Distribution: DE, NE, EC, SE, SW.

Comments: The fruit is bitter and reported poisonous while immature. The other parts of the plant are poisonous. The rootstock has been used as a cathartic.

# BIGNONIACEAE
## Trumpet Creeper Family

Plants woody tree or vine. Leaves opposite or whorled, simple or compound. Flowers irregular, with parts united; corolla funnel shaped or bell shaped; ovary superior; two to four stamens. Fruit a long, cylindrical capsule.

## *Bignonia capreolata* L.
### Cross Vine

Plants: Woody, climbing vine.

Leaves: Opposite, compound consisting of two oblong to lanceolate leaflets and a tendril arising from between them, entire, with base nearly cordate.

Inflorescence: Flowers in axillary clusters, irregular; calyx five lobed; corolla tubular, five lobed, dull red to nearly orange outside, yellow inside.

Fruit: Capsule.

Flowering Date: April–May.

Habitats: Woodlands and woodland edges.

Distribution: Throughout.

Comments: The flowers have a sweet scent.

## *Campsis radicans* (L.) Seem. ex Bureau.
### Trumpet Vine, Cow-Itch Vine, Devil's Shoe Laces, Hell Vine

Plants: Woody climbing vine.
Leaves: Opposite, pinnately compound with leaflets ovate, toothed.
Inflorescence: Flowers in terminal clusters, perfect, irregular; calyx five lobed; corolla tubular, five lobed, orange to red.
Fruit: Capsule.
Flowering Date: June–September.
Habitats: Waste sites, woodland edges, thickets, fence rows.
Distribution: Throughout.
Comments: Handling the plant may cause dermatitis. The vine is reported to contain a narcotic substance. The plant, originally cultivated, has become naturalized.

## *Catalpa bignonioides* Walt.
### Catalpa, Lady Cigar, Indian Bean, Catawba Tree, Hardy Catalpa

Plants: Tree to well over 100 feet tall.
Leaves: Opposite or occasionally whorled, simple, petiolate, ovate, entire, acuminate, with base cordate or nearly so.
Inflorescence: Panicle; flowers perfect, irregular; calyx two lobed; corolla tubular, bilabiate, five lobed, with the lobes crenate, white, marked inside with yellow line and purple spots.
Fruit: Capsule.
Flowering Date: May–June.
Habitats: Roadsides, woods, stream banks.
Distribution: DE, NE, EC, SE, SW.
Comments: A dermatitis may develop after handling the plant. It has been reported that smelling the flowers may be poisonous to some people.

# BORAGINACEAE
Forget-Me-Not Family

Plants annual, biennial, or perennial and usually very hairy. Leaves alternate. Inflorescence helicoid; calyx five lobed; corolla bell shaped, rotate, funnel-shaped, or tubular; ovary superior; five stamens. Fruit a schizocarp of four mericarps.

## *Cynoglossum virginianum* L.
### Wild Comfrey, Hound's Tongue

Plants: Upright, hairy biennial or perennial.

Leaves: Basal and alternate on the stem; basal leaves petiolate, elliptic, entire; upper leaves ovate to lanceolate, sessile, clasping, entire.

Inflorescence: Coiled clusters; flowers perfect, regular; calyx five lobed; corolla salverform, five lobed, blue.

Fruit: Schizocarp.

Flowering Date: April–June.

Habitats: Mixed woods and hardwoods.

Distribution: NE, EC.

Comments: The plant contains an alkaloid that has a narcotic effect.

## *Heliotropium indicum* L.
### Turnsole, Indian Heliotrope

Plants: Upright, branching, hairy annual.

Leaves: Alternate, simple, petiolate, ovate to lanceolate, entire, with base cuneate.

Inflorescence: Coiled clusters; flowers perfect, regular; calyx five lobed; corolla tubular, five lobed, blue; stamens bright yellow.

Fruit: Schizocarp.

Flowering Date: July–November.

Habitats: Waste sites, roadsides, old fields.

Distribution: Throughout.

## *Lithospermum caroliniense* (Gmel.) MacM.
### Orange Puccoon, Hoary Puccoon

Plants: Upright, glandular perennial.
Leaves: Alternate, simple, hairy, lanceolate, entire.
Inflorescence: Coiled clusters; flowers perfect, regular; calyx five lobed; corolla tubular to funnelform, five lobed, orange to yellow.
Fruit: Schizocarp.
Flowering Date: April–June.
Habitat: Dry, rocky woods.
Distribution: NE, EC, SE.

## *Mertensia virginica* (L.) Pers.
### Blue Bells, Virginia Cowslip

Plants: Upright, glabrous perennial.
Leaves: Basal and alternate; basal leaves elliptic to ovate, petiolate, entire; upper leaves ovate to oblong, entire, short petiolate to sessile.
Inflorescence: Coiled cluster; flowers perfect, regular; calyx five parted; corolla funnelform to nearly trumpet shaped, blue or occasionally pink to white.
Fruit: Schizocarp.
Flowering Date: March–June.
Habitat: Alluvial woods.
Distribution: Known only from Tishomingo County.

# BRASSICACEAE [= CRUCIFERAE]
## Mustard Family

Plants annual or perennial. Leaves basal, alternate or nearly opposite, simple, dissected or lobed. Four sepals; four petals; two, four, or six stamens. Fruit a one-seeded silicle.

### *Barbarea vulgaris* R. Br.
### Yellow Rocket

Plants: Upright, branching, glabrous annual or biennial.

Leaves: Basal and alternate on the stem, simple, petiolate, reduced upward, with basal leaves dissected or lobed.

Inflorescence: Raceme; flowers perfect, regular; four sepals; four petals, yellow; six stamens.

Fruit: Silique or silicle.

Flowering Date: April–June.

Habitats: Roadsides, fields, pastures.

Distribution: DE, NE, EC.

### *Cardamine bulbosa* (Schreb.) B.S.P.
### Bitter Cress, Spring Cress

Plants: Upright, glabrous perennial.

Leaves: Basal and alternate on the stem, simple; basal leaves petiolate, elliptic to orbicular, entire or slightly toothed; stem leaves reduced, entire or toothed, or dissected, sessile or short petiolate, often auriculate.

Inflorescence: Raceme; flowers perfect, regular; four sepals; four petals, white; six stamens.

Fruit: Silique.

Flowering Date: March–May.

Habitats: Alluvial woods, marshes, wet ditches.

Distribution: DE, NE, EC, SE, SW.

Comments: The roots are edible and may be used as a horseradish substitute. The leaves may be eaten as a salad.

### *Cardamine diphylla* (Michx.) Wood
**Toothwort**

Plants: Upright, glabrous to slightly hairy perennial with distinctly jointed rhizomes.

Leaves: Whorled or nearly so, usually three per stem, petiolate, palmately dissected with three to five divisions and divisions lobed or toothed; basal leaves, when present, similar to stem leaves.

Inflorescence: Raceme or panicle; flowers perfect, regular; four sepals; four petals, white; six stamens.

Fruit: Silique.

Flowering Date: March–May.

Habitats: Rich wooded slopes, alluvial woods.

Distribution: NE, EC.

### *Cardamine concatenata* (Michx.) Ahles
**Toothwort**

Plants: Upright, essentially glabrous perennial with jointed rhizomes.

Leaves: Basal or nearly opposite, usually three, petiolate, simple, usually ternately or palmately dissected to base, with segments narrowly lanceolate to ovate, toothed.

Inflorescence: Panicle; flowers perfect, regular; four sepals; four petals, white; six stamens.

Fruit: Silique.

Flowering Date: April–May.

Habitats: Rocky wooded slopes, rock ledges.

Distribution: NE.

### *Nasturtium officinale* R. Br.
**Water Cress**

Plants: Aquatic, upright to sprawling, glabrous perennial.

Leaves: Alternate, simple, pinnately dissected, with segments oval to lanceolate and entire to slightly toothed.

Inflorescence: Raceme; flowers perfect, regular; four sepals; four petals, white; six stamens.

Fruit: Silique.

Flowering Date: April–August.

Habitats: Streams, springs.

Distribution: DE, NE, EC, SW.

Comments: Water Cress was introduced from Europe. The leaves are edible as a salad.

# BUXACEAE
## Allegheny Spurge Family

Plants perennial, stoloniferous. Leaves alternate, spotted, persisting through the winter. Inflorescence a spike with the male flowers toward the tip and the female flowers toward the base; sepals and petals absent; ovary superior; four stamens. Fruit a six-seeded capsule.

### *Pachysandra procumbens* Michx.
### Allegheny Spurge

Plants: Sprawling, monoecious, essentially glabrous perennial; woody at the base.

Leaves: Alternate, evergreen, simple, ovate to obovate, with margins toothed.

Inflorescence: Spike; flowers imperfect; male flowers toward the tip and female flowers toward the base; sepals and petals absent; four stamens.

Fruit: Capsule.

Flowering Date: March–April.

Habitat: Woods.

Distribution: NE, EC, SW.

## CABOMBACEAE [= NYMPHAEACEAE]
## Cabomba Family

Plants aquatic perennial from rhizomes. Leaves alternate and floating. Flowers axillary and solitary; three sepals; three petals; ovary superior; three to twenty stamens. One nutlike fruit with several seeds.

*Brasenia schreberi* Gmel.
**Water Shield**

Plants: Aquatic, glabrous perennial with rhizomes.
Leaves: Alternate, floating, simple, peltate, long petiolate, elliptic, coated with mucilage below water surface, entire.
Inflorescence: Flowers solitary, axillary, pedunculate, perfect, regular; three sepals; three petals; perianth purplish; twelve to twenty stamens.
Fruit: Nutlike.
Flowering Date: June–October.
Habitats: Lakes, ponds, marshes, slow-moving streams.
Distribution: NE, EC, SW.

# CACTACEAE
## Cactus Family

Plants perennial, with segmented, succulent, spiny stems that become woody toward the base. Leaves fall early; usually absent. Sepals and petals similar; ovary inferior; many stamens. Fruit a spiny berry.

## *Opuntia humifusa* Raf.
**Prickly Pear**

Plants: Succulent, evergreen perennial; stem flattened, fleshy, segmented, and becoming woody toward base.

Leaves: Usually lacking because leaves are promptly shed; spines and tufts of hairlike spines form in the old leaf axes.

Inflorescence: Flowers clustered on the terminal stem segment, perfect, regular; sepals numerous; petals numerous, yellow, often reddish at the base.

Fruit: Berry.

Flowering Date: May–June.

Habitats: Dry rocky woods, rock outcrops, sandy open areas.

Distribution: DE, CO, NE, EC, SE.

Comments: The hairlike spines can be irritating for some time once they penetrate the skin.

# CAESALPINACEAE
## Caesalpinia Family

Plants annual or perennial herb, shrub, or tree. Leaves alternate, simple or compound. Flowers usually irregular, often appearing nearly regular; five to many stamens. Fruit a legume (pod).

### *Cassia marilandica* L.
**Wild Senna, Maryland Senna**

Plants: Upright, glabrous perennial.
Leaves: Alternate, petiolate, pinnately compound, with leaflets oblong to elliptic and acute or obtuse.
Inflorescence: Axillary racemes or terminal panicles; flowers irregular, perfect; five sepals; five petals, yellow; six to seven stamens.
Fruit: Legume.
Flowering Date: July–August.
Habitats: Roadsides, edges of woods.
Distribution: DE, EC.

### *Cassia obtusifolia* L.
**Sicklepod**

Plants: Upright, hairy annual.
Leaves: Alternate, petiolate, pinnately compound, with leaflets obovate, entire, having tip rounded or slightly notched.
Inflorescence: Flowers axillary clusters, irregular, perfect; five sepals, five petals, dull yellow to tan; six or seven stamens.
Fruit: Legume.
Flowering Date: July–September.
Habitats: Roadsides, waste sites.
Distribution: NE, EC.

### *Chamaecrista fasciculata* (Michx.) Greene
**Partridge Pea**

Plants: Upright, nearly glabrous annual with a taproot.
Leaves: Alternate, pinnately compound, sensitive (leaflets fold upon touch), with leaflets linear to oblong and acuminate.
Inflorescence: Flowers in axillary clusters, perfect, irregular; five sepals; five petals, yellow, more than 1 cm long; ten stamens.
Fruit: Legume.
Flowering Date: June–September.
Habitats: Prairies, roadsides, fields, woodland edges.
Distribution: Throughout.
Comment: *C. nictitans* has petals that are less than 1 cm long.

# CALYCANTHACEAE
## Sweet Shrub Family

Plants an aromatic shrub. Leaves opposite. Sepals and petals similar, maroon; many stamens. Fruit one-seeded achenes enclosed by a fleshy receptacle.

## *Calycanthus floridus* L.
### Sweet Shrub, Spicebush

Plants: Aromatic shrub.
Leaves: Opposite, simple, petiolate, lanceolate, entire, acuminate.
Inflorescence: Flowers solitary, perfect, regular; perianth cup shaped; sepals and petals similar, numerous, maroon to reddish brown; stamens numerous.
Fruit: Achenes, enclosed by a fleshy receptacle.
Flowering Date: March–June.
Habitats: Stream edges, mixed woods, clearings, swampy woods.
Distribution: CO, SE.

# CAMPANULACEAE
Bellflower Family

Plants annual, biennial, or perennial. Leaves alternate. Five sepals; corolla regular or irregular; ovary inferior or nearly so; five stamens. Fruit a many-seeded capsule.

## *Campanula americana* L.
### Tall Bluebell, American Bellflower

Plants: Upright, glabrous to hairy biennial with a taproot; stems simple to branched.

Leaves: Alternate, simple, petiolate, elliptic to lanceolate, with margins toothed and base attenuate.

Inflorescence: Raceme; flowers perfect, regular, bell shaped, subtended by leafy bracts; five sepals; five petals, blue.

Fruit: Capsule.

Flowering Date: June–September.

Habitats: Woodland edges; reported to be associated with basic soils.

Distribution: NE, EC.

Comment: Young plants can be cooked as greens.

## *Lobelia cardinalis* L.
**Cardinal Flower**

Plants: Upright, usually hairy perennial.

Leaves: Alternate, simple, petiolate, elliptic to lanceolate, acuminate, with margins toothed and base attenuate.

Inflorescence: Raceme; flowers perfect, irregular, subtended by leafy bracts; five sepals; corolla bilabiate, with upper lip two lobed and lower lip three lobed, scarlet red.

Fruit: Capsule.

Flowering Date: July–October.

Habitats: Edges of springs and streams.

Distribution: NE, EC, SE, SW.

## *Lobelia puberula* Michx.
**Blue Lobelia**

Plants: Upright, hairy perennial.

Leaves: Alternate, simple, petiolate, elliptic to oblanceolate, acuminate, with margins toothed and base attenuate.

Inflorescence: Raceme; flowers perfect, irregular, subtended by leafy bracts; five sepals; corolla bilabiate, with upper lip two lobed and lower lip three lobed, bright blue.

Fruit: Capsule.

Flowering Date: July–October.

Habitats: Edges of streams and springs, woods.

Distribution: NE, EC.

Comments: *L. siphilitica* L. has an auriculated calyx.

## *Lobelia spicata* Lam.
### Spiked Lobelia

Plants: Upright, glabrous to slightly
hairy perennial.

Leaves: Alternate, simple, sessile or
nearly so, oblong to elliptic, with
margins toothed or nearly entire, tip
obtuse, and base cuneate.

Inflorescence: Raceme; flowers perfect,
irregular; calyx five lobed; corolla
bilabiate, with upper lip two lobed
and lower lip three lobed, light to
dark blue.

Fruit: Capsule.

Flowering Date: June–November.

Habitats: Edges of streams.

Distribution: NE, EC.

Comments: *L. inflata* L. has densely
hairy stems and inflated corollas.

## *Triodanis perfoliata* (L.)
Nieuw.
### Venus' Looking Glass

Plants: Upright, glabrous annual.

Leaves: Alternate and in basal rosettes,
simple; rosette leaves petiolate,
ovate; stem leaves ovate, with margins toothed and base cordate, clasping.

Inflorescence: Spike or raceme; flowers
perfect, regular, subtended by ovate
leaflike bracts, reduced toward the
tip; calyx five lobed, with segments
lanceolate; corolla five lobed, rotate,
light blue to violet.

Fruit: Capsule, with pores below the
midpoint.

Flowering Date: April–June.

Habitats: Yards, fields, roadsides.

Distribution: DE, NE, EC, SE.

Comments: *T. biflora*, a variation of *T.
perfoliata*, has sessile leaves but they
are not clasping. It also has pores
near the apex of the capsule.

# CAPPARACEAE
## Caper Family

Plants annual. Leaves alternate, palmate. Four sepals; four petals; ovary superior; six to many stamens. Fruit a many-seeded capsule.

## *Cleome spinosa* Jacq.
### Spider Flower

Plants: Upright, glabrous or hairy annual.

Leaves: Alternate, simple and compound, petiolate; compound leaves palmate, with segments lanceolate; simple leaves of raceme lanceolate to ovate, petiolate to sessile, with base cuneate or truncate to slightly cordate.

Inflorescence: Raceme; flowers irregular, perfect, with long peduncle, subtended by leaflike bracts; four sepals; four petals, clawed; six stamens, longer than the petals.

Fruit: Capsule.

Flowering Date: June–November.

Habitats: Woods, roadsides.

Distribution: NE, EC.

Comments: Native of South America.

# CAPRIFOLIACEAE
Honeysuckle Family

Plants perennial herb, shrub, or small tree. Leaves opposite, simple or compound. Flowers regular to irregular; calyx five lobed; corolla five lobed; ovary inferior; five stamens. Fruit a berry or drupe.

*Lonicera japonica* Thunb.
**Japanese Honeysuckle**

Plants: Woody, glabrous to hairy, climbing vine.

Leaves: Opposite, simple, evergreen, petiolate, ovate to elliptic, entire, acute, with base rounded.

Inflorescence: Flowers in axillary clusters, perfect, irregular; calyx five parted; corolla bilabiate, white fading to yellow; five stamens.

Fruit: Spherical berry.

Flowering Date: April–August.

Habitats: Fence rows, roadside thickets, waste sites.

Distribution: Throughout.

Comments: Native of Asia.

## *Lonicera sempervirens* L.
### Coral Honeysuckle, Trumpet Honeysuckle

Plants: Woody, climbing vine.
Leaves: Opposite, simple; lower leaves elliptic or ovate to obovate, sessile or nearly so, entire; leaves subtending the inflorescence perfoliate, acute to rounded, entire.
Inflorescence: Flowers in terminal clusters, perfect, regular or nearly so; calyx five lobed, inconspicuous; corolla tubular, five lobed, red with yellow inside; five stamens.
Fruit: Berry.
Flowering Date: March–September.
Habitats: Yards, roadside thickets, woods.
Distribution: CO, EC, SE, SW.
Comments: Escaped from cultivation.

## *Triosteum angustifolium* L.
### Horse Gentian, Yellow-Flowered Horse Gentian

Plants: Upright, hairy perennial.
Leaves: Opposite, lower leaves and leaves at top sessile and petiolate, lanceolate, entire; middle leaves perfoliate, lanceolate, entire.
Inflorescence: Flowers axillary, few, perfect; calyx five lobed; corolla irregular, five lobed, yellow; five stamens.
Fruit: Drupe.
Flowering Date: April–May.
Habitats: Deciduous or mixed rich woods, alluvial woods.
Distribution: NE, EC.

# CARYOPHYLLACEAE
## Pink Family

Plants annual or perennial. Leaves opposite or whorled. Five sepals; five petals, absent in some; ovary superior; stamens one to ten or absent. Fruit a many-seeded capsule or one-seeded utricle.

### *Paronychia erecta* (Chapm.) Shinn.
**Square Flower**

Plants: Prostrate, hairy annual with a taproot.
Leaves: Opposite, sessile, narrowly lanceolate to linear, entire.
Inflorescence: Square terminal clusters; flowers perfect; five sepals, white; petals absent; two to five stamens.
Fruit: Utriclelike.
Flowering Date: June–October.
Habitats: Dunes, gulf beaches.
Distribution: CO.

### *Saponaria officinalis* L.
**Bouncing Bet, Soapwort**

Plants: Upright, glabrous perennial forming clumps.
Leaves: Opposite, simple, sessile, elliptic to lanceolate, entire, acute, with base cuneate.
Inflorescence: Flowers in terminal clusters, perfect, regular; five sepals; five petals, rotate, white or pinkish white; ten stamens.
Fruit: Capsule.
Flowering Date: May–October.
Habitats: Roadsides, fields, waste sites, yards.
Distribution: DE, NE, EC.
Comments: Native of Europe. A soapy lather will form when the plant is mixed with water. The plant is reported to be poisonous.

## *Silene stellata* (L.) Ait. f.
**Starry Campion**

Plants: Upright, branching, hairy perennial.
Leaves: Whorl of four and some opposite, simple, sessile, lanceolate to elliptic, entire, acuminate, with base
rounded.
Inflorescence: Flowers terminal, solitary, perfect, regular; sepals united;
five petals, fringed, white; ten stamens.
Fruit: Capsule.
Flowering Date: July–September.
Habitats: Rocky woods.
Distribution: NE, EC.

## *Silene virginica* L.
**Fire Pink**

Plants: Upright to ascending, branching, hairy perennial.
Leaves: Opposite and basal, simple;
basal leaves spatulate to oblanceolate, entire; stem leaves sessile, lanceolate, entire.
Inflorescence: Open and racemelike or
paniclelike; flowers perfect, regular,
on peduncle, sticky to touch; five sepals; five petals, notched, bright red.
Fruit: Capsule.
Flowering Date: April–July.
Habitats: Woods, rocky bluffs and
ledges.
Distribution: NE.
Comments: Easily cultivated.

## *Stellaria pubera* Michx.
**Giant Chickweed, Great
Chickweed**

Plants: Upright to ascending, hairy perennial with a rhizome.
Leaves: Opposite, simple, sessile, elliptic to lanceolate, entire, acute, with
base cuneate.
Inflorescence: Flowers terminal, solitary, perfect, regular, on peduncles;
five sepals; five petals, deeply parted
(therefore appearing to be ten petals),
white; five stamens.
Fruit: Capsule.
Flowering Date: April–June.
Habitat: Rocky wooded slopes.
Distribution: NE.
Comments: Easily cultivated.

# CELASTRACEAE
## Staff-tree Family

Plants a vine, shrub, or small tree. Leaves opposite. Four to five sepals; four to five petals; ovary superior; four to five stamens. Fruit a capsule.

*Euonymus americanus* L.
**Strawberry Bush**

Plants: Shrub to 6 feet tall.
Leaves: Opposite, simple, petiolate, lanceolate, acute, with margins toothed and base cuneate.
Inflorescence: Flowers axillary, on peduncles, regular; five petals, greenish.
Fruit: Leathery capsule.
Flowering Date: May–June.
Habitats: Woods, swampy woods.
Comments: Easily grown from seed.

# CHENOPODIACEAE
Goosefoot Family

Plants annual or perennial, some becoming woody. Leaves alternate or opposite. Three to five sepals; petals absent; one to five stamens. Fruit a utricle.

## *Salicornia virginica* L.
### Glasswort

Plants: Stems fleshy, glabrous, lying on the ground, becoming woody.

Leaves: Opposite, reduced to scales.

Inflorescence: Spike; flowers perfect, very inconspicuous; sepals present, greenish; petals absent; one to two stamens.

Fruit: Utricle.

Flowering Date: March–November.

Habitat: Salt marshes.

Distribution: CO.

Comments: *S. bigelovii* Torr. is similar but is an annual and has erect stems.

# CLETHRACEAE
## White Alder Family

Plants a shrub or small tree. Leaves alternate. Five sepals; five petals, white; ovary superior; ten stamens. Fruit a capsule.

## *Clethra alnifolia* L.
### White Alder, Sweet Pepperbush

Plants: Shrub or small tree.
Leaves: Alternate, simple, short petiolate, elliptic to oblanceolate, acute, with margins toothed and base cuneate.
Inflorescence: Terminal raceme or panicle; flowers perfect, regular; five sepals; five petals, white; ten stamens.
Fruit: Capsule.
Flowering Date: May–July.
Habitats: Pinelands, savannas.
Distribution: Coastal.

# CLUSIACEAE [= HYPERICACEAE]
## St. John's Wort Family

Plants annual, perennial, or biennial herb or shrub. Leaves opposite. Two to five sepals; four to five petals, usually yellow to cream; ovary superior; five to many stamens. Fruit a many-seeded capsule.

### *Hypericum brachyphyllum* (Spach) Steud.
**St. John's Wort**

Plants: Shrub to 4 feet tall.
Leaves: Simple, sessile, linear, with margins rolled inward and axillary branchlets.
Inflorescence: Flowers axillary or clustered on branches, perfect, regular; five sepals; five petals.
Fruit: Capsule.
Flowering Date: June–September.
Habitats: Savannas, pinelands.
Distribution: CO, SW.

### *Hypericum crux-andreae* (L.) Crantz
**St. Peter's Wort**

Plants: Shrub to 3 feet tall.
Leaves: Simple, sessile, elliptic to ovate, entire, with tip obtuse and base cuneate to clasping.
Inflorescence: Flowers axillary, solitary or clustered, perfect, regular; four sepals; four petals; three to four styles.
Fruit: Capsule.
Flowering Date: June–October.
Habitats: Savannas, pinelands, mixed woods.
Distribution: CO, NE, EC, SE.
Comments: *H. hypericoides* (St. Andrew's Cross) has two styles.

*Hypericum denticulatum*
  Walt.
**St. John's Wort**

Plants: Upright, glabrous perennial.
Leaves: Simple; elliptic or lanceolate to
  nearly linear; sessile; entire; base
  rounded, truncate, attenuate, or
  clasping; acute to acuminate.
Inflorescence: Terminal cluster; flow-
  ers perfect, regular; five sepals; five
  petals; three styles.
Fruit: Capsule.
Flowering Date: June–September.
Habitats: Savannas, pinelands, fields.
Distribution: NE, EC, SE, CO.

*Hypericum galioides* Lam.
**St. John's Wort**

Plants: Upright, glabrous shrub.
Leaves: Simple, oblanceolate, short petiolate, entire, acute, with base attenuate; leaves with scattered
  depressions, appearing as dots; axillary leaflets present.
Inflorescence: Axillary clusters; flowers perfect, regular; five sepals; five
  petals, having rounded tips with a
  small tooth on one side; three styles.
Fruit: Capsule.
Flowering Date: June–September.
Habitats: Savannas, pinelands, stream
  banks, swamps, woods.
Distribution: CO.

*Hypericum gentianoides* (L.)
  B.S.P.
**Pineweed**

Plants: Upright, freely branching annual.
Leaves: Simple, sessile, linear to sub-
  late, entire, acute, less than 6 mm
  long.
Inflorescence: Flowers terminal and
  solitary and alternate on ascending
  branches, perfect, regular; five sepals, less than 3 mm long; five petals.
Fruit: Capsule.
Flowering Date: July–October.
Habitats: Pinelands, hardwoods, mixed
  woods, roadsides, rock outcrops.
Distribution: Throughout.
Comments: *H. drummondii* is similar
  but has leaves longer than 6 mm and
  sepals longer than 3 mm.

## *Hypericum prolificum* L.
### St. John's Wort

Plants: Shrub to 6 feet tall.
Leaves: Simple, nearly sessile, elliptic to oblong, entire, with tip obtuse to acute and base cuneate.
Inflorescence: Flowers in axillary or terminal clusters, perfect, regular; five petals.
Fruit: Capsule.
Flowering Date: June–August.
Habitats: Rocky woods, open areas.
Distribution: NE, EC.

## *Hypericum punctatum* Lam.
### St. John's Wort

Plants: Upright, glabrous perennial.
Leaves: Simple, sessile, elliptic to lanceolate, black dotted, entire, with tip rounded and base often clasping.
Inflorescence: Flowers in terminal cluster, perfect, regular; five sepals, black spotted; five petals, black spotted.
Fruit: Capsule.
Flowering Date: June–September.
Habitats: Roadsides, ditches, old fields, woods.
Distribution: NE, EC.

## *Hypericum suffruticosum*
## Adams & Robson
### St. John's Wort

Plants: Sprawling shrub.
Leaves: Simple, oblong to obovate, short petiolate, entire, acute, with base attenuate.
Inflorescence: Flowers solitary or occasionally in small clusters, regular, perfect; usually two sepals; four petals; two styles.
Fruit: Capsule.
Flowering Date: April–June.
Habitat: Pinelands.
Distribution: CO.

## CONVOLVULACEAE
Morning Glory Family

Plants annual or perennial, prostrate to climbing or trailing, usually with milky sap (latex); parasitic in *Cuscuta*. Leaves simple, alternate. Sepals evenly overlapping; corolla salverform, funnel shaped or wheel shaped; ovary superior; five stamens. Fruit a capsule.

### *Calystegia sepium* (L.) R. Br.
**Hedge Bindweed**

Plants: Prostrate or climbing, glabrous to hairy perennial with rhizomes.

Leaves: Triangular, entire, acuminate, with base sagittate.

Inflorescence: Flowers axillary, solitary, subtended by two large bracts; calyx five lobed; corolla bell shaped or funnel shaped, white or pink.

Fruit: Capsule.

Flowering Date: May–August.

Habitats: Roadsides, ditches, disturbed and waste sites.

Distribution: NE, EC.

Comments: Roots are reported to be poisonous.

### *Convolvulus arvensis* L.
**Field Bindweed, Small Bindweed**

Plants: Prostrate or climbing, hairy perennial with a rhizome.

Leaves: Triangular to ovate, entire, with base truncate to hastate.

Inflorescence: Flowers axillary, one to several; calyx five lobed; corolla bell shaped, white, often tinged with pink.

Fruit: Capsule.

Flowering Date: June–December.

Habitats: Fields, disturbed sites.

Distribution: DE, EC.

Comments: Roots are reported to be poisonous.

## *Cuscuta gronovii* Willd.
### Dodder, Love Vine

Plants: Parasitic, glabrous annual; stems orange or yellow-orange and twining on host plant.
Leaves: Leafless.
Inflorescence: Paniclelike clusters; flowers perfect, regular; calyx five parted; corolla bell shaped, fringed, white or greenish white.
Fruit: Capsule.
Flowering Date: August–October.
Habitats: Parasitic on chlorophyllous plants along roadsides, edges of lakes, marshes, and streams.
Distribution: NE, EC, SE.

## *Ipomoea coccinea* L.
### Red Morning Glory, Scarlet Starglory

Plants: Prostrate or climbing, glabrous annual.
Leaves: Ovate to heart shaped, entire to slightly toothed, acuminate.
Inflorescence: Flowers solitary to several, axillary; calyx five lobed; corolla salverform, scarlet red, often whitish to yellowish in throat.
Fruit: Capsule.
Flowering Date: August–December.
Habitats: Fence rows, roadsides, waste sites.
Distribution: Throughout.

## *Ipomoea pandurata* (L.) Mey.
### Man- Root, Wild Potato Vine, Man-Of-The-Earth

Plants: Prostrate to climbing, glabrous to hairy perennial with an enlarged root.
Leaves: Ovate, entire, acuminate to acute, with base rounded, truncate, or cordate.
Inflorescence: Flowers solitary or several, axillary; calyx five- lobed; corolla tips acute to acuminate, white, purple within.
Fruit: Capsule.
Flowering Date: May–August.
Habitats: Roadsides, fields, woods, fence rows, thickets, waste areas.
Distribution: Throughout.

## *Ipomoea purpurea* (L.) Roth
**Common Morning Glory**

Plants: Prostrate to climbing, hairy annual.

Leaves: Ovate, entire, acuminate, with base cordate.

Inflorescence: Flowers solitary to several, axillary; calyx five lobed, with segments linear; corolla bell shaped, purple, pink, or white.

Fruit: Capsule.

Flowering Date: July–September.

Habitats: Fields, roadsides, fence rows, thickets, waste sites.

Distribution: Throughout.

Comments: *I. hederacea* is similar, but the leaves are usually three lobed.

## *Ipomoea quamoclit* L.
**Cypress Vine**

Plants: Prostrate to climbing, glabrous annual.

Leaves: Pinnately divided, with segments linear.

Inflorescence: Flowers solitary to several, axillary; calyx five lobed; corolla salverform, scarlet red.

Fruit: Capsule.

Flowering Date: July–September.

Habitats: Roadsides, yards, fields, thickets, fence rows, waste sites.

Distribution: CO.

Comments: Introduced from tropical America.

## *Ipomoea sagittata* Poir.
**Morning Glory**

Plants: Trailing or twining, glabrous perennial.

Leaves: Triangular, entire, acuminate, with base sagittate or hastate.

Inflorescence: Flowers solitary, axillary; calyx five lobed; corolla funnel shaped, white, pink, lavender, or purple.

Fruit: Capsule.

Flowering Date: July–September.

Habitats: Roadsides, prairies, salt marshes, dunes.

Distribution: CO.

## *Ipomoea stolonifera* (Cyr.) Gmel.
### Beach Morning Glory

Plants: Trailing, glabrous perennial.
Leaves: Ovate to oblong, entire, with tip rounded and base truncate to cordate.
Inflorescence: Flowers solitary, axillary; calyx five lobed; corolla funnel shaped, white with a yellow center.
Fruit: Capsule.
Flowering Date: July–October.
Habitats: Beaches, dunes.
Distribution: CO.

## *Ipomoea trichocarpa* Ell.
### Morning Glory

Plants: Twining, slightly hairy annual.
Leaves: Ovate, entire, acuminate, with base cordate.
Inflorescence: Flowers axillary; calyx five lobed; corolla funnel shaped, usually pink or purple, occasionally white.
Fruit: Capsule.
Flowering Date: July–October.
Habitat: Roadsides.
Distribution: CO, SE, EC.

## *Jacquemontia tamnifolia* (L.) Griseb.
### Tie Vine

Plants: Prostrate, hairy annual.
Leaves: Alternate, simple, petiolate, ovate, entire, acuminate, with base cordate.
Inflorescence: Head; flowers subtended by leafy bracts; five sepals; corolla funnel shaped, blue.
Fruit: Capsule.
Flowering Date: June–December.
Habitats: Ditches, waste sites, fields.
Distribution: Throughout.

## CORNACEAE
Dogwood Family

Plants a small tree. Leaves simple, usually opposite. Four sepals; corolla four-lobed, greenish yellow to white; ovary inferior; four stamens. Fruit a drupe.

*Cornus florida* L.
**Flowering Dogwood**

Plants: Small tree.
Leaves: Opposite, simple, short petiolate, elliptic, entire, acuminate, with base cuneate.
Inflorescence: Headlike cluster subtended by four large, white, petallike bracts; flowers perfect, regular; four sepals; four petals, greenish yellow; four stamens.
Fruit: Red drupe.
Flowering Date: March–April.
Distribution: Throughout.
Comments: The inner bark was once used as a remedy for fevers and malaria. The wood is extremely hard and used for making handles, spindles, and several other products.

# CRASSULACEAE
## Stonecrop Family

Plants annual or perennial and succulent. Leaves simple, alternate or whorled. Four to seven sepals; four to seven petals; eight to fourteen stamens. Fruit an aggregate of follicles or capsule.

### *Sedum ternatum* Michx.
### Stonecrop, Orpine, Widow's Crosses

Plants: Upright, hairy, succulent perennial.

Leaves: Alternate and whorled, simple, sessile, elliptic to spatulate, fleshy, entire.

Inflorescence: Terminal, helicoid cluster; flowers perfect, regular, subtended by a leafy bract; five sepals; ten petals, white; five stamens.

Fruit: Follicle.

Flowering Date: April–June.

Habitats: Moist rocky ledges of deciduous or mixed woods.

Distribution: NE.

# CYRILLACEAE
Titi or Cyrilla Family

Plants shrub or small tree. Leaves simple, alternate, somewhat leathery in texture. Five sepals, white; five petals, white; ovary superior; five stamens. Fruit drupelike or nutlike.

## *Cliftonia monophylla* (Lam.) Britt. ex Sarg.
### Black Titi, Buckwheat Tree

Plants: Shrub or small tree.
Leaves: Alternate, simple, sessile or nearly so, elliptic to oblanceolate, leathery, entire, with base cuneate and tip acute or sometimes having a small notch.
Inflorescence: Raceme; flowers perfect, regular; five sepals; five petals, white to pinkish, with base clawed; five stamens.
Fruit: Dry drupe.
Flowering Date: May–July.
Habitat: Bogs.
Distribution: CO.

## *Cyrilla racemiflora* L.
### Leatherwood, Titi

Plants: Shrub or small tree.
Leaves: Alternate, simple, short petiolate, evergreen to deciduous, obovate to spatulate, entire, acute or rounded, with base attenuate or cuneate.
Inflorescence: Drooping racemes; flowers perfect, regular; five sepals, white; five petals, white; five stamens.
Fruit: Drupelike.
Flowering Date: May–July.
Habitats: Savannas, pinelands.
Distribution: CO, SE.

# DROSERACEAE
## Sundew Family

Plants annual or perennial. Leaves in basal rosettes or alternate, with glandular hairs that catch insects. Five sepals; five petals; ovary superior; five stamens. Fruit a many-seeded capsule.

## *Drosera brevifolia* Pursh
**Sundew**

Plants: Upright, glandular perennial.
Leaves: Basal, spatulate, glandular, with petioles less than ¾ inch long.
Inflorescence: Scapose; flowers perfect, regular; five sepals; five petals, pink or white.
Fruit: Capsule.
Flowering Date: April–June.
Habitats: Savannas, wet ditches, pinelands.
Distribution: CO, EC.
Comments: *D. intermedia* Hayne has spatulate, glandular leaves with petioles 2 or more inches long.

## *Drosera tracyi* Macfar.
**Thread-Leaf Sundew**

Plants: Upright, glandular perennial.
Leaves: Basal, filiform, glandular.
Inflorescence: Scapose, helicoid; flowers perfect, regular, one-sided on the scape; five sepals; five petals, pink to light purple.
Fruit: Capsule.
Flowering Date: June–September.
Habitats: Savannas, pinelands, bogs.
Distribution: CO.

# ERICACEAE
## Heath Family

Plants shrub or tree. Leaves simple, alternate. Four to five sepals, united; four to five petals, united; ovary inferior or superior; four to ten stamens. Fruit a capsule or berry.

### *Kalmia latifolia* L.
**Mountain Laurel, Mountain Ivy**

Plants: Large shrub.
Leaves: Alternate, simple, short petiolate, leathery, evergreen, elliptic to lanceolate, entire, acute, with base cuneate.
Inflorescence: Terminal or axillary clusters; flowers perfect, regular, glandular, and sticky to touch; calyx five lobed; corolla rotate, white or pink, usually with purple spots; ten stamens, attached to the corolla until maturity.
Fruit: Capsule.
Flowering Date: April–June.
Habitats: Rocky dry woods, sandy woods, stream banks.
Distribution: CO, EC, SE.

### *Lyonia lucida* (Lam.) Koch
**Fetter-Bush**

Plants: Shrub to 5 feet tall.
Leaves: Alternate, elliptic, evergreen, nearly sessile, entire, acute, with base cuneate.
Inflorescence: Flowers in axillary racemes or clusters, perfect, regular; calyx five lobed; corolla urceolate, usually pinkish; ten stamens.
Fruit: Capsule.
Flowering Date: April–June.
Habitats: Savannas, bogs, pinelands.
Distribution: CO, SE.

## *Oxydendrum arboreum* (L.) DC.
### Sourwood

Plants: Usually small trees.
Leaves: Alternate, simple, petiolate, lanceolate, acuminate, with margins toothed at least toward the tip and base rounded to cuneate.
Inflorescence: Terminal, drooping panicle; flowers perfect, regular; calyx five lobed; corolla urceolate, five lobed, white; ten stamens.
Fruit: Capsule.
Flowering Date: June–July.
Habitats: Woodland edges along roadsides, woods, edges of streams.
Distribution: CO, NE, EC, SE.

## *Rhododendron austrinum* (Sm.) Rehd.
### Orange-Flowered Azalea

Plants: Shrub.
Leaves: Alternate, simple, short petiolate, elliptic or ovate to spatulate, entire.
Inflorescence: Flowers in a terminal cluster, perfect, irregular to nearly regular; calyx five lobed; corolla nearly salverform, yellow to yellowish orange, often reddish tinted; five to ten stamens, extending beyond the corolla.
Fruit: Capsule.
Flowering Date: March–April.
Habitats: Edges of woodland streams.
Distribution: SE.

## *Rhododendron canescens* Michx.) Sweet
### Wild Azalea, Wild Honeysuckle

Plants: Shrub.
Leaves: Alternate, simple, short petiolate, elliptic to lanceolate, entire or slightly toothed, acute, with base cuneate.
Inflorescence: Flowers in a terminal cluster, perfect, irregular to nearly regular; calyx five lobed; corolla five parted, nearly salverform, pink or white marked with pink, often with a yellow spot in the throat; five to ten stamens, extending well beyond the corolla; flowers appearing before and with the leaves.
Fruit: Capsule.
Flowering Date: March–May.
Habitats: Woods, savannas.
Distribution: NE, EC, SW, SE.

## *Rhododendron serrulatum* (Sm.) Mill.
### Summer Azalea, Swamp Azalea, Swamp Honeysuckle

Plants: Shrub.
Leaves: Alternate, simple, short petiolate, elliptic to obovate, with margins toothed and base cuneate.
Inflorescence: Flowers in a terminal cluster, perfect, irregular to nearly regular; calyx five lobed; corolla nearly salverform, white, occasionally marked with pink; five to ten stamens, extending beyond the corolla.
Fruit: Capsule.
Flowering Date: June–August.
Habitat: Swampy pinelands.
Distribution: CO, SE.

## *Vaccinium eliottii* Chapm.
### Wild Blueberry

Plants: Shrub.
Leaves: Alternate, simple, sessile, elliptic to ovate, entire, usually less than ¾ inch wide.
Inflorescence: Flowers in clusters, perfect, regular; calyx five lobed; corolla urceolate, five lobed, white to pinkish; ten stamens.
Fruit: Berry.
Flowering Date: March–May.
Habitats: Open pinelands, marshy sites, stream edges, roadsides.
Distribution: CO, NE, EC, SW, SE.
Comments: *V. pallidum* Ait. has an inflorescence of racemes and leaves more than ¾ inch wide. It is a more northern species.

## *Vaccinium stamineum* L.
### Squaw Huckleberry, Gooseberry, Deerberry

Plants: Shrub.
Leaves: Alternate, simple, sessile, elliptic, entire.
Inflorescence: Raceme; flowers perfect, regular; calyx five lobed; corolla bell shaped to rotate, five lobed, white; ten stamens, extending beyond the corolla.
Fruit: Berry.
Flowering Date: April–June.
Habitat: Dry upland woods.
Distribution: CO, NE, EC, SW, SE.
Comments: *V. arboreum* Marsh. (Sparkleberry) does not have stamens extending beyond the corolla.

# EUPHORBIACEAE
## Spurge Family

Plants annual or perennial herb or shrub; only *Euphorbia* has milky sap (latex); stinging hairs in some. Leaves simple or compound; opposite, alternate, or whorled. Calyx present or absent, when present, 2–5 lobed; corolla present or absent and, when present, five lobed; only *Euphorbia* has a cyathium; one to ten stamens. Fruit a capsule or utricle.

## *Cnidoscolus stimulosus* (Michx.) Engelm. & Gray
### Bull Nettle

Plants: Upright, perennial with stinging hairs.

Leaves: Alternate, simple, petiolate, three lobed with lobes toothed.

Inflorescence: Alternate, simple, petiolate, three lobed with lobes toothed.

Inflorescence: Flowers in a terminal cluster, imperfect, regular; calyx salverform, five lobed, white, petals absent.

Fruit: Capsule.

Flowering Date: April–August.

Distribution: CO, EC, SE.

## *Euphorbia corollata* L.
### Flowering Spurge, Tramp's Spurge, Prairie Spurge

Plants: Upright, glabrous to hairy perennial with milky sap.

Leaves: Whorled at the base and alternate or opposite near the inflorescence, simple, sessile or short petiolate, linear to elliptic, entire.

Inflorescence: Flowers in terminal cluster, imperfect, regular, with each cluster borne in a specialized involucre (cyathium, see Fig. oo, page ooo) and containing a female flower and several male flowers; sepals and petals absent; flower glands petaloid, white; ovary three lobed and conspicuously enlarged; one stamen.

Fruit: Capsule.

Flowering Date: May–September.

Habitats: Prairies, roadsides, woods, along railroad tracks, fields.

Distribution: CO, NE, EC, SW, SE.

## *Sebastiania fruticosa* (Bartr.) Fern.
### Sebastian Bush

Plants: Shrub.
Leaves: Alternate, simple, petiolate, elliptic to nearly lanceolate, entire.
Inflorescence: Terminal raceme; flowers imperfect, regular; three sepals, greenish; petals absent; three stamens.
Fruit: Capsule.
Flowering Date: May–June.
Habitats: Edges of streams, swampy woods.
Distribution: CO, EC, SE.

## *Stillingia sylvatica* Gard. ex L.
### Queen's Delight

Plants: Upright, glabrous perennial.
Leaves: Alternate, simple, sessile to short petiolate, obovate or oblanceolate to elliptic, with margins finely toothed and base attenuate.
Inflorescence: Terminal spike; flowers imperfect, regular; calyx two to three parted, yellow to yellowish green; petals absent; two stamens.
Fruit: Capsule.
Flowering Date: May–July.
Habitats: Sandy woods, sandy open areas near streams.
Distribution: CO, EC.

# FABACEAE
Pea Family

Plants annual, biennial, or perennial herb, shrub, or tree. Leaves alternate, mostly compound but a few simple. Flowers pea shaped (see Fig. 17, page 255), with the five petals consisting of a banner, two wings, and two petals fused to form a keel, or sometimes the corolla is reduced to a single petal; five to many stamens. Fruit a legume (pod); in some the legume is called a loment.

## *Amorpha fruticosa* L.
### False Indigo, Indigo Bush

Plants: Shrub.
Leaves: Alternate, pinnately compound, with leaflets oblong to elliptic and entire.
Inflorescence: Terminal cluster of racemes; calyx five lobed; one petal, consisting of only the banner, clawed, purple to violet; ten stamens, extending beyond the corolla.
Fruit: Legume.
Flowering Date: April–July.
Habitat: Stream edges.
Distribution: DE, NE, EC, SE.

## *Apios americana* Medic.
### Groundnut

Plants: Herbaceous, hairy, climbing vine with fleshy tubers.
Leaves: Alternate, pinnately compound, usually consisting of five leaflets, with leaflets ovate to lanceolate and entire.
Inflorescence: Axillary raceme; calyx four lobed; five petals, purple to brownish purple; ten stamens.
Fruit: Legume.
Flowering Date: June–August.
Habitats: Stream edges, alluvial woods.
Distribution: DE, NE, EC, SE.

### *Astragalus canadensis* L.
**Rattle Weed**

Plants: Upright, glabrous to hairy perennial.

Leaves: Alternate, pinnately compound, with leaflets oblong to elliptic and entire.

Inflorescence: Axillary raceme; calyx five lobed; five petals, creamy white or greenish white; ten stamens.

Fruit: Legume.

Flowering Date: June–August.

Habitats: Stream edges, woods.

Distribution: DE, NE, EC.

### *Baptisia lactea* (Raf.) Thieret
**White Wild Indigo**

Plants: Upright, glabrous perennial.

Leaves: Alternate, trifoliate, with leaflets elliptic to oblanceolate and entire.

Inflorescence: Terminal raceme; calyx five lobed; five petals, white.

Fruit: Legume.

Flowering Date: April–July.

Habitats: Prairies, roadsides, fields, edges of streams.

Distribution: Throughout.

### *Baptisia nuttalliana* Small
**Nuttall Indigo**

Plants: Upright, highly branching perennial.

Leaves: Alternate, trifoliate, with leaflets oblanceolate to obovate and entire.

Inflorescence: Terminal clusters or axillary and solitary; calyx five lobed; five petals, yellow.

Fruit: Legume.

Flowering Date: April–June.

Habitats: Prairies, roadsides, fields.

Distribution: SW, DE, SE, EC.

## *Centrosema virginianum* (L.) Benth.
### Butterfly Pea

Plants: Trailing or climbing, hairy perennial.

Leaves: Alternate, trifoliate, with leaflets ovate to nearly lanceolate and entire.

Inflorescence: Flowers in axillary clusters, subtended by bracts; calyx five lobed; five petals, blue or light purple to lavender, banner large, usually white in the lower center; ten stamens.

Fruit: Legume.

Flowering Date: June–August.

Habitats: Roadsides, woods, disturbed and waste sites.

Distribution: Throughout.

## *Clitoria mariana* L.
### Butterfly Pea

Plants: Trailing or climbing, glabrous to hairy perennial.

Leaves: Alternate, trifoliate, with leaflets ovate to lanceolate and entire.

Inflorescence: Flowers in axillary clusters; calyx five lobed; five petals, light blue to lavender, banner large with darker purple in the lower center; ten stamens.

Fruit: Legume.

Flowering Date: May–September.

Habitats: Rocky woods, stream edges.

Distribution: NE, EC, SW, SE.

## *Coronilla varia* L.
### Crown Vetch

Plants: Trailing, glabrous to slightly hairy perennial.

Leaves: Alternate, pinnately compound, with leaflets obovate and entire.

Inflorescence: Flowers in axillary umbels on long peduncles; calyx five lobed; five petals, clawed, pink to purple, with banner darker purple and wings whitish; ten stamens.

Fruit: Legume.

Flowering Date: June–September.

Habitat: Roadsides.

Distribution: Throughout.

Comments: Native of Europe. This species has been used to help prevent soil erosion of road banks. The seed is reported to be poisonous.

*Dalea purpurea* Vent.
**Purple Prairie Clover**

Plants: Upright to prostrate, glabrous
to hairy perennial.
Leaves: Alternate, pinnately com-
pound, with leaflets linear to nar-
rowly lanceolate.
Inflorescence: Terminal spike, elon-
gated to spherical; five petals,
purple; five stamens.
Fruit: Legume.
Flowering Date: May–September.
Habitats: Prairies, roadsides, calcar-
eous glades.
Distribution: NE, EC.
Comments: *D. candida* Michx. (White
Prairie Clover) has white flowers.

*Crotalaria spectabilis* Roth
**Rattlebox**

Plants: Upright, glabrous to hairy an-
nual with a taproot.
Leaves: Alternate, simple, obovate to
lanceolate, entire, with base cuneate
to attenuate.
Inflorescence: Terminal raceme; calyx
five lobed; five petals, bright yellow
to yellow- orange.
Fruit: Legume.
Flowering Date: July–September.
Habitats: Roadsides, waste sites.
Distribution: DE, CO, EC, SW, SE.

*Desmodium marilandicum*
(L.) DC.
**Beggar's Ticks, Beggar Lice**

Plants: Upright, glabrous to slightly
hairy perennial.
Leaves: Alternate, trifoliate, with leaflets oval to ovate, entire, acute to
rounded, and having base cuneate,
and terminal leaflet petiolate.
Inflorescence: Paniclelike; calyx two
lipped; five petals, purple; stamens
in two clusters.
Fruit: Loments of one to three slightly
obovate segments.
Flowering Date: June–September.
Habitats: Roadsides, fields, waste sites,
woods.
Distribution: Throughout.

## *Desmodium paniculatum* (L.) DC.
### Beggar's Ticks, Beggar Lice, Tick Trefoil

Plants: Upright, glabrous to slightly hairy perennial.
Leaves: Alternate, trifoliate, with leaflets narrowly to broadly lanceolate and entire.
Inflorescence: Paniclelike; calyx four lobed; five petals, purple.
Fruit: Loments of three to six triangular to nearly diamond-shaped segments.
Flowering Date: June–September.
Habitats: Woods, roadsides, fields.
Distribution: DE, NE, EC, SE.

## *Desmodium nudiflorum* (L.) DC.
### Beggar's Ticks, Beggar Lice

Plants: Upright, glabrous to slightly hairy perennial.
Leaves: Alternate, trifoliate, with leaflets ovate and entire.
Inflorescence: Raceme or paniclelike; calyx four lobed; five petals, violet, purple, or white; ten stamens.
Fruit: Loments of one to three nearly ovate segments.
Flowering Date: July–September.
Habitat: Woods.
Distribution: NE, EC.

## *Erythrina herbacea* L.
### Coral Bean

Plants: Upright, perennial herb or shrub.
Leaves: Alternate, trifoliate, with leaflets triangular or hastate, entire or shallowly lobed, and having base truncate or slightly cordate.
Inflorescence: Terminal raceme; five petals, red, with banner elongated (almost tubular) and wings and keel much smaller; ten stamens.
Fruit: Legume.
Flowering Date: May–July.
Habitats: Sandy woods and open areas.
Distribution: CO, EC.

## *Lespedeza capitata* Michx.
### Bush Lespedeza

Plants: Upright perennial.
Leaves: Alternate, trifoliate, with leaf-
    lets oblong to elliptic, silvery, entire.
Inflorescence: Axillary raceme; calyx
    five lobed; five petals, reddish purple
    to purple.
Fruit: Legume.
Flowering Date: August–October.
Habitats: Roadsides, fields, woods.
Distribution: Throughout.

## *Lespedeza virginica* (L.) Britt.
### Slender Bush Clover

Plants: Upright, glabrous to slightly
    hairy perennial.
Leaves: Alternate, trifoliate, with leaf-
    lets linear to oblong and entire.
Inflorescence: Axillary raceme; calyx
    five lobed; five petals, yellowish with
    a purplish spot.
Fruit: Legume.
Flowering Date: July–September.
Habitats: Roadsides, fields, woods.
Distribution: Throughout.

## *Lupinus villosus* Willd.
### Lupine

Plants: Upright, hairy perennial with a
    taproot.
Leaves: Alternate, simple, lanceolate,
    very hairy, entire, with base atten-
    uate.
Inflorescence: Raceme; calyx four
    lobed; five petals, light to dark blue,
    with banner having a purple spot.
Fruit: Legume.
Flowering Date: April–May.
Habitats: Sandy roadsides and pine-
    lands.
Distribution: EC.
Comments: *L. diffusus* is similar, but
    the banner has a cream-colored, oc-
    casionally white, spot.

## *Melilotus officinalis* (L.) Pall.
### Yellow Sweet Clover

Plants: Upright, glabrous to slightly
hairy biennial.
Leaves: Alternate, trifoliate, with leaf-
lets obovate to oblanceolate and hav-
ing toothed margins.
Inflorescence: Axillary raceme; five
petals, yellow; ten stamens.
Fruit: Legume.
Flowering Date: April–November.
Habitats: Roadsides, waste sites.
Distribution: Throughout.
Comments: *M. alba* (White Sweet Clo-
ver) has white flowers.

## *Psoralea psoralioides* (Walt.)
### Cory
### Samson's Snakeroot, Scurf Pea

Plants: Upright, hairy perennial with a
taproot.
Leaves: Alternate, trifoliate, with leaf-
lets lanceolate and entire.
Inflorescence: Spikelike raceme; calyx
5-lobed; five petals, purple; ten sta-
mens.
Fruit: Legume.
Flowering Date: May–July.
Habitats: Prairies, roadsides, fields.
Distribution: NE, EC, SE.

## *Pueraria lobata* (Willd.) Ohwi
**Kudzu**

Plants: Trailing and climbing herbaceous vine.

Leaves: Alternate, trifoliate, with leaflets ovate to nearly round and entire or lobed.

Inflorescence: Axillary panicle; calyx 5-lobed; five petals, light to dark purple.

Fruit: Legume.

Flowering Date: July–October.

Habitats: Roadsides, woods.

Distribution: Throughout.

Comments: Native of China.


## *Rhynchosia tomentosa* (L.) H. & A.
**Snoutbean**

Plants: Upright, hairy perennial.

Leaves: Alternate, trifoliate, with leaflets ovate to oblong.

Inflorescence: Axillary or terminal raceme; flowers perfect; five petals, yellow; stamens in two series, one a cluster of nine and the other having one.

Fruit: Legume.

Flowering Date: June–August.

Habitats: Woods, fields, open sites, roadsides.

Distribution: Throughout.

## *Robinia pseudoacacia* L.
### Black Locust

Plants: Trees bearing spines.

Leaves: Alternate, pinnately compound, with leaflets elliptic to ovate and entire.

Inflorescence: Axillary, drooping racemes; five petals, clawed, white, with banner having a yellowish spot; stamens united.

Fruit: Legume.

Flowering Date: April–June.

Habitats: Disturbed sites, woodland edges, yards.

Distribution: Throughout.

Comments: The inflorescence can be cooked as a fritter or made into a drink. The wood is extremely hard and has been used for such products as fence posts, ladders, and handles.

## *Robinia hispida* L.
### Bristly Locust

Plants: Shrub with bristly twigs of previous years' growth.

Leaves: Alternate, pinnately compound, with leaflets elliptic to ovate and entire.

Inflorescence: Axillary cluster of racemes; five petals, rose to reddish purple; stamens united.

Fruit: Legume.

Flowering Date: July–October.

Habitats: Roadsides, waste sites, woods.

Distribution: NE, EC.

## *Sesbania macrocarpa* Muhl. ex Raf.
### Sesbania

Plants: Upright, annual covered with a whitish coating that rubs off.
Leaves: Alternate, pinnately compound, with leaflets linear to oblong and entire.
Inflorescence: Flowers in axillary clusters; banner yellowish speckled with purplish brown or dark red and wings and keel yellowish.
Fruit: Legume.
Flowering Date: June–September.
Habitats: Wet roadside ditches, fields, marshes, sand bars of rivers.
Distribution: Throughout.

## *Sesbania punicea* (Cav.) Benth.
### Red Rattlebox

Plants: Shrub.
Leaves: Alternate, pinnately compound, with leaflets linear to oblong and entire.
Inflorescence: Axillary raceme; calyx purplish to reddish; five petals, reddish orange to reddish purple; ten stamens.
Fruit: Legume.
Flowering Date: June–September.
Habitats: Savannas, roadsides, ditches, waste sites.
Distribution: DE, CO, SE.

## *Sesbania vesicaria* (Jacq.) Ell.
### Bladder Pod

Plants: Upright, glabrous to hairy annual.
Leaves: Alternate, pinnately compound, with leaflets elliptic or oblong and entire.
Inflorescence: Raceme; calyx purplish to reddish; five petals, reddish purple to nearly orange; ten stamens.
Fruit: Legume.
Flowering Date: June–September.
Habitats: Roadsides, ditches, waste sites.
Distribution: Throughout.

## *Stylosanthes biflora* (L.) B.S.P.
### Pencil Flower

Plants: Upright to sprawling, hairy perennial.
Leaves: Alternate, trifoliate, with leaflets elliptic to lanceolate and entire.
Inflorescence: Flowers in a terminal cluster; five petals, yellow; ten stamens.
Fruit: Legume.
Flowering Date: June–August.
Habitats: Roadsides, woods, prairies.
Distribution: CO, NE, EC, SE, SW.

## *Tephrosia virginiana* (L.) Pers.
### Goat's Rue, Catgut, Hoary Pea

Plants: Upright, hairy perennial.
Leaves: Alternate, pinnately compound, with leaflets elliptic to oblong and entire.
Inflorescence: Flowers in terminal and axillary clusters; five petals with banner cream colored or whitish and keel and wings pink to rose.
Fruit: Legume.
Flowering Date: May–June.
Habitats: Prairies, rocky roadsides, glades, and woods.
Distribution: Throughout.

## *Trifolium arvense* L.
### Rabbit-Foot Clover

Plants: Upright, hairy annual.
Leaves: Alternate, trifoliate, with leaflets linear to narrowly lanceolate and entire.
Inflorescence: Terminal and axillary heads; five petals, off-white, rose, or pinkish.
Fruit: Legume.
Flowering Date: April–August.
Habitat: Roadsides.
Distribution: Throughout.

## *Trifolium incarnatum* L.
**Crimson Clover**

Plants: Upright, hairy annual.
Leaves: Alternate, trifoliate, with leaf-
lets obovate to lanceolate and having
finely toothed margins.
Inflorescence: Terminal and axillary
heads; five petals, red.
Fruit: Legume.
Flowering Date: April–June.
Habitats: Fields, roadsides.
Distribution: Throughout.
Comments: Native of Europe.

## *Trifolium pratense* L.
**Red Clover**

Plants: Upright, glabrous to hairy pe-
rennial.
Leaves: Alternate, trifoliate, with leaf-
lets elliptic to obovate and having
toothed margins.
Inflorescence: Terminal and axillary
heads; five petals, rose to light
purple.
Fruit: Legume.
Flowering Date: April–October.
Habitats: Waste sites, roadsides, fields.
Distribution: Throughout.
Comments: Native of Europe.

## *Vicia caroliniana* Walt.
**White-Flowered Vetch**

Plants: Sprawling, hairy perennial.
Leaves: Alternate, pinnately com-
pound, with leaflets elliptic and ter-
minal leaflet modified into tendrils.
Inflorescence: Flowers in axillary clus-
ters; five petals, white; ten stamens.
Fruit: Legume.
Flowering Date: April–June.
Habitats: Woods.
Distribution: NE, EC, SE, SW.

## *Vicia grandiflora* Scop.
**Large-Flowered Vetch**

Plants: Sprawling, hairy annual.
Leaves: Alternate, pinnately compound, with leaflets obovate and terminal leaflet modified into a tendril.
Inflorescence: Flowers in axillary clusters; five petals, pale yellow, with the banner often tinted purple; ten stamens.
Fruit: Legume.
Flowering Date: April–June.
Habitats: Roadsides, waste sites.
Distribution: DE, NE, EC, SE, SW.

## *Vicia villosa* Roth
**Smooth Vetch**

Plants: Trailing or climbing, slightly hairy annual or perennial.
Leaves: Alternate, pinnately compound, with leaflets linear to elliptic and leaflet modified into a tendril.
Inflorescence: Flowers in axillary clusters; five petals, purple; ten stamens.
Fruit: Legume.
Flowering Date: May–September.
Habitats: Fence rows, roadsides, waste sites.
Distribution: DE, NE.

## *Wisteria frutescens* (L.) Poir.
**Wisteria**

Plants: Climbing, woody vine.
Leaves: Alternate, pinnately compound, with leaflets ovate to oblong and entire.
Inflorescence: Flowers in terminal racemes; five petals, blue to violet; ten stamens, in two series, one a cluster of nine and the other having one.
Fruit: Legume.
Flowering Date: April–June.
Habitats: Woodland edges, woods, roadsides, stream edges.
Distribution: CO, SE, DE, EC, NE.

# FUMARIACEAE
Fumitory Family

Plants annual, biennial, or perennial. Leaves alternate or basal, dissected or lobed. Flowers irregular; two sepals; four petals in two series, with the outer series sac shaped or spurred; ovary superior; six stamens. Fruit a capsule.

## *Corydalis flavula* (Raf.) DC.
### Pale Corydalis

Plants: Upright to prostrate, glabrous annual.
Leaves: Alternate, pinnately dissected, with segments highly dissected.
Inflorescence: Terminal and axillary racemes; flowers perfect; two sepals; corolla irregular, with upper petal spurred and saccate, pale yellow.
Fruit: Capsule.
Flowering Date: March–May.
Habitats: Alluvial woods, rocky wooded slopes.
Distribution: DE, EC.

## *Dicentra cucullaria* (L.) Bernh.
### Dutchman's Breeches

Plants: Upright, glabrous perennial.
Leaves: Basal, petiolate, ternately or pinnately dissected or lobed.
Inflorescence: Raceme; flowers perfect, irregular; two sepals; four petals, with outer two spurred at the base and inner two spatulate; corolla white.
Fruit: Capsule.
Flowering Date: March–April.
Habitat: Wooded slopes.
Distribution: NE.

# GENTIANACEAE
## Gentian Family

Plants annual or perennial. Leaves simple; basal, alternate, opposite, or whorled. Four to thirteen sepals, united at the base; four to thirteen petals, united at least at the base; stamens the same number as the petals. Fruit a capsule.

### *Gentiana saponaria* L.
### Bottle Gentian, Soapwort Gentian

Plants: Upright, glabrous perennial.
Leaves: Opposite, simple, short petiolate or sessile, elliptic to lanceolate, entire, with base attenuate.
Inflorescence: Flowers mostly in a terminal cluster, appearing closed; calyx lobed; corolla tubular to funnelform, purple; four to five stamens.
Fruit: Capsule.
Flowering Date: September–November.
Habitats: Stream edges, alluvial woods, roadside ditches.
Distribution: NE.

### *Gentiana villosa* L.
### Samson's Snakeroot

Plants: Upright, hairy perennial.
Leaves: Opposite, simple, sessile, elliptic, entire, acute, with base attenuate.
Inflorescence: Flowers mostly in a terminal cluster; calyx lobed; corolla tubular to funnelform, whitish green to yellowish green; four to five stamens.
Fruit: Capsule.
Flowering Date: August–November.
Habitats: Dry sandy pinelands, sandy roadsides, dry woods.
Distribution: NE, EC.

## *Obolaria virginica* L.
**Pennywort**

Plants: Upright, glabrous perennial.
Leaves: Opposite, simple, sessile, with lower leaves reduced and upper leaves obovate, entire.
Inflorescence: Flowers in terminal and axillary clusters, subtended by two leafy bracts; calyx absent; corolla tubular, separate in part, white or whitish purple.
Fruit: Capsule.
Flowering Date: March–April.
Habitats: Wooded slopes, dry woods.
Distribution: NE, EC.

## *Sabatia bartramii* Wilbur
**Rose-Gentian, Marsh Pink**

Plants: Upright, glabrous perennial.
Leaves: Opposite, sessile; lower leaves spreading, spatulate to oblanceolate, entire; upper leaves usually appressed to the stem, becoming narrowly lanceolate to linear upward, entire.
Inflorescence: Flowers in terminal or axillary clusters; calyx lobed; corolla rotate, deeply parted into seven to twelve lobes, rose to pink with a yellow spot bordered by red at the base of each lobe.
Fruit: Capsule.
Flowering Date: June–August.
Habitats: Savannas, wet pinelands, ditches.
Distribution: CO.
Comments: *S. gentianoides* Ell. is similar, but the flowers are subtended by leafy bracts and stem leaves that are linear and clasping. *S. dodecandra* (L.) B.S.P. has leaves that are lanceolate to oblong from base to apex, and its flowers are not subtended by leafy bracts.

## *Sabatia campestris* Nutt.
### Prairie Pink, Marsh Pink, Rose Pink, Bitter Bloom

Plants: Upright, alternate-branching, glabrous annual, with angled and winged stems.

Leaves: Alternate, simple, ovate to lanceolate, entire, acute, with base cuneate.

Inflorescence: Flowers in a terminal cluster; flowering branches alternate; calyx lobed; corolla rotate, five parted, pale to dark pink with a yellow center; five stamens.

Fruit: Capsule.

Flowering Date: July–September.

Habitats: Woodlands, prairies, roadsides.

Distribution: DE, NE, EC.

Comments: *S. angularis* (L.) Pursh. has clasping leaf bases while *S. brachiata* Ell. does not. Both species have inflorescence branches that are opposite.

## *Sabatia macrophylla* Hook.
### White Sabatia

Plants: Upright, branching perennial.

Leaves: Opposite, simple, sessile, elliptic to lanceolate, entire.

Inflorescence: Flowers in terminal clusters; calyx lobed; corolla rotate, five parted, white.

Fruit: Capsule.

Flowering Date: June–July.

Habitat: Moist pinelands.

Distribution: CO.

## *Sabatia stellaris* Pursh
**Marsh Pink**

Plants: Upright, glabrous annual.
Leaves: Opposite, simple, entire; lanceolate, elliptic, or linear to filiform.
Inflorescence: Flowers terminal or axillary, usually solitary, sometimes
clustered; calyx lobed; corolla rotate,
five parted, pink with yellow at the
base bordered by a red line that is
bordered by white.
Fruit: Capsule.
Flowering Date: July–October.
Habitats: Salt and brackish marshes,
innerdune depressions.
Distribution: CO.

## *Swertia caroliniensis* (Walt.) Ktze.
**Columbo**

Plants: Upright, glabrous perennial
with thick roots.
Leaves: Basal and whorled, sessile;
basal leaves lanceolate to oblanceolate, entire; upper leaves similar, in
whorls of three to nine.
Inflorescence: Panicle; calyx four
lobed; corolla rotate, four parted
nearly to base, whitish with green
streaks and a prominent green spot
(gland) at the base of each corolla
lobe; four stamens.
Fruit: Capsule.
Flowering Date: May–June.
Habitats: Woodlands, calcareous outcrops, open areas.
Distribution: NE, EC.
Comments: The roots have been used
medicinally as a tonic, emetic, and
cathartic.

# GERANIACEAE
## Geranium or Stork's-bill Family

Plants annual or perennial. Leaves alternate or opposite, simple and palmately or pinnately divided or compound. Five sepals; five petals; ten stamens. Fruit a capsule terminated by a long beak, hence the name stork's bill.

## *Geranium maculatum* L.
### Wild Geranium

Plants: Upright, hairy perennial with rhizomes.

Leaves: Alternate, simple, sessile and petiolate, with margins deeply dissected and toothed.

Inflorescence: Flowers in a terminal cluster, perfect, regular; five sepals; five petals, pink or purplish, whitish toward the base.

Fruit: Elongated, beaklike.

Flowering Date: April–June.

Habitats: Rocky slopes, ravine bottoms.

Distribution: NE, EC.

Comments: The roots have been used medicinally for treatment of diarrhea and as a gargle for mouth sores.

# HYDRANGEACEAE
Hydrangea Family

Plants shrub or woody vine. Leaves simple, opposite. Plants with both perfect and sterile flowers; perfect flowers with a five-lobed calyx and five white petals; ovary inferior; eight to ten stamens. Fruit a capsule.

## *Hydrangea arborescens* L.
### Wild Hydrangea, Seven- Bark

Plants: Shrub.
Leaves: Opposite, simple, petiolate, acute to acuminate; ovate, oval, or lanceolate; margins toothed; base cuneate or slightly cordate to slightly truncate.
Inflorescence: Flowers in terminal clusters of both perfect and sterile flowers; perfect flower regular with five white petals and eight to ten stamens that extend beyond the petals; sterile flowers with a calyx of three to four greenish to white, petaloid lobes.
Fruit: Capsule.
Flowering Date: May–July.
Habitats: Woods, ravines, stream edges.
Distribution: NE, EC, DE.

## *Hydrangea quercifolia* Bartr.
### Oak-Leaf Hydrangea

Plants: Shrub.
Leaves: Opposite, simple, petiolate, lobed, whitish below, with base truncate or cuneate; leaves similar in appearance to leaves of some oak species.
Inflorescence: Flowers in a terminal, compact cluster of both perfect and sterile flowers; perfect flowers inconspicuous, with five white petals and numerous stamens; sterile flowers consisting of a calyx with petaloid lobes, white turning pinkish with age.
Fruit: Capsule.
Flowering Date: April–June.
Habitat: Mixed Woods.
Distribution: NE, EC.

# HYDROPHYLLACEAE
## Waterleaf Family

Plants annual or perennial. Leaves simple, alternate. Calyx five lobed or deeply divided; corolla five lobed, rotate or bell shaped; ovary superior; five stamens. Fruit a capsule.

### *Phacelia dubia* (L.) Trel.
**Hairy Phacelia**

Plants: Upright to nearly prostrate, hairy annual.

Leaves: Alternate, simple, petiolate, with margins pinnately divided and segments toothed.

Inflorescence: Flowers in a terminal cluster, perfect, regular; calyx parted; corolla bell shaped, five parted nearly to base, purple or blue, rarely white; five stamens.

Fruit: Capsule.

Flowering Date: April–May.

Habitats: Roadsides, fields, woods.

Distribution: NE, EC.

### *Hydrolea ovata* Nutt.
**Hydrolea**

Plants: Upright, hairy perennial with spines.

Leaves: Alternate, simple, nearly sessile, ovate, entire, acute, with base cuneate.

Inflorescence: Terminal panicle; flowers perfect, regular; calyx parted; corolla bell shaped, parted nearly to base, blue to bluish purple; five stamens.

Fruit: Capsule.

Flowering Date: June–September.

Habitats: Ditches with standing water, river bottoms, swamps, stream edges, ponds.

Distribution: DE, CO, EC, SW, SE.

## ILLICIACEAE
Anise Family

Plants a shrub or small tree with a rosin odor. Leaves evergreen, alternate, simple. Sepals and petals similar, deep red. Fruit an aggregate of one-seeded follicles.

*Illicium floridanum* Ellis
**Anise Tree, Stinkbush**

Plants: Shrub to small tree.
Leaves: Alternate, simple, petiolate, elliptic to lanceolate, entire, mostly acute, with base cuneate to attenuate.
Inflorescence: Flowers axillary, solitary, having a peduncle, perfect, regular; three to six sepals, deciduous; eighteen or more petals, deep maroon; numerous stamens.
Fruit: Flattened, wheel-shaped follicle.
Flowering Date: March–April.
Habitats: Wooded slopes, wet forest, swampy woods.
Distribution: CO, EC, SW, SE.

# LAMIACEAE [= LABIATAE]
## Mint Family

Plants annual or perennial, with square stems; some species
have the distinctive scent of mint. Leaves simple, opposite or
in rosettes. Flowers irregular to nearly regular; corolla five
lobed, bilabiate; ovary superior; two to four stamens. Fruit
a schizocarp of four mericarps (nutlets).

### *Collinsonia canadensis* L.
**Horse Balm, Rich Weed,
Citreonella Horse Balm**

Plants: Upright, glabrous to slightly
hairy perennial with tuberous roots.
Leaves: Opposite, simple, ovate to elliptic, acute to acuminate, with margins toothed and base rounded, truncate, or cuneate.
Inflorescence: Flowers in a terminal
cluster, perfect; calyx bilabiate,
lobed; corolla yellow; two stamens,
extending beyond the corolla.
Fruit: Schizocarp.
Flowering Date: July–September.
Habitats: Woods, bases of wooded
bluffs.
Distribution: Throughout.
Comments: The flowers have a lemon
odor. The rootstock has been used
medicinally as a remedy for kidney
and urinary problems.

### *Cunila origanoides* (L.) Britt.
**Dittany**

Plants: Upright, glabrous to hairy perennial.
Leaves: Opposite, simple, sessile or
short petiolate, ovate to lanceolate,
acute, with margins toothed and
base truncate or rounded.
Inflorescence: Flowers in terminal and
axillary clusters; calyx irregular to
nearly regular; corolla purple, pink,
or lavender; two stamens, extending
beyond the corolla.
Fruit: Schizocarp.
Flowering Date: August–September.
Habitat: Dry rocky woods.
Distribution: NE.
Comments: The leaves can be used for
making a mint tea. It was once used
medicinally for treating fevers, headaches, and snake bites.

## *Glechoma hederacea* L.
### Gill-Over-The-Ground, Ground Ivy

Plants: Sprawling to ascending perennial, rooting at the nodes.
Leaves: Opposite, simple, petiolate, cordate to kidney shaped, with margins toothed, tip obtuse.
Inflorescence: Flowers in axillary or terminal clusters, irregular; corolla blue, purple, or violet; four stamens.
Fruit: Schizocarp.
Flowering Date: March–June.
Habitats: Waste and disturbed sites, yards, roadsides.
Distribution: NE.

## *Hyptis alata* (Raf.) Shinn.
### Hyptis

Plants: Upright, hairy perennial.
Leaves: Opposite, simple, petiolate to sessile, lanceolate, acute, with margins toothed and base cuneate to attenuate.
Inflorescence: Axillary, heads on peduncles and subtended by leafy bracts; calyx irregular, five lobed; corolla one lipped, pink to lavender; four stamens, extending beyond the corolla.
Fruit: Schizocarp.
Flowering Date: June–August.
Habitats: Wet ditches, moist woodlands.
Distribution: CO.

*Lycopus americanus* Muhl. ex Bart.
## American Bugle Weed, Water Horehound

Plants: Upright, glabrous or essentially glabrous perennial.
Leaves: Opposite, simple, petiolate, elliptic to ovate, acute to acuminate, with margins toothed and base attenuate.
Inflorescence: Flowers in axillary clusters; calyx regular, five lobed; corolla nearly regular, five lobed, white or dull white; two or four stamens, extending beyond the corolla.
Fruit: Schizocarp.
Flowering Date: June–November.
Habitats: Moist woods, marshes, edges of lakes and ponds.
Distribution: Throughout.

## *Lamium amplexicaule* L.
## Henbit

Plants: Upright annual.
Leaves: Opposite, simple, petiolate, ovate to kidney shaped, with margins toothed, tip obtuse to rounded, and base truncate.
Inflorescence: Flowers in axillary clusters subtended by sessile, nearly horizontal leaves; calyx regular, five lobed; corolla light purple, with lower lip spotted with darker purple; four stamens.
Fruit: Schizocarp.
Flowering Date: March–May.
Habitats: Yards, roadsides, waste areas.
Distribution: Throughout.

## *Lamium purpureum* L.
## Henbit, Dead Nettle

Plants: Upright annual.
Leaves: Opposite, simple, petiolate, triangular to lanceolate, acuminate, with margins toothed and base cordate to truncate.
Inflorescence: Flowers in axillary clusters subtended by petiolate, drooping leaves; calyx regular, five lobed; corolla lavender, with lower lip spotted with darker purple; four stamens.
Fruit: Schizocarp.
Flowering Date: March–May.
Habitats: Yards, roadsides, waste sites.
Distribution: Throughout.

### *Mentha spicata* L.
**Spearmint**

Plants: Upright, glabrous to slightly hairy perennial with rhizomes.

Leaves: Opposite, simple, mostly sessile, lanceolate, acute to acuminate, with margins toothed and base cuneate to rounded.

Inflorescence: Spikelike, terminal and axillary; calyx regular or nearly so, five lobed; corolla nearly regular, four lobed, white marked with lavender; four stamens, extending beyond the corolla.

Fruit: Schizocarp.

Flowering Date: June–November.

Distribution: Throughout.

Comments: *M. piperita* L. (Peppermint) has leaves with definite petioles.

### *Monarda citriodora* Cerv. ex Lag.
**Lemon Mint**

Plants: Upright, hairy perennial.

Leaves: Opposite, simple, petiolate to nearly sessile, lanceolate, acute, with margins toothed and base cuneate to attenuate.

Inflorescence: Terminal, heads subtended by numerous purple, leafy bracts, heads spaced on the flower stalk; calyx regular, five lobed; corolla whitish to lavender; two stamens, extending beyond the corolla.

Fruit: Schizocarp.

Flowering Date: June–July.

Habitat: Calcareous outcrops.

Distribution: CO, EC.

## *Monarda fistulosa* L.
### Wild Bergamot, Bee Balm, Horsemint

Plants: Upright, glabrous to hairy perennial.

Leaves: Opposite, simple, petiolate, ovate to lanceolate, acuminate, with margins toothed, base truncate, rounded, or sometimes slightly cordate.

Inflorescence: Terminal head subtended by whitish to pinkish bracts; calyx regular; corolla pink, purple, or occasionally white, with lower lip spotted with dark purple; two stamens, extending beyond the corolla.

Fruit: Schizocarp.

Flowering Date: June–September.

Habitats: Prairies, roadsides, woodland edges, wooded slopes.

Distribution: NE, EC.

Comments: A tea made from the leaves has been used medicinally for the remedy of colic.

## *Monarda punctata* L.
### Dotted Monarda

Plants: Upright, glabrous to hairy perennial.

Leaves: Opposite, simple, petiolate, ovate to lanceolate, acuminate, with margins toothed and base rounded to cuneate.

Inflorescence: Terminal heads subtended by numerous pink to lavender, leafy bracts, heads spaced on the stem; calyx regular; corolla yellow spotted with purple; two stamens, extending beyond the corolla.

Fruit: Schizocarp.

Flowering Date: July–September.

Habitats: Rocky woods, sandy areas.

Distribution: NE, EC, SW, SE.

## *Perilla frutescens* (L.) Britt.
### Beef-Steak Plant

Plants: Upright, freely branching, hairy annual.

Leaves: Opposite, simple, petiolate, ovate, acute, with margins toothed and base cuneate to rounded.

Inflorescence: Terminal or axillary raceme or terminal panicle; calyx bilabiate; corolla white to lavender; four stamens, extending beyond the corolla.

Fruit: Schizocarp.

Flowering Date: August–October.

Habitats: Roadsides, woods, pastures.

Distribution: DE, NE, EC.

*Prunella vulgaris* L.
**Self- Heal, Heal-All,**

Plants: Upright, hairy perennial.
Leaves: Opposite, simple, petiolate, elliptic to lanceolate, entire to slightly
toothed, acute to obtuse, with base
cuneate to rounded.
Inflorescence: Terminal or axillary
spikes subtended by leaflike bracts,
with axillary spikes on peduncles;
calyx irregular; corolla blue to violet,
occasionally white, with lower lip
often spotted with dark purple.
Fruit: Schizocarp.
Flowering Date: April–November.
Habitats: Roadsides, prairies, waste
and disturbed sites, woods.
Distribution: NE, EC, SW, SE.
Comments: The plant has been used
medicinally to cure many ailments.
Some Indians thought it was a cure
for all ailments, which gives it the
name Heal-all.

*Physostegia virginiana* (L.)
Benth.
**False Dragonhead, Obedient
Plant**

Plants: Upright, nearly glabrous perennial with rhizomes.
Leaves: Opposite, simple, sessile, elliptic to lanceolate, acuminate, with
margins toothed and base attenuate.
Inflorescence: Terminal and axillary
spikes or racemes; calyx five lobed;
corolla white to deep pink, spotted
with reddish purple; four stamens.
Fruit: Schizocarp.
Flowering Date: June–September.
Habitats: Prairies, roadsides, bogs.
Distribution: NE, EC, SW, SE.

## *Pycnanthemum albescens* T. & G.
### Mountain Mint

Plants: Upright, freely branching, hairy perennial with rhizomes.

Leaves: Opposite, simple, petiolate, strongly whitened near top, ovate to lanceolate, entire to slightly toothed, acute to acuminate, with base cuneate to rounded.

Inflorescence: Terminal and axillary heads on peduncles; calyx lobed; corolla white to lavender spotted with purple; four stamens, usually extending beyond the corolla.

Fruit: Schizocarp.

Flowering Date: June–August.

Habitats: Savannas, pinelands, hardwoods, roadsides.

Distribution: Throughout.

## *Pycnanthemum tenuifolium* Schrad.
### Slender Mountain Mint

Plants: Upright, glabrous perennial with rhizomes.

Leaves: Opposite, simple, sessile, linear to narrowly lanceolate, entire.

Inflorescence: Flowers in terminal clusters; calyx nearly regular; corolla white to pinkish; four stamens, usually extending beyond the corolla.

Fruit: Schizocarp.

Flowering Date: June–August.

Habitats: Prairies, roadsides.

Distribution: NE, EC, SE.

## *Salvia azurea* Lam.
### Blue Sage

Plants: Upright, hairy perennial.

Leaves: Opposite, simple, petiolate, linear to lanceolate, entire to toothed, with base decurrent.

Inflorescence: Paniclelike or racemelike; calyx bilabiate; corolla blue; two or four stamens.

Fruit: Schizocarp.

Flowering Date: August–October.

Habitats: Rocky roadsides, prairies, along railroad tracks, rocky woods.

Distribution: NE, EC.

## *Salvia coccinea* Buchoz. ex Epling
**Red Sage**

Plants: Upright, glabrous to slightly hairy perennial.

Leaves: Opposite, simple, ovate, petiolate, acute, with margins toothed and base cordate to truncate.

Inflorescence: Paniclelike or racemelike; calyx bilabiate; corolla red; two stamens, extending beyond the corolla.

Fruit: Schizocarp.

Flowering Date: May–November.

Habitats: Waste sites, roadsides.

Distribution: CO.

## *Salvia lyrata* L.
**Lyre-Leaved Sage, Cancer Weed**

Plants: Upright, glabrous to slightly hairy perennial.

Leaves: Basal rosette and one to two pairs on the stem; basal leaves elliptic to obovate, petiolate, with margins entire, toothed or lobed and base attenuate.

Inflorescence: Paniclelike, terminal; calyx bilabiate; corolla light blue, purple or white; two or four stamens.

Fruit: Schizocarp.

Flowering Date: April–June.

Habitats: Yards, fields, roadsides, woods.

Distribution: Throughout.

## *Scutellaria integrifolia* L.
**Skullcap**

Plants: Upright perennial.

Leaves: Opposite, simple, petiolate, triangular to ovate, with margins toothed, tip obtuse to acute, and base truncate to cuneate.

Inflorescence: Raceme; calyx bilabiate; corolla blue to purple; four stamens, extending beyond the corolla.

Fruit: Schizocarp.

Flowering Date: May–July.

Habitats: Roadsides, woods.

Distribution: Throughout.

## *Scutellaria parvula* Michx.
### Skullcap

Plants: Upright, hairy perennial from
    moniliform stolons.
Leaves: Opposite, simple, sessile,
    ovate, entire to slightly toothed,
    acute to obtuse, with base truncate,
    cordate, or rounded.
Inflorescence: Raceme; calyx bilabiate;
    corolla blue; four stamens.
Fruit: Schizocarp.
Flowering Date: April–May.
Habitats: Woods, fields, roadsides.
Distribution: Northern half of state.

## *Teucrium canadense* L.
### Wood Sage, American
### Germander

Plants: Upright, hairy perennial with
    square rhizomes.
Leaves: Opposite, simple, petiolate, el-
    liptic to lanceolate, acute, with mar-
    gins toothed and base cuneate or
    rounded.
Inflorescence: Terminal or branched ra-
    ceme; calyx five lobed; corolla one
    lipped, pink to lavender; four sta-
    mens, extending beyond the corolla.
Fruit: Schizocarp.
Flowering Date: June–August.
Habitats: Prairies, woods, ditches.
Distribution: DE, NE, EC.

## *Trichostema dichotomum* L.
### Blue Curls, Bastard Pennyroyal

Plants: Upright, hairy annual with a
    taproot.
Leaves: Opposite, simple, sessile and
    petiolate, elliptic to lanceolate, en-
    tire to toothed, with base cuneate to
    attenuate.
Inflorescence: Flowers terminal, soli-
    tary; calyx bilabiate; corolla blue to
    violet, often spotted with purple;
    four stamens, long exerted, curled.
Fruit: Schizocarp.
Flowering Date: August–November.
Habitats: Sandy pinelands, rocky
    woods, old fields.
Distribution: Throughout.

# LENTIBULARIACEAE
## Butterwort or Bladderwort Family

Plants annual or perennial, aquatic and terrestrial. Leaves in basal rosettes or whorled and alternate; aquatic species have leaves that are finely dissected with bladders for trapping small aquatic insects. Calyx bilabiate; corolla five lobed and bilabiate, saclike or spurred; two stamens. Fruit a many-seeded capsule.

*Pinquicula lutea* Walt.
**Butterwort**

Plants: Upright, hairy perennial.
Leaves: Basal rosette, sessile, ovate to elliptic, acute to acuminate, with margins entire and usually curled inward.
Inflorescence: Flowers terminal, solitary, perfect, irregular to nearly regular; calyx five lobed; corolla two lipped, five lobed, spurred, yellow; two stamens.
Fruit: Capsule.
Flowering Date: April–May.
Habitats: Savannas, pinelands.
Distribution: CO.

*Pinquicula caerulea* Walt.
**Butterwort**

Plants: Upright, glandular perennial.
Leaves: Basal rosette, sessile, ovate to elliptic, acute to acuminate, with margins entire and usually curled inward.
Inflorescence: Flowers terminal, solitary, perfect, irregular to nearly regular; calyx five lobed; corolla two lipped, five lobed, spurred, blue to whitish blue; two stamens.
Fruit: Capsule.
Flowering Date: April–May.
Habitats: Savannas, bogs.
Distribution: CO.

## *Utricularia inflata* Walt.
**Bladderwort**

Plants: Carnivorous annual without
roots; scape with a whorl of inflated
branchlets; floating.

Leaves: Godfrey and Wooten indicate
that this genus does not have leaves
but has only a stem system that is
somewhat leaflike.

Inflorescence: Flowers terminal, several, perfect, irregular; calyx two
lobed; corolla two lipped, spurred,
yellow.

Fruit: Capsule.

Flowering Date: May–November.

Habitats: Roadside ditches with standing water, ponds, pools, swamps, wet
savannas.

Distribution: CO.

Comments: Several other species of
this genus are terrestrial.

## *Utricularia juncea* Vahl
**Bladderwort**

Plants: Carnivorous annual without
roots; scape without a whorl of inflated branchlets; terrestrial.

Leaves: See *U. inflata* Walt.

Inflorescence: Flowers terminal, several, perfect, irregular; calyx two
lobed; corolla two lipped, spurred,
yellow.

Fruit: Capsule.

Flowering Date: May–November.

Habitats: Wet roadside ditches, wet savannas.

Distribution: CO.

## LINACEAE
Flax Family

Plants annual, biennial, or perennial. Leaves opposite or alternate, simple. Five sepals; five petals; five stamens. Fruit a capsule.

### *Linum medium* (Planch.) Britt.
**Flax**

Plants: Upright, glabrous, branching annual or perennial.

Leaves: Upper leaves alternate and lower leaves opposite, simple, sessile, linear.

Inflorescence: Panicle; flowers perfect, regular; five sepals; five petals, yellow; five stamens.

Fruit: Capsule.

Flowering Date: May–August.

Habitats: Prairies, calcareous glades, rocky woods.

Distribution: EC.

# LOGANIACEAE
## Jessamine Family

Plants perennial herb or woody vine. Leaves opposite or alternate. Calyx four to five lobed; corolla four to five lobed; ovary superior; four to five stamens. Fruit a many-seeded capsule.

## *Gelsemium sempervirens* (L.) J. St. Hil.
### Yellow Jessamine

Plants: High-climbing vine.
Leaves: Opposite, simple, petiolate, evergreen, lanceolate, entire, acute to acuminate, with base cuneate to rounded.
Inflorescence: Flowers in axillary clusters, sometimes solitary, perfect, regular; five sepals; corolla five lobed, nearly rotate, bright yellow; five stamens.
Fruit: Capsule.
Flowering Date: March–May.
Habitats: Fence rows, woods, thickets, disturbed sites.
Distribution: CO, NE, EC, SW, SE.

## *Spigelia marilandica* L.
### Indian Pink, Pink Root

Plants: Upright, glabrous perennial.
Leaves: Opposite, simple, short petiolate, ovate to lanceolate, entire, acute to acuminate, with base rounded to cuneate.
Inflorescence: Terminal, helicoid cluster; flowers perfect, regular; five sepals; corolla five lobed, funnelform, scarlet red outside and yellow inside; five stamens.
Fruit: Capsule.
Flowering Date: May–July.
Habitats: Roadsides, woods.
Distribution: NE, EC, SE.

## LYTHRACEAE
Loosestrife Family

Plants annual or perennial. Leaves opposite, alternate, or whorled; simple. Calyx four to six lobed; petals absent, four, or six; ovary superior; eight to twelve stamens. Fruit a many-seeded capsule.

### *Ammannia coccinea* Rottb.
**Tooth-Cup**

Plants: Upright, branching annual.
Leaves: Opposite, simple, sessile, linear to lanceolate, entire.
Inflorescence: Flowers axillary, several, perfect, regular; calyx lobed; four petals, pink to purple.
Fruit: Capsule.
Flowering Date: July–October.
Habitat: Marshes.
Distribution: Throughout.

## *Cuphea viscosissima* Jacq.
### Waxweed

Plants: Upright, hairy annual.

Leaves: Opposite, simple, petiolate, elliptic to lanceolate, entire, acute to somewhat acuminate, with base cuneate to rounded.

Inflorescence: Flowers axillary or terminal cluster, perfect; calyx six lobed; six petals, purple; twelve stamens.

Fruit: Capsule.

Flowering Date: July–October.

Habitats: Wet ditches, wet woods, stream edges, lakes.

Distribution: EC.

## *Decodon verticillatus* (L.) Ell.
### Water Loosestrife, Water Willow, Swamp Loosestrife

Plants: Upright, hairy perennial; becoming shrubby.

Leaves: Opposite or whorled, simple, petiolate, lanceolate, entire, acuminate, with base cuneate.

Inflorescence: Flowers in axillary clusters, perfect, regular; calyx lobed; six petals, crinkly, purple or pink.

Fruit: Capsule.

Flowering Date: July–September.

Habitats: Wet ditches, pools, marshes, edges of lakes.

Distribution: NE, EC.

# MAGNOLIACEAE
## Magnolia Family

Plants tree. Leaves alternate, simple. Three or more sepals;
three or more petals; ovary superior; many stamens. Fruit an
aggregate of follicles or samaras.

### *Liriodendron tulipifera* L.
**Tulip Tree, Yellow Poplar**

Plants: Trees.

Leaves: Alternate, simple, petiolate,
with margins lobed, tip truncate or
truncate and notched, and base truncate to slightly cordate.

Inflorescence: Flowers terminal, solitary, perfect, regular; three sepals, becoming reflexed; six petals, yellowish green; numerous stamens.

Fruit: Samaras.

Flowering Date: April–June.

Habitat: Woods.

Distribution: CO, NE, EC, SW, SE.

### *Magnolia acuminata* L.
**Cucumber Tree**

Plants: Trees.

Leaves: Alternate, simple, short petiolate, elliptic to ovate, entire, acuminate, with base cuneate to slightly
cordate; leaves are deciduous.

Inflorescence: Flowers terminal, solitary, perfect, regular; three sepals;
numerous petals, off-white to yellowish white; numerous stamens.

Fruit: Aggregate of follicles.

Flowering Date: April–May.

Habitat: Woods.

Distribution: CO, NE, EC, SW, SE.

## *Magnolia grandiflora* L.
### Bull Bay

Plants: Trees.
Leaves: Alternate, simple, short petiolate, elliptic, often with rusty-
colored hairs on lower leaves, acute
or obtuse, entire, with base cuneate;
leaves evergreen.
Inflorescence: Flowers terminal, solitary, cup shaped, perfect; three sepals; numerous petals, creamy
white.
Fruit: Ellipsoid aggregate of follicles.
Flowering Date: May–June.
Habitats: Hardwoods, floodplains,
wooded ravines.
Distribution: CO, SW, SE, DE.

## *Magnolia tripetala* L.
### Umbrella Magnolia

Plants: Trees.
Leaves: Alternate, simple, short petiolate, lanceolate or ovate to oblanceolate, entire, acuminate, with base cuneate to attenuate.
Inflorescence: Flowers terminal, solitary, perfect, regular; three sepals;
numerous petals, white to off-white;
numerous stamens.
Fruit: Aggregate of follicles.
Flowering Date: April–May.
Habitat: Woods.
Distribution: SW, SE.
Comments: *M. macrophylla* Michx.
has auriculate or cordate leaf bases.

## *Magnolia virginiana* L.
### Bay Magnolia

Plants: Trees.
Leaves: Alternate, simple, short petiolate, evergreen or nearly so, elliptic
to obovate, entire, acute, with base
cuneate.
Inflorescence: Flower terminal, solitary, perfect, regular; three sepals;
numerous petals, white to off-white;
numerous stamens.
Fruit: Aggregate of follicles.
Flowering Date: April–July.
Habitats: Savannas, wet woods, boggy
stream banks.
Distribution: CO, NE, EC, SE.

# MALVACEAE
Mallow Family

Plants annual or perennial herbs or shrubs. Leaves alternate, simple, usually palmately lobed. Five sepals, united at least at the base; five petals, united at the base; ovary superior; numerous stamens; Fruit a one- to many-seeded capsule.

## *Abutilon theophrasti* Medic.
### Indian Mallow, Velvet Leaf, Butter Print

Plants: Upright, hairy annual.
Leaves: Petiolate, ovate, acuminate, velvety, entire to slightly toothed, with base cordate.
Inflorescence: Flowers axillary, solitary, or in leafy racemes; yellow-orange.
Fruit: Capsule.
Flowering Date: June–October.
Habitats: Waste sites, fields, roadsides.
Distribution: DE, EC.

## *Callirhoe papaver* (Cav.) Gray
### Poppy Mallow

Plants: Prostrate, hairy perennial with a taproot.
Leaves: Petiolate, palmately three to five lobed or dissected, with margins toothed and base mostly truncate.
Inflorescence: Flowers solitary on long peduncles, purple.
Fruit: Capsule.
Flowering Date: March–July.
Habitats: Roadsides, prairies, pinelands, fields.
Distribution: SE.

## *Hibiscus aculeatus* Walt.
### Comfort Root

Plants: Upright, hairy perennial.
Leaves: Petiolate, palmately three to
  five lobed, with lobes toothed and
  base truncate.
Inflorescence: Solitary on long pe-
  duncle, yellowish white to cream.
Fruit: Capsule.
Flowering Date: June–September.
Habitats: Savannas, roadsides, ditches,
  pinewoods.
Distribution: CO, SE, SW.

## *Hibiscus coccineus* Walt.
### Scarlet Hibiscus

Plants: Upright, glabrous perennial.
Leaves: Petiolate, lower leaves unlobed
  and upper leaves palmately three
  lobed.
Inflorescence: Flowers solitary, axillary,
  on peduncles, scarlet red; stamens
  fused and extending beyond the
  flower.
Fruit: Capsule.
Flowering Date: May–August.
Habitats: Clearings of floodplains,
  stream edges, ditches.
Distribution: CO.

## *Hibiscus lasiocarpus* Cav.
### Wooly Rose Mallow

Plants: Upright, hairy perennial.
Leaves: Petiolate, triangular to ovate,
  with margins toothed and base truncate or cuneate to slightly cordate.
Inflorescence: Flowers in terminal
  clusters, white to rose, purple toward
  the base; stamens fused and extending beyond the flower.
Fruit: Capsule.
Flowering Date: May–September.
Habitats: Moist roadside ditches, wet
  fields, other wet disturbed sites.
Distribution: DE.

### *Hibiscus militaris* Cav.
**Halberd-Leaved Marsh-Mallow**

Plants: Upright, glabrous perennial.
Leaves: Petiolate, lanceolate, acuminate, with margins toothed and base
lobed, sagittate to nearly hastate.
Inflorescence: Flowers solitary, axillary,
pink to white, dark red to purple at
the base; stamens fused and extending beyond the flower.
Fruit: Capsule.
Flowering Date: June–August.
Habitats: Wet ditches, open sites along
rivers and streams, alluvial ground.
Distribution: DE.

### *Kosteletzkya virginica* (L.)
Presl ex Gray
**Seashore Mallow**

Plants: Upright, hairy perennial.
Leaves: Petiolate, triangular to lanceolate or ovate, with margins lobed or
unlobed and toothed and base truncate to sagittate.
Inflorescence: Terminal racemes; flowers pink, lavender, or occasionally
white; stamens fused and extending
beyond the flower.
Fruit: Capsule.
Flowering Date: July–October.
Habitats: Salt, brackish, and freshwater
marshes; ditches; edges of swamps;
marshy shorelines; wet woods.
Distribution: CO.

### *Sida spinosa* L.
**Prickly Mallow**

Plants: Upright, hairy annual often
with spines.
Leaves: Petiolate, ovate to lanceolate,
acute, with margins toothed and
base rounded to cordate.
Inflorescence: Flowers solitary, axillary,
on peduncles; petals bent to one side
at the apex; yellow, yellow-orange, or
cream.
Fruit: Capsule.
Flowering Date: June–October.
Habitats: Roadsides, disturbed sites.
Distribution: Throughout.

# MELASTOMATACEAE
Melastoma Family

Plants perennial. Leaves opposite, simple. Four sepals; four petals; ovary superior; eight stamens, usually spurred. Fruit a many-seeded capsule.

*Rhexia alifanus* Walt.
**Meadow Beauty**

Plants: Upright, glabrous perennial.
Leaves: Opposite, simple, sessile to short petiolate, lanceolate to elliptic, entire, with base cuneate.
Inflorescence: Flowers in terminal clusters, perfect, regular; four sepals; four petals, deep pink; eight stamens, bent to one side near the tip.
Fruit: Capsule.
Flowering Date: May–September.
Habitats: Savannas, pinelands.
Distribution: CO.

## *Rhexia lutea* Walt.
### Yellow Rhexia

Plants: Upright, hairy perennial.
Leaves: Opposite, simple, sessile, entire to slightly toothed; linear, elliptic, or oblanceolate to obovate.
Inflorescence: Flowers in a terminal cluster, perfect, regular; four sepals; four petals, yellow; eight stamens, bent to one side near the tip.
Fruit: Capsule.
Flowering Date: April–July.
Habitats: Savannas, pinelands.
Distribution: CO.

## *Rhexia mariana* L.
### Meadow Beauty

Plants: Upright, hairy perennial with rhizomes.
Leaves: Opposite, simple, sessile, acute to acuminate; lanceolate, elliptic, or ovate to linear; margins toothed; base attenuate.
Inflorescence: Flowers in terminal clusters, perfect, regular; four sepals; four petals, mostly pale pink; eight stamens, bent to one side near the tip.
Fruit: Capsule.
Flowering Date: May–October.
Habitats: Moist ditches and meadows.
Distribution: DE, CO, EC.

# MENYANTHACEAE
Bogbean Family

## *Nymphoides peltata* (Gmel.) Ktze.
### Yellow Floating Heart

Plants: Aquatic perennial with rhizomes.

Leaves: Simple, cordate, entire, with tip rounded and petioles fused to the stem.

Inflorescence: Flowers attached just below the leaf and floating in clusters; five sepals; five petals, slightly fringed, yellow; five stamens.

Fruit: Capsule.

Flowering Date: July–September.

Habitats: Ponds, lake coves.

Distribution: SE.

Comments: *N. aquatica* (Gmel.) Ktze. has petioles and stems that are conspicuously dotted with reddish purple. *N. cordata* (Ell.) Fern. has petioles and stems that are usually not dotted with red. Both species have white flowers.

## MIMOSACEAE
Mimosa Family

Plants vine, shrub, or tree. Leaves alternate, compound. Inflorescence a compact head or spike; corolla tubular, inconspicuous; numerous stamens the most conspicuous part of the flower, extending beyond the corolla. Fruit a legume (pod).

*Desmanthus illinoensis*
(Michx.) MacM.
**Illinois Bundle Flower, Prairie
Mimosa, False Sensitive Plant**

Plants: Erect to arching, spiny perennial.

Leaves: Alternate, bipinnately compound, with leaflets linear.

Inflorescence: Axillary heads on peduncles; flowers perfect, regular; calyx lobed; corolla five parted, united at base, whitish; five stamens, whitish, extending beyond the corolla.

Fruit: Cluster of legumes.

Flowering Date: June–July.

Habitats: Prairies, calcareous glades, roadsides, fields.

Distribution: DE, CO, NE, EC.

## *Schrankia microphylla* (Dry.) MacBr.
### Sensitive Briar, Bashful Briar

Plants: Prostrate perennial with prickles.

Leaves: Alternate, bipinnately compound, with leaflets asymmetrical; fold together upon handling.

Inflorescence: Axillary heads; flowers perfect, regular; calyx lobed; corolla funnel shaped, lobed, pinkish; eight to thirteen stamens, pinkish, extending long beyond the corolla.

Fruit: Legume.

Flowering Date: June–September.

Habitats: Prairies, roadsides, calcareous glades, fields, woods.

Distribution: DE, NE, EC.

## *Neptunia lutea* (Leavenw.) Benth.
### Yellow Sensitive Plant

Plants: Sprawling perennial.

Leaves: Alternate, bipinnately compound, with leaflets linear or lanceolate to oblong.

Inflorescence: Axillary heads on peduncles; flowers perfect, regular; corolla five parted, united at base, yellow; numerous stamens, yellowish, extending beyond the corolla.

Fruit: Legume.

Flowering Date: June–September.

Habitats: Prairies, calcareous soils, pinelands, edges of salt marshes.

Distribution: NE, EC, SW.

## MONOTROPACEAE
Indian Pipe Family

Plants perennial, lacking chlorophyll, apparently saprophytic. Leaves scalelike. Sepals absent or up to five; four to five petals; ovary superior; eight to ten stamens. Fruit a capsule.

*Monotropa uniflora* L.
**Indian Pipe**

Plants: Upright perennial lacking chlorophyll; saprophyte.
Leaves: Alternate, reduced to scales.
Inflorescence: Flowers terminal, solitary, regular, perfect, drooping, bell shaped; sepals absent; five petals, white.
Fruit: Capsule.
Flowering Date: June–October.
Habitats: Dry woods, sandy woods.
Distribution: NE, EC, SE.
Comments: *M. hypopithys* L. is similar, but the entire plant is a combination of white and pink to red or yellowish and lavender. It looks like Christmas candy.

# NELUMBONACEAE
## Water Lotus Family

Plants perennial, aquatic. Leaves alternate, nearly round, emerging above the water surface. Sepals grading into petals, both numerous; ovary superior; numerous stamens. Fruit nutlike, embedded in the receptacle.

### *Nelumbo lutea* (Willd.) Pers.
**Water Lily, American Water Lotus, Yellow Nelumbo, Pond Nuts**

Plants: Aquatic perennial with rhizomes.

Leaves: Floating to emergent, round or nearly so, long petiolate, peltate, entire.

Inflorescence: Flowers terminal, solitary, on long peduncles, perfect, regular; numerous sepals, with the inner ones becoming petallike; numerous petals, off-white to cream; numerous stamens.

Fruit: Nutlike, embedded in a large flat-topped receptacle.

Flowering Date: June–September.

Habitats: Ponds, lakes, slow-moving streams.

Distribution: DE, NE.

# NYMPHAEACEAE
## Water Lily Family

Plants perennial, aquatic. Leaves submersed, emersed, or floating. Flower parts numerous, often grading into each other; four to fourteen sepals; ovary superior; fruit berrylike, many seeded.

## *Nuphar luteum* (L.) Sibth. & Sm.
### Spatter Dock, Cow Lily, Yellow Pond Lily

Plants: Aquatic perennial with rhizomes.

Leaves: Submerged, floating, or emergent; petiolate; lanceolate to nearly round; entire; base cordate.

Inflorescence: Flowers axillary, solitary, perfect, regular; five to fourteen sepals, petaloid, yellow to yellowish green, often tinged with red; numerous petals, inconspicuous; numerous stamens.

Fruit: Berrylike.

Flowering Date: April–October.

Habitats: Ponds, lakes, swamps, streams.

Distribution: CO, NE, SE.

## *Nymphaea odorata* Ait.
### Water Lily

Plants: Aquatic perennials.

Leaves: Floating, nearly orbicular, petiolate, entire, with base cordate and lower surface purple.

Inflorescence: Flowers terminal, solitary, perfect, regular; four sepals, numerous petals, white to deep pink; numerous stamens.

Fruit: Berrylike.

Flowering Date: June–September.

Habitats: Ponds, lakes, slow-moving streams.

Distribution: DE, CO, NE, EC, SE.

Comments: *N. mexicana* Zucc. has yellow flowers.

# OLEACEAE
## Olive Family

Plants shrub or tree. Leaves opposite or occasionally alternate, simple or compound. Calyx four lobed; four petals or petals absent; ovary superior; two stamens. Fruit a drupe or samara.

## *Chionanthus virginicus* L.
### Fringe-Tree, Old Man's Beard

Plants: Shrub to small tree.
Leaves: Opposite, simple, petiolate, elliptic to obovate, entire, acute, with base attenuate to cuneate.
Inflorescence: Panicle; flowers perfect, regular; four sepals, four petals, white; two stamens.
Fruit: Drupe.
Flowering Date: April–May.
Habitats: Dry woods, open rock outcrops.
Distribution: NE, EC, SW, SE.
Comments: Easily cultivated.

## ONAGRACEAE
Evening Primrose Family

Plants annual, biennial, or perennial. Leaves opposite or alternate, simple. Two to seven sepals; two to seven petals, partially united, or petals absent; ovary inferior; two to ten stamens; Fruit a capsule.

### *Gaura biennis* L.
**Morning Honeysuckle, Butterfly Flower**

Plants: Upright, hairy annual.
Leaves: Alternate, simple, petiolate, lanceolate to elliptic, with margins toothed and base attenuate.
Inflorescence: Spikelike raceme; flowers perfect, irregular; four sepals, four petals, white, slightly reflexed, clawed; eight stamens.
Fruit: Nutlike capsule.
Flowering Date: June–October.
Habitats: Along railroad tracks, prairies, calcareous glades, roadsides.
Distribution: CO, NE, EC, SW, SE.
Comments: *G. parviflora* Doug. (Velvety Gaura) has flowers in more compact spikes.

### *Ludwigia alternifolia* L.
**Seedbox**

Plants: Upright, glabrous perennial with winged or slightly winged stems.
Leaves: Alternate, simple, short petiolate, elliptic to lanceolate, entire.
Inflorescence: Flowers axillary, solitary, perfect, regular; calyx four lobed; four petals, yellow; four stamens.
Fruit: Capsule (four angled).
Flowering Date: May–October.
Habitats: Edges of ponds and lakes, ditches.
Distribution: DE, CO, NE, EC.

## *Ludwigia octovalvis* (Jacq.) Raven
### Rattlebox

Plants: Upright, glabrous to slightly hairy annual or perennial.

Leaves: Alternate, sessile or nearly so, linear, lanceolate to oblanceolate, entire, acute, with base cuneate.

Inflorescence: Flowers solitary, axillary, perfect, regular; calyx four lobed; four petals, yellow; eight stamens.

Fruit: Capsule, linear to oblong and ribbed.

Flowering Date: June–October.

Habitats: Wet ditches, stream edges, wet fields, marshes, swampy woods.

Distribution: CO.

## *Ludwigia peploides* (H.B.K.) Raven
### Floating Primrose Willow

Plants: Prostrate, floating perennial, rooting at the nodes.

Leaves: Alternate, elliptic to ovate, short petiolate, entire, with base cuneate.

Inflorescence: Flowers axillary, solitary, perfect, regular; five sepals; five petals, yellow; ten stamens.

Fruit: Capsule.

Flowering Date: May–September.

Habitats: Edges of ponds and lakes, ditches.

Distribution: CO, DE, EC.

## *Oenothera biennis* L.
### Sundrops

Plants: Upright, glabrous to hairy biennial.

Leaves: Alternate, simple, upper leaves sessile and lower leaves petiolate, lanceolate to elliptic, acute, with margins toothed and base attenuate.

Inflorescence: Flowers in a terminal cluster, perfect, regular; calyx tubular, lobed; five petals, funnel shaped; eight stamens.

Fruit: Capsule.

Flowering Date: June–October.

Habitats: Fields, roadsides, rocky woods, waste sites.

Distribution: CO, NE, EC, SW, SE.

## *Oenothera linifolia* Nutt.
### Sundrops

Plants: Upright, branching, hairy annual with a taproot.
Leaves: Alternate, simple, sessile, linear to narrowly lanceolate.
Inflorescence: Terminal spike; flowers perfect, regular; calyx lobed; four petals, yellow; four stamens.
Fruit: Capsule.
Flowering Date: May–July.
Habitats: Prairies, fields, glades, rocky woods.
Distribution: NE, EC.

## *Oenothera tetragona* Roth
### Sundrops

Plants: Upright, hairy perennial.
Leaves: Alternate, simple, mostly sessile, lanceolate to elliptic, entire to toothed, acute, with base attenuate.
Inflorescence: Flowers in a terminal cluster, perfect, regular; calyx lobed; five petals, yellow; eight stamens.
Fruit: Capsule.
Flowering Date: May–August.
Habitats: Woods, boggy areas.
Distribution: NE, EC, SW, SE.

## *Oenothera speciosa* Nutt.
### Evening Primrose; Buttercups

Plants: Upright, hairy perennial.
Leaves: Alternate, simple, sessile, elliptic to oblanceolate, nearly entire to pinnately lobed or toothed.
Inflorescence: Flowers in a terminal cluster, perfect, regular; calyx tubular; four petals, white to pink; four stamens.
Fruit: Capsule.
Flowering Date: May–August.
Habitats: Roadsides, fields, waste sites.
Distribution: Throughout.

# OROBANCHACEAE
Broom-rape Family

Plants perennial, lacking chlorophyll, a parasite. Leaves scale-like, alternate. Four to five sepals, united; corolla four to five lobed, bilabiate; ovary superior; four stamens. Fruit a many-seeded capsule.

*Conopholis americana* (L.)
  Wallr.
**Squaw Root**

Plants: Upright parasite on oak roots; lacks chlorophyll; stems yellowish brown to brown.
Leaves: Overlapping scales.
Inflorescence: Terminal spike, solitary; flowers subtended by a bract similar to the leaf scale; calyx irregular; corolla two lipped, with the upper lip notched and the lower lip three parted; four stamens, exerted.
Fruit: Capsule.
Flowering Date: March–June.
Habitat: Wooded slopes of oak forests.
Distribution: NE.

*Epifagus virginiana* (L.) Bart.·
**Beech-Drops**

Plants: Upright, perennial parasite on
beech tree roots; lacks chlorophyll;
stems purplish, occasionally yellowish.

Leaves: Reduced to scales, alternate,
reddish purple.

Inflorescence: Racemelike to spike;
flowers perfect; calyx cuplike, lobed;
corolla two lipped, four lobed, irregular; four stamens.

Fruit: Capsule.

Flowering Date: September–November.

Habitat: Woods.

Distribution: CO, NE, EC, SW.

*Orobanche uniflora* L.
**One-Flowered Cancer-Root, One-
Flowered Broom-Rape**

Plants: Upright, parasitic, glabrous perennial lacking chlorophyll; stems
white.

Leaves: Basal, usually two, clasping
and overlapping, white.

Inflorescence: Flowers solitary, perfect,
regular; calyx cup shaped, lobed; corolla tubular to salverform, five
lobed, white to purplish white; four
stamens.

Fruit: Capsule.

Flowering Date: April–May.

Habitat: Woods.

Distribution: NE, EC.

# OXALIDACEAE
## Wood Sorrel Family

Plants annual or perennial with rhizomes or bulbs. Leaves alternate, compound with three somewhat heart-shaped leaflets. Five sepals; five petals; ten stamens. Fruit a many-seeded capsule.

### *Oxalis stricta* L.
#### Wood Sorrel, Yellow Wood Sorrel, Sheep Sorrel, Lady's Sorrel

Plants: Upright, glabrous to hairy perennial with rhizomes.

Leaves: Alternate, ternately compound, petiolate, with leaflets green and often having purple or purplish markings.

Inflorescence: Flowers in a terminal, flat-topped cluster, perfect, regular; five sepals; five petals, yellow; ten stamens.

Fruit: Capsule.

Flowering Date: May–October.

Habitats: Woods, yards, roadsides.

Distribution: Throughout.

Comments: *O. dillenii* Jacq. has flowers in umbels and is more typical of lawns, gardens, and other disturbed areas. The plants contain oxalic acid which produces a dill-like taste. In small quantities it adds flavor to salads. However, in large quantities the oxalic acid can cause health problems.

### *Oxalis violacea* L.
#### Wood Sorrel, Lady's Sorrel, Violet Wood Sorrel

Plants: Upright, glabrous perennial with bulbs.

Leaves: Alternate, ternately compound, petiolate, with leaflets notched at the tip.

Inflorescence: Umbel-like; flowers perfect, regular; five sepals; five petals, purple, pink, or white; ten stamens.

Fruit: Capsule.

Flowering Date: April–May; may flower again during the fall.

Habitats: Prairies, woods.

Distribution: NE, EC.

# PAPAVERACEAE
Poppy Family

Plants annual or perennial; stems usually with milky or colored sap. Leaves alternate, sometimes appearing basal, simple or compound. Two to three sepals; four to twelve petals; ovary superior; numerous stamens. Fruit a capsule.

## *Sanquinaria canadensis* L.
**Bloodroot, Red Puccoon**

Plants: Upright perennial with rhizomes.

Leaves: Appearing basal, simple, petiolate, usually only one per flower stalk, kidney shaped, with margins palmately lobed or parted and base auriculate.

Inflorescence: Flowers solitary, perfect, regular, on peduncles; two sepals; numerous petals, white; numerous stamens.

Fruit: Capsule.

Flowering Date: March–April.

Habitats: Wooded slopes, ravines.

Distribution: NE, EC.

Comments: The entire plant produces a red sap that was once used by the American Indians as a dye source. The root is poisonous but has been used medicinally as an emetic and stimulant.

# PASSIFLORACEAE
## Passion Flower Family

Plants vine, often becoming woody. Leaves alternate, simple.
Five sepals; five petals; corona present; five stamens, elevated
on a special structure. Fruit a berry.

### *Passiflora incarnata* L.
### Passion Flower, Maypops, Apricot Vine.

Plants: Climbing, hairy vine; becoming woody.

Leaves: Alternate, simple, petiolate,
deeply palmately three lobed or occasionally five lobed, with margins
toothed.

Inflorescence: Flowers axillary, solitary,
perfect, regular; five sepals, whitish
above; five petals, blue to bluish
white; corona segments numerous,
lavender or whitish with purple
bands; five stamens, elevated well
above the petals.

Fruit: Berry, green to yellow-green
when mature.

Flowering Date: May–July.

Habitats: Roadsides, fence rows, fields,
woodland edges, waste sites.

Distribution: Throughout.

### *Passiflora lutea* L.
### Passiflora

Plants: Climbing, hairy vine.

Leaves: Alternate, simple, petiolate,
shallowly three lobed, with base
truncate.

Inflorescence: One to three axillary,
perfect, regular flowers on peduncles; five sepals; five petals, yellowish green; corona segments numerous, green to yellow-green; five
stamens, elevated above the petals.

Fruit: Berry, black when mature.

Flowering Date: June–September.

Habitats: Woods and thickets.

Distribution: Throughout.

## PLUMBAGINACEAE
Leadwort Family

Plants perennial. Leaves in basal rosettes, simple. Calyx five lobed; corolla five lobed; ovary superior; five stamens. Fruit a one-seeded utricle.

### *Limonium carolinianum* (Walt.) Britt.
**Sea Lavender**

Plants: Upright, glabrous or nearly glabrous perennial.

Leaves: Mostly basal with some alternate, petiolate, succulent, oblanceolate to spatulate, entire, with base attenuate and tip rounded, often terminated by a short point.

Inflorescence: Open panicle; flowers perfect, regular; calyx five lobed, white; corolla five lobed, lavender to purple; five stamens.

Fruit: Utricle.

Flowering Date: August–October.

Habitats: Salt and brackish marshes.

Distribution: CO.

# POLEMONIACEAE
## Phlox Family

Plants annual, biennial, or perennial. Leaves alternate or opposite. Five sepals; corolla five-parted, bell shaped or rotate or salverform; ovary superior; five stamens. Fruit a capsule.

## *Ipomopsis rubra* (L.) Wherry
**Standing Cypress**

Plants: Upright, hairy biennial.
Leaves: Alternate, simple, sessile or nearly so, pinnately divided into linear segments.
Inflorescence: Panicle; flowers perfect, regular; calyx five lobed; corolla salverform, 5 lobed, red; five stamens, extending slightly beyond the corolla.
Fruit: Capsule.
Flowering Date: June–August.
Habitats: Sandy roadsides, sandy open sites, stream edges.
Distribution: CO.

## *Phlox divaricata* L.
**Blue Phlox**

Plants: Upright perennial with rhizomes.
Leaves: Opposite, simple, sessile, linear or elliptic to lanceolate, entire.
Inflorescence: Paniclelike; flowers perfect, regular; five sepals; corolla salverform, five lobed, blue to lavender; five stamens.
Fruit: Capsule.
Flowering Date: April–May.
Habitat: Hardwoods.
Distribution: NE, EC.

## *Phlox maculata* L.
### Phlox, Wild Sweet William, Meadow Phlox

Plants: Upright perennial.
Leaves: Opposite, simple, sessile, ovate to lanceolate, entire.
Inflorescence: Paniclelike; flowers perfect, regular; five sepals; corolla salverform, five lobed, pink to lavender; five stamens.
Fruit: Capsule.
Flowering Date: June–September.
Habitats: Stream edges, alluvial woods.
Distribution: NE, EC.

## *Phlox pilosa* L.
### Prairie Phlox

Plants: Upright, hairy perennial.
Leaves: Opposite, simple, sessile, narrowly lanceolate, entire.
Inflorescence: Paniclelike; flowers perfect, regular; five sepals; corolla salverform, five lobed, purple, lavender, pink, or white; five stamens.
Fruit: Capsule.
Flowering Date: April–June.
Habitats: Prairies, roadsides, woods.
Distribution: NE, EC.

## *Polemonium reptans* L.
### Jacob's Ladder

Plants: Upright to arching, hairy perennial with a rhizome.
Leaves: Alternate, simple, sessile, pinnately divided, with segments ovate to elliptic.
Inflorescence: Flowers in a terminal cluster, perfect, regular; calyx lobed; corolla bell shaped, five lobed, blue; five stamens.
Fruit: Capsule.
Flowering Date: April–May.
Habitats: Wooded slopes and ravines.
Distribution: NE.

# POLYGALACEAE
## Candy Root Family

Plants annual, biennial, or perennial. Leaves opposite, whorled or forming rosettes, simple. Five sepals, with three small and two petallike (wings); corolla three lobed; six to eight stamens. Fruit a capsule.

### *Polygala cruciata* L.
**Candy Root, Drum Heads**

Plants: Upright annual with winged stems.
Leaves: Whorled with four per whorl, simple, sessile, linear to narrowly oblanceolate, entire.
Inflorescence: Raceme; flowers perfect, irregular; five sepals, with two petaloid and pinkish to greenish; corolla tube fringed at the apex, pinkish to whitish; eight stamens.
Fruit: Capsule.
Flowering Date: June–October.
Habitats: Bogs, savannas, pinelands.
Distribution: CO.
Comments: *P. brevifolia* Nutt. has peduncles more than 1 cm long; those of *P. cruciata* L. are less than 1 cm long.

### *Polygala grandiflora* Walt.
**Large Flower Polygala**

Plants: Upright, hairy perennial.
Leaves: Alternate, simple, sessile, linear to oblanceolate, entire.
Inflorescence: Raceme; flowers perfect, irregular; five sepals, with two petaloid and pink; corolla three lobed, pinkish.
Fruit: Capsule.
Flowering Date: May–July.
Habitats: Savannas, vegetated dunes.
Distribution: CO.

*Polygala lutea* L.
**Candy Root, Orange Polygala**

Plants: Upright biennial.
Leaves: Basal rosettes and upper leaves
    alternate, spatulate, reduced upward,
    entire.
Inflorescence: Raceme; flowers perfect,
    irregular; five sepals, with two petal-
    oid and orange; corolla three lobed,
    orange; eight stamens.
Fruit: Capsule.
Flowering Date: April–October.
Habitats: Savannas, pinelands, vege-
    tated dunes, bogs.
Distribution: CO, SE.

*Polygala incarnata* L.
**Candy Root**

Plants: Upright, glabrous annual.
Leaves: Alternate, simple, sessile,
    linear, entire.
Inflorescence: Terminal raceme; flow-
    ers perfect, irregular; five sepals,
    pink; corolla pink to reddish pink,
    fringed; eight stamens.
Fruit: Capsule.
Flowering Date: June–July.
Habitats: Pinelands, savannas, vege-
    tated dunes, fields, mixed woods.
Distribution: Throughout.

## *Polygala nana* (Michx.) DC.
### Candy Root, Bachelor's Button

Plants: Upright biennial.
Leaves: Basal rosette, simple, spatulate to oblanceolate, entire.
Inflorescence: Raceme; flowers perfect, irregular; five sepals, with two petaloid and yellowish green; corolla three lobed, yellowish green; eight stamens.
Fruit: Capsule.
Flowering Date: March–October.
Habitats: Savannas, roadsides, pinelands.
Distribution: CO, EC.

## *Polygala ramosa* Ell.
### Short Milkwort

Plants: Upright, glabrous biennial with numerous stems from the base.
Leaves: Basal rosette and alternate on the stem, with basal leaves elliptic to spatulate and stem leaves linear, entire.
Inflorescence: Flowers in a terminal, flat- topped cluster, perfect, irregular; five sepals, with two petaloid and yellowish green; corolla fringed at the apex, yellowish green; six stamens.
Fruit: Capsule.
Flowering Date: June–August.
Habitats: Savannas, pinelands.
Distribution: CO.
Comments: *P. cymosa* is similar, but the stems are usually solitary and the corolla is not fringed.

# POLYGONACEAE
## Buckwheat or Smartweed Family

Plants annual or perennial herb, vine, or shrublike; stems usually with enlarged nodes and sheathing stipules (the ocreae). Leaves alternate or whorled, simple. Calyx three to six lobed, often petal-like; petals absent; ovary superior; four to twelve stamens. Fruit a nutlet (achene by some).

### *Brunnichia ovata* (Walt.) Shinn.
**Ladies'-Eardrops**

Plants: Climbing, partly woody vine.
Leaves: Alternate, simple, ovate to broadly lanceolate, entire, acuminate, with base mostly truncate.
Inflorescence: Flowers in terminal or axillary, paniclelike cluster; calyx five lobed, yellowish green; eight stamens.
Fruit: Nutlet.
Flowering Date: June–August.
Habitats: Low wet woods, swamp forest.
Distribution: DE, NE, EC, SW.

### *Polygonum pensylvanicum* L.
**Pinkweed, Pennsylvania Smartweed**

Plants: Upright, glabrous to slightly hairy perennial.
Leaves: Alternate, simple, sessile, lanceolate, entire, with base cuneate and stipules (ocreae) sheathing the stem.
Inflorescence: Raceme; flowers perfect, regular; calyx five parted, pink; corolla absent.
Fruit: Nutlet.
Flowering Date: July–November.
Habitats: Wet ditches, wet fields, disturbed sites.
Distribution: Throughout.

# PORTULACACEAE
## Purslane Family

Plants annual or perennial, succulent or somewhat so. Leaves alternate or opposite, simple. Two sepals; four to six petals; ovary superior or nearly so; five to many stamens. Fruit a capsule.

## *Claytonia virginica* L.
### Spring Beauty

Plants: Upright, glabrous perennial with corms.

Leaves: Opposite, simple, sessile, linear to narrowly lanceolate.

Inflorescence: Raceme; flowers perfect, regular, on peduncles; two sepals; five petals, white with pink veins or pink; five stamens.

Fruit: Capsule.

Flowering Date: March–May.

Habitats: Woods, lawns, waste sites, roadsides.

Distribution: DE, NE, EC, SW, SE.

# PRIMULACEAE
Primrose Family

Plants annual or perennial; some aquatic. Leaves opposite or
in a basal rosette, simple. Five sepals, united; corolla five
lobed; ovary superior; five stamens. Fruit a capsule.

### *Dodecatheon meadia* L.
**Shooting Star**

Plants: Scapose  glabrous perennial.
Leaves: Basal rosette, simple, lanceolate to oblanceolate, entire, with
   petiole winged.
Inflorescence: Terminal, hanging cluster; flowers perfect, regular; calyx
   five lobed; corolla five parted, with
   lobes strongly reflexed, white to
   pink; five stamens.
Fruit: Capsule.
Flowering Date: March–May.
Habitats: Wooded slopes and ravines.
Distribution: NE.

### *Lysimachia lanceolata* Walt.
**Fringed Loosestrife**

Plants: Upright perennial.
Leaves: Opposite, simple, petiolate,
   lanceolate, entire, acute to acuminate, with base cuneate.
Inflorescence: Panicle, usually in
   whorls of four; flowers perfect, regular; calyx five lobed; corolla five
   lobed, rotate, with lobes often having
   a hair point; five stamens.
Fruit: Capsule.
Flowering Date: June–August.
Habitats: Alluvial woods, wet open
   sites, ditches.
Distribution: NE, EC, SW.

# RANUNCULACEAE
Buttercup Family

Plants annual or perennial. Leaves alternate, opposite, whorled, or basal; simple or compound. Numerous sepals, often petal-like; petals present or absent, regular or irregular; ovary inferior. Fruit an aggregate of achenes, follicles, or berries.

## *Actaea pachypoda* Ell.
### Baneberry, Doll's Eyes

Plants: Upright, glabrous perennial.
Leaves: Alternate, ternately or pinnately compound, with leaflets toothed and petiolate.
Inflorescence: Raceme; flowers perfect, regular; four to five sepals; three to seven petals, clawed, white; numerous stamens.
Fruit: Berry (glossy white with a black spot)
Flowering Date: April–May.
Habitats: Wooded slopes and ravines.
Distribution: NE, EC.

## *Anemone caroliniana* Walt.
### Windflower, Prairie Anemone, Carolina Anemone

Plants: Upright, hairy perennial.
Leaves: Basal, simple, petiolate, usually deeply three lobed, with lobes toothed.
Inflorescence: Flowers terminal, subtended by a pair of involucral leaves, perfect, regular; numerous sepals, petaloid, white, pinkish, or blue; petals absent; numerous stamens.
Fruit: Achene.
Flowering Date: March–April.
Habitats: Prairies, roadsides.
Distribution: EC.

## *Anemonella thalictroides* (L.) Spach
### Windflower, Rue Anemone

Plants: Upright, glabrous perennial with tuberous roots.

Leaves: Basal leaves petiolate, biternately compound, appearing simple, with segments ovate to nearly round and slightly lobed; leaves subtending flower cluster opposite or whorled, ternately compound, divided to base, appearing simple, with leaflets ovate to nearly round and slightly lobed.

Inflorescence: Flowers in a terminal cluster, perfect, regular, on peduncles; usually five to ten sepals, petaloid, white to lavender; petals absent; numerous stamens.

Fruit: Achene.

Flowering Date: March–May.

Habitats: Rocky wooded slopes and ravines.

Distribution: NE.

## *Aquilegia canadensis* L
### Columbine

Plants: Upright, hairy to glabrous perennial.

Leaves: Lower stem leaves alternate, ternately compound, with segments lobed and petiolate.

Inflorescence: Paniclelike; flowers perfect, regular, hanging upside down; five sepals; five petals, spurred, red and yellowish; numerous stamens.

Fruit: Follicle.

Flowering Date: March–May.

Habitat: Rocky bluffs.

Distribution: NE.

## *Clematis crispa* L.
### Leather-Flower, Swamp Leather-Flower

Plants: Climbing vine with angled stems.

Leaves: Opposite, pinnately compound, petiolate, with three to five leaflets, ovate and entire.

Inflorescence: Flowers terminal, solitary, perfect, regular; four sepals, spreading and reflexed at the tip, petaloid, crinkly, blue; numerous stamens.

Fruit: Achene.

Flowering Date: April–August.

Habitats: Moist ditches and woods.

Distribution: Throughout.

## *Clematis glaucophylla* Small
### Leather-Flower

Plants: Sprawling, hairy to glabrous vine with angled stems.

Leaves: Opposite, pinnately compound, petiolate, with leaflets ovate to elliptic and leathery.

Inflorescence: Flowers terminal, solitary, perfect, regular; four sepals, urn-shaped, lavender; many stamens.

Fruit: Achene.

Flowering Date: May–September.

Habitat: Woods.

Distribution: EC, SE.

## *Clematis virginiana* L.
### Virgin's Bower

Plants: Climbing, hairy vine.

Leaves: Opposite, pinnately compound, petiolate, with three leaflets that are ovate, petiolate, and having toothed margins.

Inflorescence: Flowers in axillary cluster, perfect, regular; numerous sepals, white, off- white, or yellowish white; numerous stamens.

Fruit: Achene.

Flowering Date: July–September.

Habitats: Fence rows, thickets, stream edges, moist woods.

Distribution: NE, EC, SW, SE.

## Delphinium carolinianum Walt.
### Prairie Larkspur, Carolina Larkspur, Blue Larkspur

Plants: Upright, hairy perennial with tuberous roots.

Leaves: Alternate, simple, petiolate, deeply dissected into linear segments.

Inflorescence: Raceme; flowers perfect, irregular; five sepals, with one spurred, blue; four petals, with two spurred and protruding into sepal spur and two clawed, blue to violet; numerous stamens.

Fruit: Follicle.

Flowering Date: April–July.

Habitats: Calcareous glades, prairies, rocky woods.

Distribution: EC.

## Hepatica americana (DC.) Ker - Gawl.
### Liverleaf

Plants: Upright, hairy perennial with a rhizome.

Leaves: Basal, simple, petiolate, three lobed.

Inflorescence: Flowers solitary, perfect, regular, on long peduncles; numerous sepals, lavender to violet; numerous stamens.

Fruit: Achene.

Flowering Date: February–April.

Habitats: Rocky wooded slopes and ravines.

Distribution: NE.

## Isopyrum biternatum (Raf.) T. & G.
### False Rue Anemone

Plants: Upright, glabrous perennial with a rhizome.

Leaves: Alternate, simple with two to three ternately compound, appearing simple, and having segments three lobed.

Inflorescence: Flowers terminal, solitary, perfect, regular, and subtended by sessile, leaflike bracts; five sepals, petaloid, white; petals absent; numerous stamens.

Fruit: Follicle.

Flowering Date: March–April.

Habitat: Rocky wooded slopes.

Distribution: NE.

## *Ranunculus fascicularis* Muhl. ex Bigel.
### Early Buttercup

Plants: Upright, hairy perennial.
Leaves: Alternate, simple, petiolate, dissected.
Inflorescence: Flowers axillary, solitary, perfect, regular, on peduncles; five sepals, petaloid, yellow; petals absent; numerous stamens.
Fruit: Achene.
Flowering Date: March–May.
Habitats: Roadsides, disturbed areas, woods.
Distribution: NE, EC, SW, SE.

## *Thalictrum pubescens* Pursh
### Meadow Rue, Quicksilver Weed

Plants: Upright, glabrous perennial; plants male or female (dioecious).
Leaves: Alternate, ternately or pinnately decompound, upper leaves sessile or nearly so and lower leaves distinctly petiolate; terminal leaflet three lobed.
Inflorescence: Paniclelike; flowers imperfect; sepals present; corolla absent; numerous stamens, with filaments club shaped and yellowish green to purplish.
Fruit: Achene.
Flowering Date: May–July.
Habitats: Moist woods, drainage areas of pastures, floodplains, bogs.
Distribution: NE, EC, SE.
Comments: *T. dioicum* L. has petiolate upper leaves, and it flowers from March into early April.

## *Xanthorhiza simplicissima* Marsh.
### Yellow Root

Plants: Small shrub with yellow wood and roots.
Leaves: Alternate, pinnately compound, petiolate, with leaflets ovate.
Inflorescence: Panicle; flowers perfect; five sepals, yellowish green to maroon; corolla absent; five to ten stamens.
Fruit: Follicle.
Flowering Date: April–May.
Habitat: Stream edges.

## RHAMNACEAE
Buckthorn Family

Plants shrub, tree, or woody vine. Leaves alternate or opposite, simple. Five sepals; five petals, usually clawed; five stamens. Fruit a capsule, or drupe.

### *Ceanothus americanus* L.
**New Jersey Tea, Wild Snowball**

Plants: Shrub.
Leaves: Alternate, simple, sessile or short petiolate, ovate to lanceolate, acute to acuminate, with margins toothed and base cuneate.
Inflorescence: Flowers in a terminal or axillary cluster, perfect, regular; calyx present, cup shaped; five petals, hooded and clawed, white to grayish white; five stamens, extending beyond the petals.
Fruit: Drupe.
Flowering Date: May–July.
Habitats: Prairies, open woods, roadsides.
Distribution: CO, NE, EC, SE.

### *Berchemia scandens* (Hill) Koch
**Supple Jack, Rattan Vine**

Plants: Glabrous, woody vine with reddish brown branches; plants either male or female (dioecious).
Leaves: Alternate, simple, petiolate, ovate to elliptic, entire to toothed, with base cuneate to rounded and tip obtuse.
Inflorescence: Flowers in terminal or axillary panicles, imperfect, greenish; five sepals; five petals.
Fruit: Drupe.
Flowering Date: May–June.
Habitat: Mixed woods.
Distribution: Throughout.

# ROSACEAE
## Rose Family

Plants biennial or perennial herb, shrub, tree, or woody vine. Leaves alternate, simple or compound. Four to five sepals, united; four to five petals or petals absent; ovary superior or inferior; five to many stamens. Fruit achenes, follicles, capsules, pomes, drupes, or nutlets.

### *Amelanchier arborea* (Michx. f.) Fern.
**June Berry, Shadbush, Serviceberry**

Plants: Tree.
Leaves: Alternate, simple, petiolate, ovate to oblong, acute, with margins toothed and base truncate to cuneate.
Inflorescence: Terminal raceme; flowers white.
Fruit: Pome.
Flowering Date: March–May.
Habitat: Woods.
Distribution: CO, NE, EC, SE.

### *Agrimonia pubescens* Wallr.
**Harvest-Lice, Cocklebur**

Plants: Upright, hairy perennial.
Leaves: Alternate, pinnately compound, with leaflets lanceolate, alternating in size, and having toothed margins.
Inflorescence: Raceme; flowers yellow; ten stamens.
Fruit: Nutlet.
Flowering Date: July–September.
Habitats: Dry woods, disturbed sites.
Distribution: DE, EC, NE, SE.

## *Aruncus dioicus* (Walt.) Fern.
**Goat's Beard**

Plants: Upright, glabrous to hairy perennial; plants either male or female (dioecious).
Leaves: Alternate, ternately or biternately compound, petiolate, with leaflets lanceolate to elliptic and having toothed margins.
Inflorescence: Panicle of racemes; flowers white or greenish white.
Fruit: Follicle.
Flowering Date: May–June.
Habitat: Woods.
Distribution: NE.

## *Duchesnea indica* (Andr.) Focke
**Indian Strawberry, Mock Strawberry, Snakeberry**

Plants: Sprawling, hairy perennial.
Leaves: Alternate, ternately compound, petiolate, with leaflets toothed.
Inflorescence: Flowers axillary, solitary, yellow.
Fruit: Aggregate of achenes.
Flowering Date: February–November.
Habitats: Yards, waste sites, alluvial woods.
Distribution: DE, NE, EC, SW.

## *Crataegus marshallii* Eggl.
**Parsley Haw**

Plants: Tree with spines.
Leaves: Alternate, simple, petiolate, lobed, with margins toothed.
Inflorescence: Flowers in a terminal cluster, white; stamens pink.
Fruit: Pome.
Flowering Date: April–May.
Habitat: Moist to dry woods.
Distribution: Throughout.

## *Fragaria virginiana* Duchn.
### Wild Strawberry

Plants: Stoloniferous, hairy perennial with rhizomes.
Leaves: Alternate, ternately compound, petiolate, with three toothed leaflets.
Inflorescence: Flowers in a terminal cluster, white.
Fruit: Aggregate of achenes.
Flowering Date: March–June.
Habitats: Woods, edges of woods, roadsides, fields.
Distribution: NE, EC.

## *Geum canadense* Jacq.
### Avens, Red Root

Plants: Upright, hairy perennial.
Leaves: Alternate, simple, petiolate to sessile, entire to lobed and toothed.
Inflorescence: Paniclelike; flowers white.
Fruit: Aggregate of achenes.
Flowering Date: May–November.
Habitat: Alluvial to dry woods.
Distribution: NE, EC.

## *Potentilla simplex* Michx.
### Cinquefoil, Five Finger

Plants: Sprawling, prostrate to erect, hairy perennial.
Leaves: Alternate, palmately compound, sessile, with five leaflets, that are lanceolate and have toothed margins.
Inflorescence: Flowers axillary or terminal, cream to yellow.
Fruit: Achene.
Flowering Date: April–June.
Habitats: Roadsides, waste sites, pastures, lawns.
Distribution: NE, EC.

## *Prunus angustifolia* Marsh.
**Chickasaw Plum**

Plants: Thicket- forming shrub.
Leaves: Alternate, simple, petiolate, elliptic to lanceolate, acute to acuminate, with margins toothed and base
cuneate; mature leaves have a thickened callous.
Inflorescence: Flowers white, in alternate clusters; appear before the
leaves.
Fruit: Drupe.
Flowering Date: March–April.
Habitats: Roadsides, fence rows, pastures, old fields, edges of woods.
Distribution: Throughout.
Comments: *P. americana* Marsh. produces flowers after the leaves appear.
The teeth of the mature leaves lack a
thickened callous.

## *Prunus caroliniana* (Mill.) Ait.
**Carolina Cherry**

Plants: Small to large tree.
Leaves: Alternate, simple, evergreen,
shiny, elliptic to lanceolate, entire to
toothed, acute, with base cuneate to
rounded.
Inflorescence: Axillary raceme; flowers
white; ten stamens.
Fruit: Drupe.
Flowering Date: March–April.
Habitats: Disturbed sites, roadside
thickets, woods.
Distribution: DE, EC, SW, SE.
Comments: Mostly an escape from
cultivation.

## *Prunus serotina* Ehrh.
**Wild Black Cherry**

Plants: Tree.
Leaves: Alternate, simple, petiolate,
acute to acuminate, with margins
toothed and base cuneate to rounded.
Inflorescence: Raceme; flowers perfect,
sometimes slightly irregular; white.
Fruit: Drupe.
Flowering Date: April–May.
Habitats: Yards, edges of streams and
springs, fence rows, roadsides, edges
of woods.
Distribution: Throughout.
Comments: The leaves and seeds are
considered poisonous. The bark has
been used medicinally as an astrin-
gent and for coughs and headaches.

## *Rosa laevigata* Michx.
**Wild Rose, Cherokee Rose**

Plants: Climbing, glabrous perennial with prickles.
Leaves: Alternate, ternately compound, with three leaflets that are elliptic to lanceolate and have toothed margins.
Inflorescence: Flowers solitary, white.
Fruit: Aggregate of achenes (known as a hip).
Flowering Date: March–May.
Habitats: Roadsides, woods, disturbed sites.
Distribution: CO.
Comments: *R. carolina* L. has compound leaves with five leaflets.

## *Rosa multiflora* Thunb. ex Murr.
**Multiflora Rose, Japanese Rose**

Plants: Upright shrub that is highly branched from the base.
Leaves: Alternate, pinnately compound, with seven to nine leaflets that are elliptic to obovate, acute, with toothed margins and the base cuneate to rounded.
Inflorescence: Paniclelike cluster, white.
Fruit: Aggregate of achenes (known as a hip).
Flowering Date: May–July.
Habitats: Fence rows, yards, waste sites, woodlands, pastures.
Distribution: DE, NE, EC, SW, SE.
Comments: Native of Japan.

## *Spiraea tomentosa* L.
**Hardhack, Steeple Bush**

Plants: Shrub.
Leaves: Alternate, simple, lanceolate to elliptic, short petiolate, with margins toothed.
Inflorescence: Compact panicle; flowers pink to purplish.
Fruit: Capsule.
Flowering Date: July–September.
Habitats: Edges of low woods, bogs, wet open areas.
Distribution: NE, EC.

## RUBIACEAE
### Madder or Coffee Family

Plants annual or perennial herb, shrub, or small tree. Leaves opposite or whorled. Calyx four lobed; corolla four to five lobed; ovary inferior or nearly so; four to five stamens. Fruit a capsule, drupe, berry, or nutlet.

### *Cephalanthus occidentalis* L.
**Button Bush**

Plants: Shrub.
Leaves: Opposite or whorled, ovate to elliptic, petiolate, entire.
Inflorescence: Terminal and axillary spherical heads; flower perfect, regular; calyx four lobed; corolla tubular, white; four stamens, extending beyond the corolla.
Fruit: Nutlets.
Flowering Date: June–August.
Habitats: Low moist meadows, stream edges, moist ditches, wet areas near lakes.
Distribution: Throughout.

### *Diodia teres* Walt.
**Rough Buttonweed**

Plants: Usually prostrate, occasionally erect, hairy annual.
Leaves: Opposite, simple, sessile, linear to lanceolate, entire.
Inflorescence: Flowers axillary clusters or solitary, perfect, regular; calyx four lobed; corolla salverform, four lobed, white; four stamens.
Fruit: Berry.
Flowering Date: June–December.
Habitats: Roadsides, waste sites, ditches, sandy old fields.
Distribution: Throughout.
Comments: *D. virginiana* L. has a two-lobed calyx.

## *Hedyotis crassifolia* Raf.
**Mountain Houstonia**

Plants: Upright, hairy perennial with angled stems.

Leaves: Opposite, simple, sessile, lanceolate to elliptic, entire, with base rounded.

Inflorescence: Flowers in a terminal cluster, perfect, regular; four sepals; corolla funnel shaped, four lobed, blue to lavender, with center darker lavender or red; four stamens.

Fruit: Capsule.

Flowering Date: May–July.

Habitats: Rock outcrops, roadsides, open woods.

Distribution: Mostly northern half of state.

Comments: *H. caerulea* (L.) T. & G. is similar but has lighter blue flowers with a yellow center.

## *Mitchella repens* L.
**Partridge Berry**

Plants: Prostrate, hairy to glabrous perennial.

Leaves: Opposite, simple, sessile, ovate, leathery, entire.

Inflorescence: Flowers terminal and axillary, two per node, perfect, regular; the two flowers have a fused calyx; corolla salverform, four lobed, white or occasionally pink, noticeably hairy; four stamens.

Fruit: Two fused berries turning bright red at maturity.

Flowering Date: May–June.

Habitats: Dry or moist woods.

Distribution: NE, EC, SW, SE, CO.

## *Richardia scabra* L.
**Richardia**

Plants: Decumbent, hairy annual.

Leaves: Opposite, simple, sessile or nearly so, lanceolate to elliptic, entire, acute, with base cuneate.

Inflorescence: Flowers terminal, compact cluster subtended by four ovate to lanceolate bracts, perfect, regular; calyx four lobed; corolla four lobed, white.

Fruit: Berry.

Flowering Date: June–November.

Habitats: Roadsides, waste sites, yards, savannas.

Distribution: CO.

# SANTALACEAE
## Toadflax Family

Plants perennial herb, shrub, or tree. Leaves alternate or opposite. Calyx four lobed, occasionally two lobed; corolla absent; ovary inferior; four to five stamens. Fruit a drupe.

## *Comandra umbellata* (L.) Nutt.
### Bastard Toadflax

Plants: Upright annual.
Leaves: Alternate, simple, sessile, elliptic, entire.
Inflorescence: Flowers in terminal or axillary clusters, perfect; five sepals, petaloid, greenish yellow to cream; petals absent; five stamens.
Fruit: Drupe.
Flowering Date: April–June.
Habitats: Prairies, woodland edges, roadsides.
Distribution: EC.

## *Nestronia umbellula* Raf.
### Nestronia

Plants: Dioecious shrub.
Leaves: Opposite, simple, sessile or short petiolate, ovate, entire.
Inflorescence: Flowers axillary, with imperfect female flowers solitary and male flowers clustered; flowers regular; calyx funnel shaped, four lobed in female and five lobed in male, both are yellowish green; five stamens.
Fruit: Drupe.
Flowering Date: April–May.
Habitat: Pinelands.
Distribution: EC.

# SAPINDACEAE
## Soapberry Family

Plants annual, tree, or a somewhat-woody vine. Leaves alternate and compound. Four to five sepals; four to five petals, clawed; ovary superior, eight to ten stamens. Fruit an inflated membranous capsule or drupelike.

### *Cardiospermum halicababum* L.
#### Balloon Vine

Plants: Annual or a partially woody vine.
Leaves: Alternate, biternately compound, with segments lanceolate and toothed.
Inflorescence: Flowers axillary clusters on peduncles, irregular; four sepals; four petals, white to bluish white.
Fruit: Capsule.
Flowering Date: August–September.
Habitat: Roadsides.
Distribution: EC, CO, SE.
Comments: Escaped cultivation.

# SARRACENIACEAE
## Pitcher Plant Family

Plants perennial from a rhizome. Leaves basal, modified into a hollow tube (the pitcher). One flower per flowering stem (peduncle), nodding; five sepals; five petals; ovary superior; numerous stamens. Fruit a capsule.

*Sarracenia alata* Wood
**Yellow Pitcher Plant, Yellow Trumpets**

Plants: Stem modified into an underground rhizome; no aboveground stems.

Leaves: Hollow, hooded, reddish veined.

Inflorescence: Flowers solitary, perfect, regular, on peduncle, nodding; five sepals, yellowish green; five petals, yellowish green; numerous stamens; usually begins flowering before the leaves appear.

Fruit: Capsule.

Flowering Date: March–April.

Habitats: Savannas, pinelands.

Distribution: CO

## *Sarracenia psittacina* Michx.
### Parrot Pitcher Plant, Parrot-Beaks

Plants: Stem modified into an underground rhizome; no aboveground stems.

Leaves: Hollow, somewhat flattened, erect to nearly lying on the ground, greenish with white spots and reddish veins, with hood beaklike.

Inflorescence: Flowers solitary, perfect, regular, on peduncle, nodding; five sepals, reddish; five petals, reddish; numerous stamens.

Fruit: Capsule.

Flowering Date: April–May.

Habitats: Savannas, pinelands.

Distribution: CO.

## *Sarracenia leucophylla* Raf.
### Fiddler's Trumpet, Purple Trumpets, Crimson Pitcher Plant

Plants: Stem modified into an underground rhizome; no aboveground stems.

Leaves: Hollow, hooded, greenish toward base and whitish toward apex, with red veins.

Inflorescence: Flowers solitary, perfect, regular, on peduncle, nodding; five sepals, reddish purple; five petals, reddish purple; numerous stamens.

Fruit: Capsule.

Flowering Date: April–May.

Habitats: Savannas, pinelands, bogs.

Distribution: CO.

# SAURURACEAE
## Lizard's Tail Family

Plants perennial from a rhizome, usually aquatic. Leaves alternate, simple. Flowering stalk opposite a leaf; sepals and petals absent; three to seven stamens. Fruit a capsule.

### *Saururus cernuus* L.
**Lizard's Tail**

Plants: Upright, hairy perennial with a rhizome.

Leaves: Alternate, simple, petiolate, lanceolate to nearly triangular, entire, acuminate, with base cordate.

Inflorescence: Flowers solitary raceme opposite a leaf, perfect; sepals and petals absent; three to seven stamens, white.

Fruit: Capsule.

Flowering Date: May–July.

Habitats: Wet ditches, wet lowlands, edges of streams and lakes.

Distribution: Throughout.

# SAXIFRAGACEAE
## Saxifrag Family

Plants perennial herb or shrub. Leaves alternate, opposite, calyx four or five lobed; four to five petals; ovary inferior or superior; two, four, or five stamens. Fruit a capsule or berry.

## *Heuchera americana* L.
### Alumroot

Plants: Upright perennial with rhizomes.

Leaves: Basal, simple, petiolate, ovate to nearly round, with margins lobed and toothed and base cordate.

Inflorescence: Compact panicle; flowers perfect, regular or irregular; calyx five lobed; five petals, pink or purple; five stamens, extending beyond the petals.

Fruit: Capsule.

Flowering Date: April–June.

Habitat: Crevices and ledges of rock outcrops.

Distribution: NE, EC.

## Itea virginica L.
**Virginia Willow**

Plants: Shrub.
Leaves: Alternate, simple, ovate to lan-
ceolate, acute, with margins toothed
and base cuneate.
Inflorescence: Terminal raceme; flow-
ers perfect, regular; calyx five lobed;
five petals, white; five stamens.
Fruit: Capsule.
Flowering Date: May–June.
Habitats: Stream edges and alluvial
woods.
Distribution: Throughout.

## Tiarella cordifolia L.
**Foam Flower**

Plants: Upright perennial with a rhizome.
Leaves: Basal or nearly so, simple, petiolate, ovate, with margins slightly
lobed and toothed.
Inflorescence: Terminal raceme; flowers perfect, regular; calyx lobed; five
petals, white, clawed; ten stamens,
extending beyond the flowers.
Fruit: Capsule.
Flowering Date: March–June.
Habitat: Woods.
Distribution: NE, EC.

## Saxifraga virginiensis Michx.
**Early Saxifrag**

Plants: Upright perennial.
Leaves: Basal rosette, simple, spatulate,
acute to obtuse, with margins
toothed and base long attenuate.
Inflorescence: Paniclelike, terminal;
flowers perfect, regular or nearly so;
calyx five lobed; five petals, white;
ten stamens.
Fruit: Capsule.
Flowering Date: March–May.
Habitats: Dry rocky woods and moist
woods.
Distribution: NE, EC.

# SCROPHULARIACEAE
## Figwort or Snapdragon Family

Plants annual, biennial, or perennial herb or tree. Leaves opposite, alternate, whorled or in a basal rosette; simple. Calyx irregular to nearly regular; four to five sepals; corolla irregular to nearly regular, bilabiate, four to five parted; ovary superior; two or five stamens. Fruit a capsule.

### *Agalinis purpurea* (L.) Penn.
**Gerardia, Purple Gerardia**

Plants: Upright, slightly hairy annual.

Leaves: Opposite, simple, sessile, linear to very narrowly lanceolate.

Inflorescence: Raceme, appearing paniclelike; calyx lobed; corolla bilabiate, with upper lip two lobed and lower lip three lobed, lavender to purple, with the throat lined with yellow and spotted with dark purple; four stamens; pedicel shorter than the calyx tube.

Fruit: Capsule.

Flowering Date: August–November.

Habitats: Roadsides, woodland edges, savannas, prairies.

Distribution: CO, NE, EC.

Comments: *A. linifolia* (Nutt.) Britt. is a glabrous perennial with flowers lacking yellow lines within. *A. fasciculata* (Ell.) Raf. has leaves in clusters (fascicles). *A. maritima* (Raf.) Raf. is somewhat succulent and restricted to salt marshes.

*Agalinis tenuifolia* (Vahl) Raf.
**Gerardia**

Plants: Upright, glabrous annual, often having reddish stems.

Leaves: Filiform.

Inflorescence: Raceme; calyx barely lobed; corolla bilabiate, with upper lip two lobed and lower lip three lobed, purple, with throat yellow lined; four stamens; pedicel longer than the calyx tube.

Fruit: Capsule.

Flowering Date: August–October.

Habitats: Prairies, roadsides, fields, woods.

Distribution: NE, EC, SE.

Comments: *A. obtusifolia* Raf. has yellowish green stems, leaves that are somewhat linear to spatulate, and flowers that lack a yellow- lined throat.

*Aureolaria flava* (L.) Farw.
**Smooth Foxglove**

Plants: Upright, glabrous perennial; parasitic on the roots of white oak.

Leaves: Opposite, simple, sessile, lanceolate, entire to pinnately lobed to dissected.

Inflorescence: Terminal racemes; calyx five lobed; corolla bilabiate, with upper lip two lobed and lower lip three lobed; flowers yellow; four stamens.

Fruit: Capsule.

Flowering Date: August–September.

Habitats: Dry woodland and edges, savannas, roadsides.

Distribution: NE, EC, SW.

## *Aureolaria pectinata* (Nutt.) Penn.
### Foxglove

Plants: Upright, hairy annual; parasitic on the roots of black oak.

Leaves: Basal rosette and opposite on the stem; basal leaves elliptic to lanceolate, entire; stem leaves lanceolate, pinnately parted, with lobes toothed.

Inflorescence: Flowers axillary, solitary; calyx five lobed; corolla bilabiate, with upper lip two lobed and lower lip three lobed; flowers yellow; four stamens.

Fruit: Capsule.

Flowering Date: May–September.

Habitat: Woods.

Distribution: NE, EC.

## *Castilleja coccinea* (L.) Spreng.
### Indian Paint Brush, Painted Cup, Indian Blanket

Plants: Upright, hairy annual or biennial; may be parasitic (some think this species is parasitic; others say it is not).

Leaves: Basal and alternate, simple, sessile; basal leaves elliptic, entire; stem leaves three forked or lobed or divided into linear or narrowly lanceolate segments.

Inflorescence: Spike; flowers subtended by red bracts that are usually three forked and are longer than flowers (appear to be the flower but not); calyx four lobed; corolla tubular, yellow; four stamens.

Fruit: Capsule.

Flowering Date: April–May.

Habitats: Prairies, grassy roadsides, meadows.

Distribution: NE, EC.

## *Buchnera americana* L.
### American Blue Hearts

Plants: Upright, hairy perennial.

Leaves: Opposite, simple, sessile, elliptic to lanceolate, entire to toothed, with three prominent parallel veins.

Inflorescence: Open spike; flowers usually appearing regular; calyx five lobed; corolla nearly salverform, five lobed, purple; four stamens.

Fruit: Capsule.

Flowering Date: July–September.

Habitats: Savannas, prairies, stream edges.

Distribution: CO, EC.

Comments: *B. floridana* Gand. does not have the three prominent parallel leaf veins. It is often difficult to distinguish *B. floridana* from *B. americana.*

### *Chelone obliqua* L.
**Turtlehead**

Plants: Upright, glabrous to hairy perennial.
Leaves: Opposite, simple, sessile, elliptic to lanceolate, acuminate, with margins toothed and base cuneate.
Inflorescence: Spikelike raceme; calyx five lobed; corolla bilabiate, rose to pink; four stamens.
Fruit: Capsule.
Flowering Date: October.
Habitats: Steam edges, swamp forest.
Distribution: NE.

### *Linaria canadensis* (L.) Dumont
**Toadflax**

Plants: Upright, glabrous biennial.
Leaves: Basal and opposite, alternate, or whorled; leaves linear to narrowly lanceolate.
Inflorescence: Open raceme; calyx five parted; corolla bilabiate, with upper lip two lobed and lower lip three lobed, spurred; flowers light to dark blue, occasionally white; four stamens.
Fruit: Capsule.
Flowering Date: March–May.
Habitats: Roadsides, old fields, waste sites.
Distribution: Throughout.

### *Pedicularis canadensis* L.
**Lousewort**

Plants: Upright, hairy perennial.
Leaves: Alternate and mostly basal with a few occasionally on the stem, simple, lanceolate or elliptic, lower leaves petiolate and upper leaves sessile, with margins pinnately divided.
Inflorescence: Terminal, spikelike raceme; corolla bilabiate, with upper lip two parted and hoodlike and lower lip shorter; corolla cream, yellow, sometimes purplish.
Fruit: Capsule.
Flowering Date: April–May.
Habitats: Moist woods, prairies.
Distribution: Throughout.

## Penstemon laevigatus
### Soland. ex Ait.
**Beardtongue**

Plants: Upright, glabrous to hairy perennial.

Leaves: Alternate, simple, sessile, lanceolate, entire to toothed, acuminate.

Inflorescence: Panicle; calyx five lobed; corolla bilabiate, with upper lip two lobed and lower lip three lobed; flowers lavender to purple; four stamens.

Fruit: Capsule.

Flowering Date: April–June.

Habitats: Woods, stream edges, moist woods.

Distribution: EC, SW, SE.

## Penstemon laxiflorus Penn.
**Beardtongue**

Plants: Upright, slightly hairy perennial.

Leaves: Opposite, simple, sessile, lanceolate to ovate, acuminate, with margins toothed.

Inflorescence: Panicle; calyx five lobed; corolla bilabiate, with upper lip two lobed and lower lip three lobed; flowers white to pink; four stamens.

Fruit: Capsule.

Flowering Date: April–June.

Habitats: Roadsides, prairies, woodland edges, open grassy areas.

Distribution: NE.

## Verbascum blattaria L.
**Moth Mullein**

Plants: Upright, hairy perennial.

Leaves: Basal rosettes and alternate, simple, sessile, lanceolate to oblanceolate, with margins toothed.

Inflorescence: Raceme; flowers nearly regular; calyx lobed; corolla rotate, five lobed, yellow or white; five stamens, extending beyond the corolla.

Fruit: Capsule.

Flowering Date: April–July.

Habitats: Roadsides, waste sites, woodland edges, fields, prairies.

Distribution: DE, CO, NE, EC.

## *Verbascum thapsus* L.
### Mullein, Camper's Friend

Plants: Upright, hairy perennial.
Leaves: Basal rosettes and alternate, simple, sessile, lanceolate to oblanceolate, entire.
Inflorescence: Raceme; flowers nearly regular; calyx lobed; corolla rotate, five lobed, yellow; five stamens, extending beyond the corolla.
Fruit: Capsule.
Flowering Date: June–October.
Habitats: Roadsides, disturbed and waste sites.
Distribution: Throughout.
Comments: The roots have been used medicinally as a stimulant. The large, soft leaves are welcomed when emergencies arise and no toilet paper is available.

## *Veronica arvensis* L.
### Corn Speedwell

Plants: Prostrate to erect, hairy annual.
Leaves: Opposite, simple, sessile, ovate, with margins toothed.
Inflorescence: Raceme; flowers nearly regular; four sepals, corolla four lobed, light blue with dark blue veins and a white center; two stamens.
Fruit: Capsule.
Flowering Date: March–June.
Habitats: Roadsides, yards, disturbed sites.
Distribution: Throughout.

## *Veronicastrum virginicum* (L.) Farw.
### Culver's Root

Plants: Upright, glabrous to slightly hairy perennial.
Leaves: Whorled, simple, sessile, lanceolate, entire.
Inflorescence: Terminal raceme; calyx five lobed; corolla tubular, bilabiate, with upper lip two lobed and lower lip three lobed; flowers white; two stamens, extending beyond the corolla.
Fruit: Capsule.
Flowering Date: July–August.
Habitats: Prairies, roadsides, bogs, stream edges.
Distribution: NE, EC.

# SOLANACEAE
## Nightshade Family

Plants annual or perennial herb, shrub, or woody vine. Leaves alternate, simple, with margins often spined or gland tipped. Five sepals; five petals; ovary superior; two to ten stamens. Fruit a capsule or berry.

## *Datura stramonium* L.
### Jimpson Weed

Plants: Upright, foul- smelling, nearly glabrous annual with a rhizome.

Leaves: Alternate, simple, petiolate, lanceolate, with margins toothed, tip sharp pointed, and base attenuate.

Inflorescence: Flowers terminal, solitary, perfect, regular; calyx lobed; corolla tubular to funnel shaped, 5 lobed, white to lavender; five stamens.

Fruit: Spiny capsule.

Flowering Date: July–September.

Habitats: Waste and disturbed sites, roadsides.

Distribution: Throughout.

Comments: All parts of this plant are extremely poisonous.

## *Physalis virginiana* Mill.
### Ground Cherry, Husk Tomato

Plants: Upright, glabrous to hairy perennial with rhizomes.

Leaves: Alternate, simple, petiolate, lanceolate to ovate, entire to toothed, with tip pointed and base cuneate.

Inflorescence: Axillary, solitary; flowers perfect, regular; calyx five lobed; corolla bell shaped, with tip wavy.

Fruit: Berry, partially enclosed by a papery shell (modified calyx).

Flowering Date: April–June.

Habitats: Roadsides, waste sites.

Distribution: Throughout.

## *Solanum carolinense* L.
### Horse Nettle, Bull Nettle

Plants: Upright, hairy perennial with
  spines.
Leaves: Alternate, simple, petiolate,
  ovate, shallowly lobed.
Inflorescence: Terminal raceme; flowers perfect, regular; calyx five lobed;
  corolla rotate, five lobed, white to
  purple; five stamens, extending beyond the corolla.
Fruit: Berry.
Flowering Date: May–July.
Habitats: Roadsides, waste areas, old
  fields.
Distribution: Throughout.

## *Solanum americanum* Mill.
### Black Nightshade

Plants: Upright, mostly glabrous annual.
Leaves: Alternate, simple, petiolate,
  ovate to lanceolate, acute, with margins toothed and base cuneate.
Inflorescence: Umbel-like, drooping
  clusters; flowers perfect, regular; calyx lobed; corolla rotate, usually
  with reflexed lobes, white; five stamens, extending beyond the corolla.
Fruit: Berry (contains hard granules).
Flowering Date: June–November.
Habitats: Roadsides, woodland edges,
  old fields.
Distribution: Throughout.
Comments: *S. pseudogracile* Heiser
  (Black Nightshade) is finely hairy
  and produces a fruit lacking hard
  granules. It inhabits dunes, vegetated
  dunes, sandy disturbed sites, and
  brackish marshes of the gulf coast. It
  should be assumed that all parts of
  Nightshades may be poisonous.

## *Solanum rostratum* Dun.
### Buffalo Bur, Kansas Thistle

Plants: Upright, very spiny, hairy perennial.
Leaves: Alternate, simple, petiolate,
  spiny, elliptic to obovate, with margins pinnately lobed.
Inflorescence: Raceme; flowers perfect,
  regular; calyx lobed; corolla rotate,
  five lobed, yellow; five stamens, extending beyond the corolla.
Fruit: Berry, enclosed in a spiny covering (modified calyx).
Flowering Date: July–September.
Habitat: Waste sites.
Distribution: DE, EC.

## STAPHYLEACEAE
Bladdernut Family

Plants a shrub or small tree. Leaves opposite, compound, consisting of three leaflets. Calyx five lobed; corolla four or five lobed; ovary superior; five stamens. Fruit an inflated capsule.

### *Staphylea trifolia* L.
**Bladdernut**

Plants: Shrub or small tree.
Leaves: Opposite, compound, petiolate, trifoliate with leaflets ovate to lanceolate, acute to acuminate, and having toothed margins and cuneate base.
Inflorescence: Axillary panicle; flowers perfect, regular; calyx lobed; corolla cylindrical, five lobed, greenish white; five stamens.
Fruit: Inflated capsule.
Flowering Date: April.
Habitat: Woods.
Distribution: NE, EC.

## STYRACACEAE
Styrax Family

Plants a shrub or small tree. Leaves alternate, simple. Calyx five lobed; corolla five lobed or five parted; ovary superior; eight to sixteen stamens. Fruit dry with one to three seeds.

### *Halesia diptera* Ellis
**Silverbell**

Plants: Small tree.
Leaves: Alternate, simple, petiolate, elliptic to obovate, entire to toothed, acuminate, with base cuneate.
Inflorescence: Flowers axillary from previous year's buds, perfect, regular; calyx lobed; corolla bell shaped, four lobed, white; numerous stamens.
Fruit: Capsule.
Flowering Date: April–May.
Habitat: Woodland edges.
Distribution: CO, EC, SW, SE.

### *Styrax grandifolia* Ait.
**Snowbell**

Plants: Shrub or small tree.
Leaves: Alternate, simple, short petiolate, oblanceolate or obovate to elliptic, entire, acute to apiculate, with base attenuate or cuneate.
Inflorescence: Terminal raceme; flowers perfect, regular; calyx lobed; five petals, white; ten stamens.
Fruit: Capsule.
Flowering Date: April–May.
Habitat: Dry woods.
Distribution: CO, NE, EC, SW.
Comments: *S. americana* Lam. has axillary, solitary flowers.

# SYMPLOCACEAE
## Sweetleaf Family

Plants a shrub or small tree. Leaves alternate, simple, somewhat leathery in texture. Five sepals, attached to the ovary; five petals; ovary nearly inferior; numerous stamens, in clusters, conspicuous. Fruit a drupe.

### *Symplocos tinctoria* (L.) L'Her.
**Sweetleaf, Horse Sugar**

Plants: Shrub or small tree.

Leaves: Alternate, simple, petiolate, leathery, lanceolate, entire, acute to acuminate, with base cuneate.

Inflorescence: Flowers in axillary clusters, perfect, regular; calyx lobed; five petals, yellow; numerous stamens, extending beyond the petals, yellowish green; flowers appear before the leaves.

Fruit: Drupe.

Flowering Date: March–May.

Habitats: Stream edges, dry or alluvial woods.

Distribution: Throughout.

# THEACEAE
## Tea or Camellia Family

Plants a shrub or tree. Leaves alternate, simple. Five sepals; five petals, white; ovary superior; Numerous stamens; Fruit a capsule.

### *Gordonia lasianthus* (L.) Ellis
**Loblolly Bay**

Plants: Shrub.
Leaves: Alternate, simple, nearly ses-sile, elliptic to oblanceolate, acute to short acuminate, with margins toothed and base cuneate to rounded.
Inflorescence: Flowers axillary, solitary, perfect, regular; five sepals; five pet-als, white; numerous stamens.
Fruit: Capsule.
Flowering Date: July–September.
Habitats: Moist woods, bogs, roadsides.
Distribution: CO.

### *Stewartia malachodendron* L.
**Silky Camellia**

Plants: Shrub.
Leaves: Alternate, simple, short petio-late, elliptic, acute, with margins toothed and base cuneate.
Inflorescence: Flowers solitary, axillary, perfect, regular; five sepals; five pet-als, white to off-white; numerous stamens, attached to petals.
Fruit: Capsule.
Flowering Date: May–June.
Habitats: Moist woods and stream edges.
Distribution: CO.

# VALERIANACEAE
## Valerian Family

Plants annual with equally forked branches. Leaves opposite
and in a basal rosette, simple. Calyx absent or nearly so; corolla five lobed, funnel shaped; ovary superior; three stamens.
Fruit a one-seeded, leathery nutlet.

### *Valerianella radiata* (L.) Dufr.
**Corn Salad**

Plants: Upright, somewhat succulent
  annual; stems dichotomously
  branched.
Leaves: Basal rosette, and opposite on
  stem, simple, sessile, spatulate, entire, with tip rounded to truncate and
  base attenuate.
Inflorescence: Flowers in terminal
  clusters, perfect, regular, subtended
  by leaflike bracts; calyx absent or
  nearly so; corolla funnel shaped to
  rotate, five lobed, white; three stamens.
Fruit: Nutlet.
Flowering Date: April–June.
Habitats: Abandoned lots, old fields,
  waste sites, woodland edges, along
  railroad tracks.
Distribution: Throughout.

# VERBENACEAE
Vervain Family

Plants annual or perennial herb, shrub, or tree. Leaves opposite or whorled, simple or compound. Calyx two to five parted; corolla four or five lobed, rotate or salverform; ovary superior; four stamens. Fruit a schizocarp, drupe, or utricle.

## *Callicarpa americana* L.
### Beauty Berry, French Mulberry

Plants: Herbs becoming shrubs.
Leaves: Opposite or nearly so, simple, petiolate, ovate to broadly lanceolate, acuminate to acute, with margins toothed and base cuneate.
Inflorescence: Flowers in axillary clusters on peduncles, perfect, irregular to nearly regular; calyx five lobed; corolla five parted, funnel shaped to nearly salverform, pinkish to lavender; four stamens.
Fruit: Drupe.
Flowering Date: June–July.
Habitats: Roadsides, woods, disturbed sites.
Distribution: NE, EC, CO, SW, SE.

## *Phyla lanceolata* (Michx.) Greene
### Fog Fruit

Plants: Upright, hairy perennial rooting at the nodes, with stems sometimes four angled.
Leaves: Opposite, simple, petiolate, ovate to lanceolate, acute, with margins toothed and base cuneate.
Inflorescence: Terminal head; flowers perfect, irregular; calyx parted; corolla salverform, five lobed, pink, lavender, or occasionally white; four stamens.
Fruit: Schizocarp.
Flowering Date: June–November.
Habitats: Wet ditches, edges of lakes and streams.
Distribution: Throughout.
Comments: *P. nodiflora* (L.) Greene has leaves that are oblanceolate to obovate or spatulate with an obtuse to rounded tip.

## *Verbena brasiliensis* Vell.
### Brazilian Vervain

Plants: Upright, highly branched perennial with angled stems.

Leaves: Opposite, simple, sessile, lanceolate, acute, with margins toothed and base attenuate and not clasping.

Inflorescence: Terminal spike; flowers perfect, irregular; calyx five lobed; corolla salverform, five lobed, bluish purple; four stamens.

Fruit: Schizocarp.

Flowering Date: May–October.

Habitats: Roadsides, waste and disturbed sites.

Distribution: Throughout.

Comments: *V. bonariensis* L. has at least some leaves that are partly clasping the stem.

## *Verbena rigida* Spreng.
### Verbena

Plants: Upright, hairy perennial.

Leaves: Opposite, simple, sessile, lanceolate, clasping, with margins toothed and tip spined.

Inflorescence: Spike; flowers perfect, irregular; calyx five lobed; corolla salverform, five lobed with lobes notched, purple to violet; four stamens.

Fruit: Schizocarp.

Flowering Date: March–September.

Habitats: Roadsides, waste sites.

Distribution: CO, EC, SW, SE.

## *Verbena tenuisecta* Briq.
### Moss Verbena

Plants: Upright to sprawling perennial rooting at the nodes.

Leaves: Opposite, simple, sessile, triangular, deeply dissected into nearly linear segments.

Inflorescence: Solitary spikes; flowers perfect, irregular; calyx five lobed; corolla salverform, five lobed, lavender to purple.

Fruit: Schizocarp.

Flowering Date: March–November.

Habitat: Roadsides.

Distribution: EC, SW, SE, CO.

# VIOLACEAE
## Violet Family

Plants annual or perennial. Leaves alternate and often appearing basal, simple. Flowers irregular; five sepals; five petals; ovary superior. Fruit a capsule.

### *Hybanthus concolor* (Forst.) Spreng.
**Green Violets**

Plants: Upright, glabrous to hairy perennial.

Leaves: Alternate, simple, sessile, elliptic to lanceolate, entire or occasionally toothed, long acuminate, with base attenuate.

Inflorescence: Flowers in axillary cluster, perfect, irregular; five sepals; five petals; five stamens.

Fruit: Capsule.

Flowering Date: April–June.

Habitat: Alluvial woods.

Distribution: NE.

### *Viola floridana* Brainerd
**Common Violet**

Plants: Upright, glabrous perennial with rhizomes.

Leaves: Basal, simple, petiolate, ovate, with margins toothed, tip rounded, and base truncate to cordate.

Inflorescence: Flowers terminal, solitary, perfect, irregular, on long peduncles; five sepals; five petals, with bottom petal spurred, usually bluish to violet, occasionally white; five stamens.

Fruit: Capsule.

Flowering Date: February–November.

Habitats: Alluvial woods, stream edges, woods.

Distribution: Throughout.

## *Viola lanceolata* L.
### Lance-Leaved Violet

Plants: Upright, glabrous or nearly glabrous perennial with rhizomes.
Leaves: Basal, simple, petiolate, with
margins toothed and base attenuate.
Inflorescence: Flowers terminal, solitary, perfect, irregular, on long peduncles; five sepals; five petals, with
bottom petal spurred, white with
purple veins; five stamens.
Fruit: Capsule.
Flowering Date: March–June.
Habitats: Sandy woods, savannas.
Distribution: CO.
Comments: *V. primulifolia* L. is similar but has leaves with cuneate to
truncate bases.

## *Viola pedata* L.
### Bird's Foot Violet, Pansy Violet, Hens and Roosters

Plants: Upright, hairy perennial with
rhizomes.
Leaves: Basal, simple, petiolate, palmately dissected, occasionally lobed.
Inflorescence: Flowers terminal, solitary, perfect, irregular; five sepals;
five petals, with bottom petal
spurred; upper two petals blue, violet, or white and lower three petals
blue, violet, or white (can be any
combination; most often all petals
blue to violet); five stamens.
Fruit: Capsule.
Flowering Date: March–May.
Habitats: Prairies, roadsides, rocky
open woods.
Distribution: NE, EC, SW, SE.

## *Viola pubescens* Ait.
### Yellow Violet

Plants: Upright, glabrous to hairy perennial with rhizomes.
Leaves: Basal, simple, petiolate, ovate,
entire to toothed, with tip rounded
and base truncate to cordate.
Inflorescence: Flowers terminal, solitary, perfect, irregular; five sepals;
five petals, yellow, with bottom petal
spurred, occasionally purple veined;
five stamens.
Fruit: Capsule.
Flowering Date: March–May.
Habitat: Rocky woods.
Distribution: NE, EC, SW, SE.
Comments: According to some au-
thors, this species is synonymous
with *V. eriocarpa* Schwein. and *V.
pensylvanica* Michx.

## *Viola rafinesquii* Greene
**Johnny-Jump-Up, Wild Pansy**

Plants: Upright, glabrous to slightly
  hairy perennial with rhizomes.
Leaves: Alternate, simple, petiolate,
  lanceolate to ovate or spatulate, entire or slightly toothed; stipules are
  leaflike and pinnately divided.
Inflorescence: Flowers terminal, solitary, perfect, irregular; five sepals;
  five petals, usually lavender and becoming whitish toward the base,
  marked with purple veins and a yellowish center, with spur not prominent; five stamens.
Fruit: Capsule.
Flowering Date: March–May.
Habitats: Yards, old fields, roadsides,
  pastures.
Distribution: NE, EC, DE.

## *Viola rostrata* Pursh
**Violets**

Plants: Upright, glabrous to slightly
  hairy perennial with rhizomes.
Leaves: Alternate, simple, petiolate,
  ovate, acute to short acuminate, with
  margins toothed and base cordate.
Inflorescence: Flowers terminal, solitary, perfect, irregular; five sepals;
  five petals, usually lavender to violet, deep purple in the center, veins
  darker pigmented, with spur prominent; five stamens.
Fruit: Capsule.
Flowering Date: April–May.
Habitats: Moist ledges of vertical rock,
  rich woods.
Distribution: NE.

## *Viola sagittata* Ait.
**Violets**

Plants: Upright, glabrous to slightly
  hairy perennial.
Leaves: Alternate, simple, petiolate,
  lanceolate to ovate, acute to acuminate, with margins toothed and base
  sagittate.
Inflorescence: Flowers terminal, solitary, perfect, irregular; five sepals;
  five petals, violet or bluish violet and
  white toward the base, with spur
  prominent; five stamens.
Fruit: Capsule.
Flowering Date: March–May.
Habitats: Woods, fields.
Distribution: NE, EC.

ACHENE. One-seeded indehiscent fruit in which the outer layer is fused to the seed (example: sunflower seeds).

ACUMINATE. Tapering to a long or short point, with the sides of the point pinched in, setting it off abruptly from the lower portion of the body.

ACUTE. Tapering to the tip with the sides at the tip forming an angle less than a right angle.

ADVENTITIOUS. Roots derived from stems or leaves.

AGGREGATE FRUIT. A headlike cluster of fruits on a common receptacle (example: strawberry).

ALLUVIAL. Composed of soil deposited by a river or by other moving water.

ALTERNATE LEAVES. One leaf per node.

ANNUAL. A plant that completes its life cycle in one growing season.

ANTHER. The part of the male organ (stamen) where pollen is produced.

APEX. The tip or top.

ATTENUATE. Gradually narrowing to the base.

AURICLE. An earlobe-shaped projection or appendage at the base of some leaves and petals.

AURICULATE. Having an auricle(s).

AXIL. The angle between a stem or leaf and its axis.

AXILLARY. Within the axil.

BANNER. The upper petal of the pea-shaped flower of the Fabaceae family.

BASAL. Related to or situated at the base.

BASIC. As related to soils, rich in alkaline minerals.

BEACH. That portion of the coastline lying between the lowest tide and the highest tide and composed of sand.

BERRY. A fleshy fruit with numerous seeds (example: tomato).

BIENNIAL. A plant that completes its life cycle in two years.

BILABIATE. Having a corolla with two lips (examples: members of the mint and snapdragon families).

BIPINNATE LEAF. A leaf that is divided into segments (leaflets), with each segment divided again into segments. Twice compound.

BLADDER. An inflated, thin-walled structure.

BLADE. The expanded, flat portion of a leaf or petal.

BOG.   A wetland area in which organic matter accumulates as peat.

BRACKISH.   Water that is intermediate between saltwater and freshwater.

BRACT.   A leaflike structure just below (subtending) an inflorescence or a flower. The structure is smaller than and usually dissimilar to the stem leaves.

BULB.   An underground stem surrounded by fleshy modified leaves or scales (example: onion).

CALCAREOUS.   Being rich in calcium; pertaining to limestone or chalk. Growing on calcium-rich soils.

CALLUS.   A hard protuberance.

CALYX.   The collective term for all the sepals of a flower; the outer series of the perianth.

CALYX TUBE.   The part of the calyx where the sepals are fused.

CAMPANULATE.   Bell shaped.

CAPITATE.   A headlike or compact, spherical cluster of flowers.

CAPSULE.   A dry fruit that is dehiscent and many seeded and develops from two or more carpels (examples: iris, morning glory).

CARPEL.   A single pistil. There may be one per flower (simple pistil) or two or more per flower (compound pistil).

CATHARTIC (PURGATIVE).   A compound that stimulates evacuation of substances from the body.

CHLOROPHYLL.   The green pigment of plants.

CLASPING.   Having the lower part of a leaf blade partially or wholly surround the stem.

CLAVATE.   Club shaped.

CLAW.   The narrow base or stalk of some petals.

COAST.   An area of land adjacent to an ocean or sea.

COLUMN.   Filaments that are united. In orchids, the central part of the flower formed by the union of the stamens, style, and stigma.

COMPLETE.   A flower that contains sepals, petals, stamen(s), and pistil(s).

COMPOUND.   Composed of two or more similar structures.

COMPOUND LEAF.   A leaf that is divided into two or more distinct segments.

CORDATE.   Heart shaped and attached between lobes.

CORM.   A thickened, short, upright underground stem, often covered with thin, dry leaves (example: gladiolus).

COROLLA.   All the petals of a flower; the inner floral series of the perianth.

CORONA (CROWN). An outgrowth between the stamens and corolla.

CORYMB. A relatively flat-topped, open inflorescence.

CRENATE. Having toothed leaf margins with rounded teeth.

CUNEATE. Wedgeshaped.

DECIDUOUS. Having organs, such as leaves, that fall off at the end of a growing season.

DECOMPOUND. Divided more than once.

DECURRENT. Extending down from the point of attachment.

DEHISCENT. Opening by pores or slits in dry fruits; the anthers' opening to shed pollen.

DENTATE. Having triangular teeth at right angles to the edge of the structure.

DICHOTOMOUS. Two branched, with branches equal or nearly equal in length.

DIOECIOUS. Containing flowers of only one sex; the male (staminate) flowers and female (pistillate) flowers are on separate plants.

DISC FLOWER. The tubular flowers of the Asteraceae.

DISSECTED. Usually, deeply divided into segments; used in reference to leaves.

DIVIDED. Deeply lobed, nearly to the midrib.

DRUPE. A one-seeded, fleshy fruit (example: plum).

DUNE. A mound of loose sand deposited by wind.

ELLIPTIC. Being widest in the center.

EMARGINATE. Having a notched apex, used in reference to leaves and petals.

ENTIRE. Having no teeth or lobes on the margin, as in a leaf's edge.

EPIPHYTIC. Being nonparasitic but still growing on another plant.

EQUITANT. Overlapping in two ranks.

ESTUARY. An inlet from a sea or an ocean where freshwater and saltwater mix.

EVERGREEN. Bearing green leaves throughout the year or for a number of years.

FASCICLE. A bundle or cluster of leaves.

FILAMENT. Threadlike structure; portion of the stamen that supports the anther.

FILIFORM. Leaves are threadlike.

FLATWOODS. A relatively flat, wooded area.

FLOODPLAIN. A lowland area near a water source that is subject to periodic flooding.

FOLLICLE. A dry fruit that contains more than one seed and splits along the suture at maturity.

FORB.   Any herbaceous plant other than a sedge, rush, or grass.

FUNNELFORM.   Funnel shaped, with the tube widening toward the top.

FUSIFORM.   Broadest at the middle and tapering in both directions.

GLABROUS.   Without hairs.

GLADES.   Small openings in the forest, usually on hillsides; the soils are relatively shallow and supporting, underground rock is often exposed.

GLAND.   A secreting organ.

GLAUCOUS.   Covered with a whitish or bluish waxy substance.

HARDWOODS.   Forested areas dominated by oak and/or hickory.

HASTATE.   Leaves that are arrowhead shaped, with the lobes pointing outward.

HEAD.   A dense cluster of flowers on a common receptacle.

HELICOID.   Spiraled.

HERBACEOUS.   Having the characteristics of an herb.

HIP.   The fruit of a rose, formed by the enlargement and increased fleshiness of the floral cup.

HORN.   A tapering appendage similar in shape to a cattle horn.

HYPANTHIUM.   A structure formed by the fusion of sepals, petals, and stamens.

IMPERFECT FLOWER (UNISEXUAL).   A flower containing either stamens or pistils but not both.

INDEHISCENT.   Not opening by suture lines or pores.

INFERIOR OVARY.   Ovary situated below the sepals, petals, and stamens.

INFLORESCENCE.   The flowering part of a plant. It may consist of one flower or many flowers.

INNERDUNE.   Between two dunes.

INTERNODE.   The portion of a stem between two nodes.

INVOLUCRE.   A whorl of separate or fused leaves or bracts subtending an inflorescence or a flower.

IRREGULAR FLOWER (ZYGOMORPHIC).   A flower that can be divided into only two parts that are mirror images of each other.

LABIATE.   Being composed of two opposed parts (for example, as in the mint family's flowers' two upper petals being opposed to the three lower petals); used in reference to flowers.

LANCEOLATE.   Lance shaped; several times longer than broad and widest at the base.

LEAFLET.   One of the divisions of a compound leaf.

LEGUME (POD). A dry fruit that contains more than one seed and splits along two sutures.

LIGULE. A flat, straplike body.

LINEAR. Narrow with parallel sides, as in a leaf.

LIP. The upper and lower segments of a labiate flower.

LOBE. A rounded segment of an organ, as on a leaf or petal.

LOMENT. A legume that is constricted into a linear series of segments, each containing one seed.

MARGIN. An edge, as in a leaf's edge.

MARSH. An area of land that is constantly saturated with water; marshes may be freshwater or saltwater.

MERICARP. The individual carpel of a schizocarp; the portions of a fruit, each individually appearing as a fruit.

MIXED WOODS. A forest in which several different species are dominant or compete for dominance.

MONOECIOUS. Containing flowers of both sexes; the male (staminate) flowers and female (pistillate) flowers are separate but on the same plant.

NETTED VENATION. The veins of a leaf form a network (reticulated).

NODE. The point on a stem where a leaf, branch, or flower originates.

NUT. A hard, one-seeded fruit that does not split.

NUTLET. A small nut; often applied to any small, dry, nutlike fruit or seed, such as the hard mericarp of some species.

OBCORDATE. Heart shaped but attached at the point.

OBLANCEOLATE. Lance shaped but attached at the tapered end.

OBLIQUE. With unequal sides.

OBLONG. Two to four times longer than wide with parallel sides.

OBOVATE. Egg shaped but attached at the narrow end.

OBTUSE. Nearly rounded; blunt.

OCREA. A tube formed by the fusion of a pair of stipules.

OPPOSITE. Leaves, stems, or flowers located at the same level and on opposite sides of the supporting structure.

OVAL. Broadly elliptical, with the width more than one-half the length.

OVARY. The part of the pistil that bears the ovule (future seed).

OVATE. Egg shaped and attached at the widest end.

OVOID. A three-dimensional, egg-shaped figure.

PALMATE. Having three or more veins or leaflets arise from a common point, either the base of a leaf (veins) or the tip of a petiole (leaflets).

PANICLE. A compound raceme.

PAPPUS.  The modified calyx of the Asteraceae, composed of bristles or scales.

PARALLEL VENATION.  The veins of a leaf are arranged parallel to one another.

PARASITE.  An organism that is nutritionally dependent upon another organism for completion of its life cycle.

PEDICEL.  The stalk of a single flower.

PEDUNCLE.  The main stalk of an entire inflorescence.

PELTATE.  Having the petiole attached at the center; refers to leaves.

PERENNIAL.  A plant that continues to grow for more than two years.

PERFECT FLOWER (BISEXUAL).  A flower containing both stamens and pistils.

PERFOLIATE.  Having two or more opposite or whorled leaves fused into a collarlike structure around a stem.

PERIANTH.  The collective term for the calyx and corolla together or either one if one is absent.

PETAL(S).  The sterile part of the flower that forms a series of usually pigmented structures just above the sepals; the petals collectively are termed corolla.

PETALOID.  Petal-like; often applied to the sepals and bracts.

PETIOLATE.  Having a petiole.

PETIOLE.  The stalk of a leaf.

PINELANDS.  Forest in which pines are essentially the only trees; most of other woody plants consist of shrubs and vines.

PINNATE.  An elongated axis with branches, leaflets, or veins arising along both sides (like a bird's feather).

PISTIL.  The female part of a flower, consisting of an ovary, style, and stigma.

PLICATE.  Folded lengthwise into pleats (like a fan).

POME.  A fruit from an inferior ovary consisting of a berry-like structure fused to a fleshy receptacle known as a hypanthium (examples: apple, pear).

PRAIRIE.  In the southeast, an open and relatively extended area characterized by big and little bluestem, Indian grass, and other tallgrass vegetation.

PRICKLE.  A sharp-pointed, usually small outgrowth of the bark or epidermis.

PROSTRATE.  Lying on the ground.

RACEME.  A single inflorescence with stalked flowers arranged along an elongated stem.

RACHIS.  The axis of a compound leaf or inflorescence.

RAY FLOWER.  The ligulate (strap-shaped) corolla of the Asteraceae.

RECEPTACLE. The usually expanded portion of a flower stalk on which the floral parts are attached.

RECURVED. Curved downward or backward.

REFLEXED. Bent abruptly downward.

REGULAR FLOWER (ACTINOMORPHIC). A flower in which a line bisecting the flower through the center will produce symmetrical halves; radially symmetrical.

RHIZOME. An underground horizontal stem.

ROCK OUTCROPS. Area in which bedrock is exposed.

ROSETTE. A circular arrangement of leaves at the base of the plant.

ROTATE. Wheel-shaped, with a short tube.

SACCATE. Sac shaped or pouch shaped.

SAGITTATE. Having arrowhead-shaped leaves, with the leaf lobes pointing downward or backward.

SALT FLAT. A nearly unvegetated area in or near a salt marsh.

SALT MARSH. A marsh subject to periodic flooding by saltwater.

SALVERFORM. A flower with a long, slender tube that flares at the tip.

SAMARA. A dry, winged fruit that does not split open at maturity.

SAPROPHYTE. A plant that usually lacks chlorophyll and lives on dead organic material.

SCAPOSE. Having a leafless flowering stem.

SCHIZOCARP. An ovary with two or more seed chambers (locule) in which the seed chambers separate at maturity (example: maple).

SEPAL(S). The sterile part of the flower that forms the usually green outer series of structures; the sepals collectively are termed the calyx.

SERRATE. Sharp toothed.

SESSILE. Lacking a stalk; usually in reference to certain leaves.

SHEATH. A tubular envelope.

SHRUB. A woody plant with several stems arising from a common base; smaller than a tree.

SILICLE. A short silique that is usually as long as it is broad or broader.

SILIQUE. A dry fruit with two seed chambers separated by a false partition (example: members of the mustard family).

SIMPLE. Consisting of only one part.

SOLITARY. Alone; one.

SPADIX. A thick, fleshy spike densely covered with imperfect flowers.

SPATHE.   A bract that encloses or sheaths an inflorescence.

SPATULATE.   Spoon shaped; broadest at the apex and tapering to the base.

SPIKE.   An inflorescence with sessile flowers along an elongated axis.

SPINE.   A sharp-pointed, rigid outgrowth from the wood of the stem.

SPUR.   A hollow, saclike or tubular extension from a petal or sepal.

STAMEN.   The male part of a flower, consisting of a filament and the pollen-producing anther.

STERILE.   Not producing pollen or eggs.

STIGMA.   The part of the pistil located at the tip; usually receives the pollen.

STIPULE.   An appendage at the base of the petiole or leaf.

STOLON.   A trailing, above ground stem that roots at the tip.

STOLONIFEROUS.   Having stolons.

STYLE.   The stalklike part of the pistil between the ovary and stigma.

SUBTEND.   To occupy a lower position than and be adjacent to another structure.

SUBULATE.   Awl shaped.

SUCCULENT.   Fleshy or spongy and filled with water.

SUPERIOR OVARY.   An ovary situated above the stamens, petals, and sepals.

SWAMP.   A low, wooded area under the influence of freshwater, with saturated soils or standing water.

SYNONYMS (SYNONYMOUS).   Two or more scientific names applied to the same plant (taxon).

TAPROOT.   The primary root; often fleshy.

TENDRIL.   A twining or clasping structure derived from a modified stem, leaf, or part of a leaf, by which some plants climb.

TERMINAL.   At the end point.

TERNATE.   Arranged in threes.

TERRESTRIAL.   A plant growing from the soil.

THORN.   A rigid, sharp-pointed structure originating from wood and differing from a spine by the presence of vascular tissue.

TRAILING.   Lying on the ground but not rooting.

TRIFOLIATE.   A compound leaf consisting of three leaflets, all arising from a common point.

TRIPINNATE.   A leaf that is three times pinnate.

TRUNCATE.   With the tip or base squared (horizontal); usually referring to leaves.

TUBE. A hollow cylindrical structure; usually in reference to a flower.

TUBER. A thickened, short underground stem or branch of a stem serving as a storage organ (examples: potato, some orchids).

TUBULAR. Having a tube.

TWINING. Climbing by coiling around a support.

UMBEL. A rounded or flat-topped inflorescence with the pedicels of the flowers arising from a common point.

URCEOLATE. Urn shaped; cylindrical or ovoid and contracted at the mouth.

UTRICLE. A bladderlike body; dry, thin-walled, one-seeded fruit.

VINE. A climbing plant.

WHORLED. With three or more leaves or flowers at a single node, arranged in a circle around the stem.

WING. The lateral petals of the Fabaceae; a thin expansion of the surface of an organ.

**Plant Parts, Shapes, and Arrangements**

Vascular plants (those that contain the water-, mineral-, and food-conducting tissues, xylem and phloem) are highly variable in size from nearly microscopic to several hundred feet or more in height. They may have a simple stem with one or few flowers or have numerous branches with hundreds of flowers. Their leaves can be simple (such as those of elm and maple) to highly modified (such as those of pitcher plants and cacti). The flowers are even more variable; they may be found in myriad shapes and colors.

This section's purpose is to present some of the basic flower and leaf parts, shapes, and arrangements. The illustrations will help in understanding terminology presented in the text.

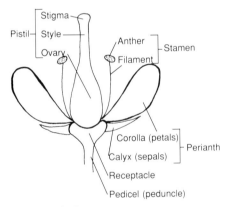

Fig. 1 Typical Flower

**Flower Symmetry**

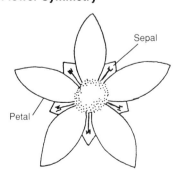

Fig. 2 Regular (Actinomorphic)

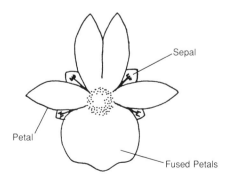

Fig. 3 Irregular (Zygomorphic)

**Flower Shapes**

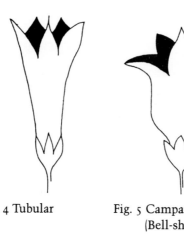

Fig. 4 Tubular

Fig. 5 Campanulate
(Bell-shaped)

Fig. 6 Funnelform

Fig. 7 Salverform

Fig. 8 Rotate

Fig. 9 Urceolate
(Urn-shaped)

**Ovary Position**

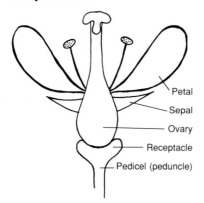

Fig. 10 Ovary Inferior

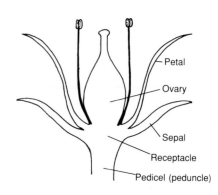

Fig. 11 Ovary Superior

## Special Flower Shapes

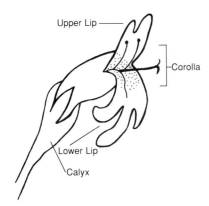

Fig. 12 Bilabiate (Scrophulariaceae)

Fig. 13 Head (Asteraceae)

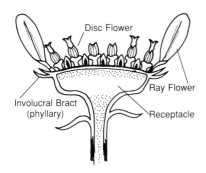

Fig. 14 Head (Longitudinal Section)

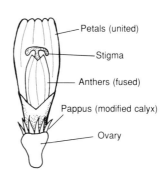

Fig. 15 Ray or Ligulate Flower

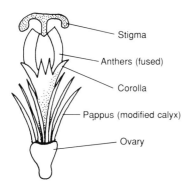

Fig. 16 Disc or Tubular Flower

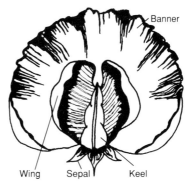

Fig. 17 Pea-shaped Flower (Fabaceae)

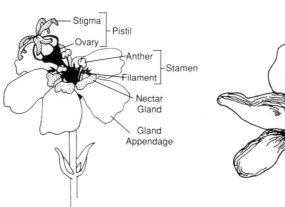

Fig. 18 Cyathium (Euphorbia)

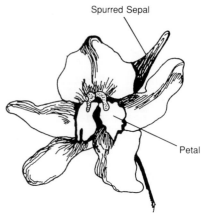

Fig. 19 Irregular Flower (Ranunculaceae)

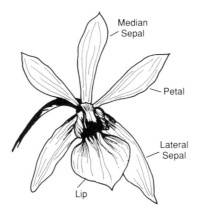

Fig. 20 Irregular Flower
(Orchidaceae)

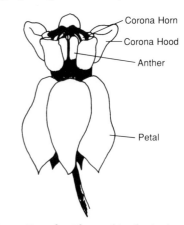

Fig. 21 Regular Flower (Asclepias)

**Inflorescence Types**

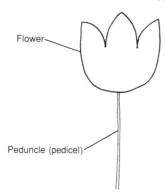

Fig. 22 Scapose

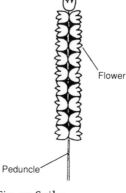

Fig. 23 Spike

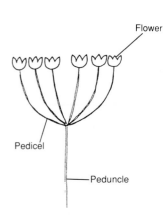

Fig. 24 Umbel

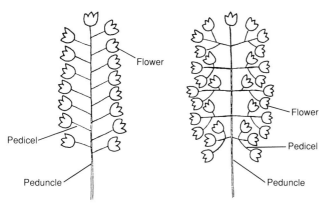

Fig. 25 Raceme        Fig. 26 Panicle

## Leaf Arrangement

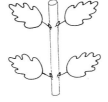

Fig. 27 Whorled        Fig. 28 Opposite        Fig. 29 Alternate        Fig. 30 Rosette

## Leaf Types

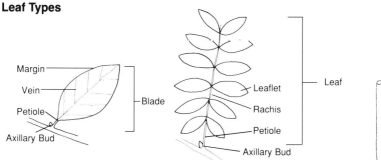
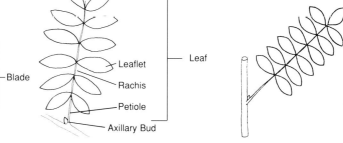

Fig. 31 Simple        Fig. 32 Compound        Fig. 33 Pinnately Compound

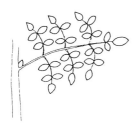
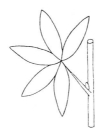

Fig. 34 Bipinnately Compound  Fig. 35 Palmately Compound    Fig. 36 Ternately Compound
                                                              (Trifoliate)

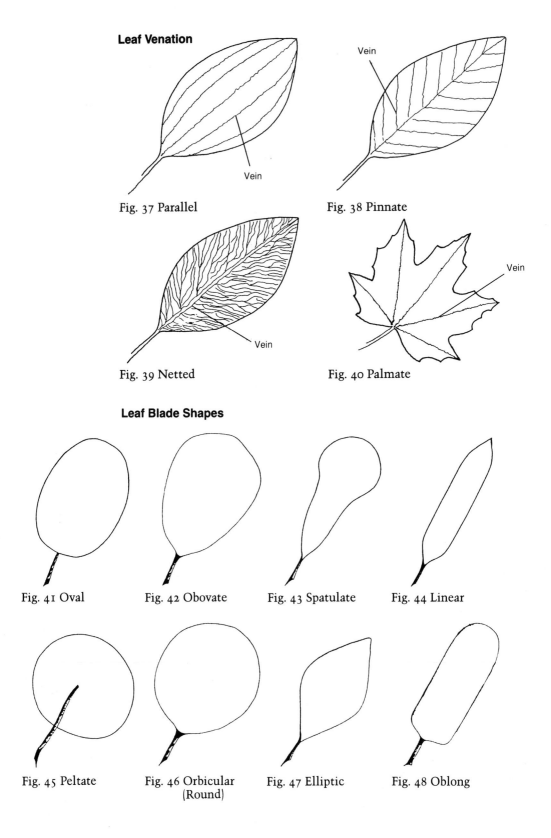

**Leaf Venation**

Fig. 37 Parallel

Fig. 38 Pinnate

Fig. 39 Netted

Fig. 40 Palmate

**Leaf Blade Shapes**

Fig. 41 Oval

Fig. 42 Obovate

Fig. 43 Spatulate

Fig. 44 Linear

Fig. 45 Peltate

Fig. 46 Orbicular (Round)

Fig. 47 Elliptic

Fig. 48 Oblong

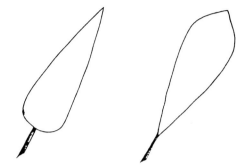

Fig. 49 Lanceolate     Fig. 50 Oblanceolate

## Leaf Margins

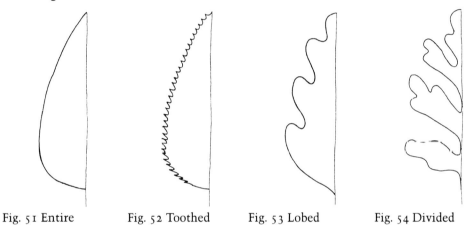

Fig. 51 Entire     Fig. 52 Toothed     Fig. 53 Lobed     Fig. 54 Divided

## Leaf Apexes

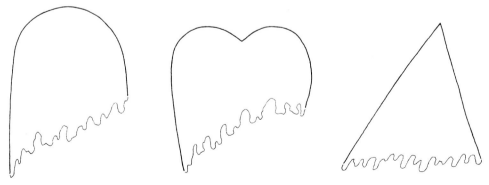

Fig. 55 Round     Fig. 56 Emarginate     Fig. 57 Acute

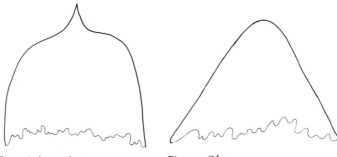

Fig. 58 Acuminate          Fig. 59 Obtuse

**Leaf Bases**

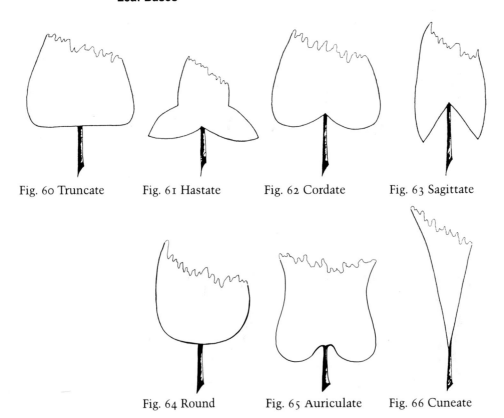

Fig. 60 Truncate     Fig. 61 Hastate     Fig. 62 Cordate     Fig. 63 Sagittate

Fig. 64 Round     Fig. 65 Auriculate     Fig. 66 Cuneate

# Selected References

Bare, J. E. 1979. *Wildflowers and Weeds of Kansas.* The Regents Press of Kansas, Lawrence.

Barkeley, T. M. 1968. *A Manual of the Flowering Plants of Kansas.* The Kansas State University Endowment Association, Manhattan.

———. (ed.). 1986. *Flora of the Great Plains.* University Press of Kansas, Lawrence.

Clewell, A. F. 1985. *Guide to the Vascular Plants of the Florida Panhandle.* Florida State University Press, Tallahassee.

Correll, D. S., and M. C. Johnston. 1979. *Manual of the Vascular Plants of Texas.* The University of Texas, Dallas.

Cronquist, A. 1980. *Vascular Flora of the Southeastern United States.* Vol. 1, *Asteraceae.* The University of North Carolina Press, Chapel Hill.

———. 1981. *An Integrated System of Classification of Flowering Plants.* Columbia University Press, New York City.

Gledhill, D. 1985. *The Names of Plants.* Cambridge University Press, Cambridge, England.

Godfrey, R. K., and J. W. Wooten. 1981. *Aquatic and Wetland Plants of Southeastern United States: Dicotyledons and Monocotyledons.* The University of Georgia Press, Athens.

Harrington, H. D., and L. W. Durrell. 1981. *How to Identify Plants.* (2nd ed.). Ohio University Press, Athens.

Kartesz, J. T., and R. Kartesz. 1980. *A Synonymized Checklist of the Vascular Flora of the United States, Canada, and Greenland.* Vol. 2, *The Biota of North America.* The University of North Carolina Press, Chapel Hill.

Lewis, W. H., and M. P. F. Elvin-Lewis. *Medical Botany.* John Wiley & Sons, New York City.

Lincoln, R. J., G. A. Boxshall, and P. F. Clark. 1982. *A Dictionary of Ecology, Evolution, and Systematics.* Cambridge University Press, Cambridge, England.

Lowe, E. N. 1921. *Plants of Mississippi.* Mississippi State Geological Survey, Jackson.

Luer, C. A. 1975. *The Native Orchids of the United States and Canada.* The New York Botanical Garden, New York City.

McDaniel, S. 1983. *Pearl River Basin Native Woody Plants Species.* The Crosby Arboretum Foundation, Picayune, Mississippi.

Molenbrock, R. H. 1975. *Guide to the Vascular Flora of Illinois.* Southern Illinois University Press, Carbondale and Edwardsville.

Oosting, H. J. *The Study of Plant Communities.* W. H. Freeman and Company, San Francisco.

Radford, A. E., H. E., Ahles, and C. R. Bell. 1968. *Manual of the Vascular Flora of the Carolinas.* The University of North Carolina Press, Chapel Hill.

Small, J. K. 1933. *Manual of the Southeastern Flora.* The University of North Carolina Press, Chapel Hill.

Steyermark, J. A. 1963. *Flora of Missouri.* The Iowa State University Press, Ames.

# Additional Regional Wildflower Field Guides

Ajilvsgi, G. 1984. *Wildflowers of Texas.* Shearer Publications, Bryan, TX.

Batson, W. T. 1987. *Wildflowers in the Carolinas.* University Press of South Carolina, Columbia.

Bell, C. R., and B. J. Taylor. 1982. *Florida Wildflowers and Roadside Plants.* Laurel Hill Press, Chapel Hill, NC.

Brown, C. A. 1972. *Wildflowers of Louisiana and Adjoining States.* Louisiana State University Press, Baton Rouge.

Dean, B. E., A. Mason, and J. L. Thomas. *Wildflowers of Alabama and Adjoining States.* The University of Alabama Press, Tuscaloosa.

Gupton, O. W., and F. C. Swope. 1986. *Wild Orchids of the Middle Atlantic States.* The University of Tennessee Press, Knoxville.

Hunter, C. G. 1984. *Wildflowers of Arkansas.* Ozark Society Books, Little Rock.

Justice, W. S., and C. R. Bell. 1968. *Wildflowers of North Carolina.* The University of North Carolina Press, Chapel Hill.

Loughmiller, C., and L. Loughmiller. 1984. *Texas Wildflowers: A Field Guide.* University of Texas Press, Austin.

Molenbrock, R. H. 1987. *Wildflowers.* Macmillan Co., New York.

Smith, A. I. 1979. *A Guide to Wildflowers of the Mid-South.* Memphis State University Press, Memphis.

Summers, B. 1981. *Missouri Orchids.* Missouri Department of Conservation, Jefferson City.